THE HUMAN EMBRYO *IN VITRO*

The Human Embryo In Vitro explores the ways in which UK law engages with embryonic processes under the Human Fertilisation and Embryology Act 1990 (as amended), the intellectual basis of which has not been reconsidered for almost thirty years. McMillan argues that in regulating 'the embryo' – that is, a processual liminal entity in itself – the law is regulating for uncertainty.

This book offers a fuller understanding of how complex biological processes of development and growth can be better aligned with a legal framework that purports to pay respect to the embryo while also allowing its destruction. To do so it employs an anthropological concept, liminality, which is itself concerned with revealing the dynamics of process. The implications of this for contemporary regulation of artificial reproduction are fully explored, and recommendations are offered for international regimes on how they can better align biological reality with social policy and law.

CATRIONA A. W. MCMILLAN is a Senior Research Fellow in Medical Law and Ethics at the University of Edinburgh. Her research focuses on the intersection of health law, ethics, and society, particularly the regulation of reproduction, and advances in health technologies.

This series of books – formerly called Cambridge Law, Medicine and Ethics – was founded by Cambridge University Press with Alexander McCall Smith as its first editor in 2003. It focuses on the law's complex and troubled relationship with medicine across both the developed and the developing world. In the past twenty years, we have seen in many countries increasing resort to the courts by dissatisfied patients and a growing use of the courts to attempt to resolve intractable ethical dilemmas. At the same time, legislatures across the world have struggled to address the questions posed by both the successes and the failures of modern medicine, while international organisations such as the WHO and UNESCO now regularly address issues of medical law. It follows that we would expect ethical and policy questions to be integral to the analysis of the legal issues discussed in this series. The series responds to the high profile of medical law in universities, in legal and medical practice, as well as in public and political affairs. We seek to reflect the evidence that many major health-related policy and bioethics debates in the UK, Europe and the international community over the past two decades have involved a strong medical law dimension. With that in mind, we seek to address how legal analysis might have a trans-jurisdictional and international relevance. Organ retention, embryonic stem cell research, physician-assisted suicide and the allocation of resources to fund health care are but a few examples among many. The emphasis of this series is thus on matters of public concern and/or practical significance. We look for books that could make a difference to the development of medical law and enhance the role of medico-legal debate in policy circles. That is not to say that we lack interest in the important theoretical dimensions of the subject, but we aim to ensure that theoretical debate is grounded in the realities of how the law does and should interact with medicine and health care.

Series Editors

Professor Graeme Laurie, *University of Edinburgh*
Professor Richard Ashcroft, *Queen Mary University of London*

Books in the Series

Heather Widdows

The Connected Self: The Ethics and Governance of the Genetic Individual

Amel Alghrani, Rebecca Bennett and Suzanne Ost

Bioethics, Medicine and the Criminal Law Volume I: The Criminal Law and Bioethical Conflict: Walking the Tightrope

Danielle Griffiths and Andrew Sanders

Bioethics, Medicine and the Criminal Law Volume II: Medicine, Crime and Society

Margaret Brazier and Suzanne Ost

Bioethics, Medicine and the Criminal Law Volume III: Medicine and Bioethics in the Theatre of the Criminal Process

Sigrid Sterckx, Kasper Raus and Freddy Mortier

Continuous Sedation at the End of Life: Ethical, Clinical and Legal Perspectives

A. M. Viens, John Coggon and Anthony S. Kessel

Criminal Law, Philosophy and Public Health Practice

Ruth Chadwick, Mairi Levitt and Darren Shickle

The Right to Know and the Right Not to Know: Genetic Privacy and Responsibility

Eleanor D. Kinney

The Affordable Care Act and Medicare in Comparative Context

Katri Lõhmus

Caring Autonomy: European Human Rights Law and the Challenge of Individualism

Catherine Stanton and Hannah Quirk

Criminalising Contagion: Legal and Ethical Challenges of Disease Transmission and the Criminal Law

Sharona Hoffman

Electronic Health Records and Medical Big Data: Law and Policy

Barbara Prainsack and Alena Buyx

Solidarity in Biomedicine and Beyond

Camillia Kong

Mental Capacity in Relationship

Oliver Quick

Regulating Patient Safety: The End of Professional Dominance?

Thana C. de Campos

The Global Health Crisis: Ethical Responsibilities

Jonathan Ives, Michael Dunn and Alan Cribb

Empirical Bioethics: Theoretical and Practical Perspectives

Alan Merry and Warren Brookbanks

Merry and McCall Smith's Errors, Medicine and the Law (second edition)

Donna Dickenson

Property in the Body: Feminist Perspectives (second edition)

THE HUMAN EMBRYO *IN VITRO*

Breaking the Legal Stalemate

CATRIONA A. W. MCMILLAN

University of Edinburgh

CAMBRIDGE
UNIVERSITY PRESS

University Printing House, Cambridge CB2 8BS, United Kingdom

One Liberty Plaza, 20th Floor, New York, NY 10006, USA

477 Williamstown Road, Port Melbourne, VIC 3207, Australia

314–321, 3rd Floor, Plot 3, Splendor Forum, Jasola District Centre, New Delhi – 110025, India

79 Anson Road, #06–04/06, Singapore 079906

Cambridge University Press is part of the University of Cambridge.

It furthers the University's mission by disseminating knowledge in the pursuit of education, learning, and research at the highest international levels of excellence.

www.cambridge.org
Information on this title: www.cambridge.org/9781108844109
DOI: 10.1017/9781108933421

First published 2021

A catalogue record for this publication is available from the British Library.

Library of Congress Cataloging-in-Publication Data
Names: McMillan, Catriona A. W., author.
Title: The human embryo in vitro : breaking the legal stalemate/ Catriona A. W. McMillan, University of Edinburgh.
Description: Cambridge, United Kingdom ; New York, NY : Cambridge University Press, 2021. | Series: Cambridge bioethics and law | Based on author's thesis (doctoral - University of Edinburgh, 2018) issued under title: Human embryo in vitro : a processual entity in legal stasis. | Includes bibliographical references and index.
Identifiers: LCCN 2021000448 (print) | LCCN 2021000449 (ebook) | ISBN 9781108844109 (hardback) | ISBN 9781108933421 (ebook)
Subjects: LCSH: Fetus – Legal status, laws, etc. – Great Britain. | Human reproductive technology – Law and legislation – Great Britain.
Classification: LCC KD744.U53 M36 2021 (print) | LCC KD744.U53 (ebook) | DDC 342.4108/5–dc23
LC record available at https://lccn.loc.gov/2021000448
LC ebook record available at https://lccn.loc.gov/2021000449

ISBN 978-1-108-84410-9 Hardback

For Dad.

CONTENTS

FOREWORD

Graeme T. Laurie
Professorial Fellow, Edinburgh Law School

It is with considerable pleasure and pride that I write the foreword for this monograph authored by Dr McMillan. As she indicates in the introduction to the work, her research was supported by a Wellcome Senior Investigator Award – *Confronting the Liminal Spaces of Human Health Research* – of which I had the privilege of being Principal Investigator (2014–2021, WT103360MA). This was the Liminal Spaces Project (www.liminalspaces.ed.ac.uk/). And, while it is an all-too-common feature of contemporary academia that researchers are held to account for their worth through numbers of publications, quality metrics, and research assessment exercises, there is still much that is not captured about the process of being involved in a research team and in producing a work of calibre such as this. Indeed, given that a central feature of the contribution of this work is to invite readers to consider the importance of *processual* regulation in dealing with the human embryo, I consider it fitting that I share with readers the experience for Dr McMillan and me in being supported by Wellcome in this project and in the *process* of producing this excellent monograph.

First, I want to signal our considerable appreciation of the flexibility that Wellcome funding affords. Because of this, I was able to employ Dr McMillan as a research assistant while she was undertaking her doctorate and also to provide partial funding support for the doctoral studies, even although this plan had not been part of the original proposal to the funder. This meant that Dr McMillan became a full member of the Liminal Spaces Project, and this was to the mutual benefit of Dr McMillan and the existing team in many ways over the ensuing years. Not only was Dr McMillan able to present and test her core ideas contained in this book at numerous international conferences, but she also benefitted from extensive and sustained interactions with other members of the team who were also working with the anthropological concept of liminality that sits at the heart of this work. Our collective contributions were considerably enhanced as a result, and it is a testament to Dr McMillan's hard work and commitment that she was eventually appointed as Senior Research Fellow on the project. For those interested in metrics and meritocracy, all of this ultimately led to Dr McMillan securing a British Academy Postdoctoral Fellowship. It is important that these stories are told.

As to the present work, the contributions to scholarship are myriad and profoundly challenging to the ways in which law currently constructs the idea of the 'human embryo'. As a paradigm example of a liminal entity – neither one thing nor another, and 'trapped' in a state of in-betweenness betwixt proto-person and laboratory artefact – the embryo, as it is treated in law, is a perfect illustration of law's constant struggle in regulating human health research to deliver on the twin objectives of both protecting what is human and promoting scientifically sound, socially valuable research. Yet the particular contribution of this monograph goes beyond revealing the deep-rooted moral ambivalence that lies at the heart of the existing regulatory regime to suggest ways to move through and out of that permanent state of uncertainty. Indeed, many would argue that this is a regulatory state of unsustainable hypocrisy. It is here that Dr McMillan's insights through the lens of liminality – with its focus on recognising the importance of process and the processual and the need to move through and out of states of liminality towards clearly defined end points – throw into stark relief how law's bounded approach to regulation is at serious odds with the biological and processual realities of human development from its earliest stages. In seeking ways through and out of this impasse, Dr McMillan develops her notion of processual regulation, the contours of which are fully explored herein. Moreover, in the spirit of genuinely significant and impactful scholarship, it is important to recognise that this concept of processual regulation has value and application beyond the realm of the embryo and into other areas of human experience and regulation. We look forward to Dr McMillan's future scholarship in this regard.

But to remain with the current work, and as further indication of the value of being involved with an interdisciplinary team of scholars working in and around related concepts, it is also important to recognise how the Wellcome funding supported Dr McMillan to engage with projects and colleagues outside the legal realm to draw from parallel discourses about the ontology of the human embryo. In this regard, the Liminal

Spaces Project was a joint funder of the Uncanny Bodies Project that led to an anthology of fiction and non-fiction inspired by Freud, cyborgs, and the history of Edinburgh, published by Luna Press in 2020 (Edited by P. Goldschmidt, G. Haddow, and F. Mazanderani). Dr McMillan's involvement in this project considerably enriched the development of Part II of this book, which further contextualises law's ambivalence towards the embryo against other literatures – most particularly the 'gothic' – and relative to ongoing discussions about the 'uncanniness' of the embryo. Furthermore, in once again bringing a liminal lens to these literatures, the monograph helps us to get past the rather jarring 'So What?' question. It is by these means that the reader is brought to Part III where the legal, regulatory, and social implications of this research are fully explored.

In sum, Dr McMillan is to be commended for deftly weaving together an intricate patchwork of novel insights about the legal status of the embryo. As a stand-alone work in its own right, I recommend this book to a range of scholars and practitioners who are rightly concerned about how we should treat the embryo *right*. While there is manifestly no obligation to agree with the conclusions that are reached, I wager that Dr McMillan's analysis will be difficult to ignore in the ongoing debates, and I am confident that it will contribute significantly to how we see the human embryo *in vitro* in the future.

ACKNOWLEDGEMENTS

I am grateful to Wellcome Trust for supporting this research as part of a senior research fellowship and PhD on the Senior Investigator Award entitled *Confronting the Liminal Spaces of Health Research Regulation* (WT103360MA).

Many thanks are owed to those who have read various iterations of this research over the past few years, especially Sarah Chan and Mary Neal for their thoughtful feedback on an earlier version of this work. My heartfelt thanks are owed to Gillian Black for her encouragement and support throughout the writing process. I also thank Bobby Lindsay and Rebecca Richards for their helpful comments on this book as in its final stages.

I consider myself very lucky to have carried out this research as part of the Liminal Spaces Project, alongside a team of brilliant colleagues and friends who I am grateful to for their encouragement over the past few years: Edward Dove, Agomoni Ganguli-Mitra, Isabel Fletcher, Emily Postan, Samuel Taylor-Alexander, Nayha Sethi, and Annie Sorbie. I especially thank Graeme Laurie, who led the project, without whom this work would not have been possible. I am particularly grateful for his dedication, support, and invaluable advice throughout.

Finally, I thank my father for his unwavering support and encouragement.

TABLE OF CASES

UK Cases

A (children) (conjoined twins: surgical separation) [2001] Fam 147.

Attorney-General's Reference (No 3 of 1994) [1998] AC 245.

Burton v. *Islington Health Authority and De Martell* v. *Merton and Sutton Health Authority* [1993] QB 204.

C and another v. *S and others* [1987] 1 All ER 1230.

Cohen v. *Shaw* 1992 SLT 1022.

CP (A Child) v. *First-Tier Tribunal (Criminal Injuries Compensation)* [2014] EWCA Civ 1554.

Evans v. *Amicus Healthcare Ltd*, [2004] EWCA Civ 727.

Kelly v. *Kelly* 1997 SC 285.

MB (an Adult: Medical Treatment), Re (1997) 38 BMLR 175 CA.

McWilliams v. *Lord Advocate* 1992 SLT 1045.

Nurse v. *Yerworth* (1674) 3 Swanston 608.

Paton v. *British Pregnancy Advisory Service* [1979] QB 276.

R (Quintavalle) v. *Secretary of State for Health* [2001] All ER 1013.

R (Quintavalle) v. *Secretary of State for Health* [2002] EWCA Civ 29, [2002] QB 628.

R (Quintavalle) v. *Secretary of State for Health* [2003] UKHL 13 [2003] 2 AC 687.

R v. *Bergmann and Ferguson* [1948] 1 BMJ 1008.

R v. *Bourne* [1939] 1 KB 687.

R v. *Newton and Stungo* [1958] CrimLR 469.

R v. *Trilloe* (1842) Car & M 650.

R v. *Reeves* (1839) 9 Car & P 25.

Re F (in utero) [1988] 2 All ER 193.

Re S (Adult: Refusal of Treatment) [1992] 4 All ER 671.

Re T (Adult: Refusal of Medical Treatment) [1992] 411 ER 649.

Rex v. *Goodhall* (1846) 1 Den CC 187.

Rex v. *Scudder* (1828) 1 Mood CC 216.

Rochdale Healthcare (NHS) Trust v. *C* [1997] 1 FCR 274.

Royal College of Nursing v. *Department of Health and Social Security* [1981] AC 800.

St George's Healthcare NHS Trust v. *S* [1998] All ER 673, [1998] 3 WLR 936.

Stuart v. *Reid* 2014 Rep LR 107.

The Town of Stirling v. *the Unfreemen in Falkirk and Kilsith* (1672) 2 Bro Sup 642.

ECHR

Brüggemann and Scheuten v. *Federal Republic of Germany* (1981) 3 EHRR 344.
Evans v. *UK* (2008) 46 EHRR 34.
Paton v. *UK* (1981) 3 EHRR 408.
Vo v. *France* (2005) 40 EHRR 12.

ECJ

Brüstle v. *Greenpeace* (C-34/10) [2012] All ER EC 809.

Australia

Attorney-General (ex rel Kerr) v. *T* [1983] 1 Qd R 404.

Canada

Tremblay v. *Daigle* [1989] 2 S.C.R. 530.

USA

Davis v. *Davis*, 842 S.W.2d 588, 597 (Tenn. 1992).
Kaas v. *Kaas*, 91 N.Y.2d 554 (N.Y. Ct. App. 1998).
Roe v. *Wade*, 410 U.S. 113 (1973).

TABLE OF LEGISLATION

UK Statutes

Statutory Instruments

ABBREVIATIONS

ART	assisted reproductive technology
AWT	artificial womb technology
CNR	cell nuclear replacement
ECHR	European Convention on Human Rights
ECtHR	European Court of Human Rights
ECJ	European Court of Justice
ESCs	embryonic stem cells
GMC	General Medical Council
HCSTC	House of Commons Science and Technology Committee
HFEA	Human Fertilisation and Embryology Authority
HRC Act	Human Reproductive Cloning Act 2001
ILP Act	Infant Life Preservation Act 1929
iPSCs	induced pluripotent stem cells
IVF	*in vitro* fertilisation
IVG	*in vitro* gametogenesis
MRT	mitochondrial replacement therapy
OAP Act	Offences against the Person Act (year as indicated)
PGD	preimplantation genetic diagnosis
SCR	stem cell research
UCP Bill	Unborn Child Protection Bill 1985
1803 Act	Lord Ellenborough's Act 1803
1967 Act	Abortion Act 1967
1967 Act (as amended)	Abortion Act 1967 (as amended by the Human Fertilisation and Embryology Act 2008)
1990 Act	Human Fertilisation and Embryology Act 1990
1990 Act (as amended)	Human Fertilisation and Embryology Act 1990 (as amended by the Human Fertilisation and Embryology Act 2008)
2008 Act	Human Fertilisation and Embryology Act 2008

~

Introduction

I.1 Background

In 1978, Louise Brown was the first child to be born through *in vitro* fertilisation (IVF).[1] Since then, the embryo *in vitro*, born from an assemblage of biological and technological matters, has generated complex ontological and moral questions for the law. As medical science marches forward, commonly held constructions of the embryo are becoming increasingly problematic. The physical contexts in which the embryo can exist are growing and changing, as are its possible *teleologies*.[2] The politics of fertility have been extended to new heights[3] with the harnessing, control, and enhancement of reproductive genetic procedures in the biotechnology industry. 'The embryo' – and the legal, moral, and social connotations surrounding it – is not the same 'embryo' it was over 30 years ago.

The Human Fertilisation and Embryology Act 1990 (the 1990 Act) is the key piece of legislation on the embryo *in vitro* in the United Kingdom. Yet, because of the changes and opportunities facilitated by the 1990 Act, reproduction and research have been defined and redefined,[4] in legal, cultural, social, political, and even economic senses. Arguably, its influence on our spheres of understandings in this domain can be grouped under three broad headings:

1. On the embryo *in vitro* itself
2. On science (persons and practices, e.g. research practices and researchers)

---

[1] The procedure whereby an egg is fertilised by a sperm outside of the body.

[2] For the purposes of this book, this term is used to highlight the reproductive and research ends for regulated embryos *in vitro*. This is discussed in detail in Chapter 6.

[3] S. Franklin, 'Postmodern Procreation: A Cultural Account of Assisted Reproduction' in F. Ginsburg and R. Rapp (eds.), *Conceiving The New World Order: The Global Politics of Reproduction* (University of California Press, 1995), 326.

[4] Ibid.

1

3. On the family (in the broadest sense, e.g. donors, potential parents, hypothetical mothers, and hypothetical children).

The regulation of emerging technologies may be described as the governance of processes in persistent flux, and in some cases, it is the regulation of what we do not yet know or fully understand. Reconciling process with progress, therefore, has not been easy. Nonetheless, the regulation of the embryo *in vitro*, and all the practices that law currently allows are, in essence, regulating for processes of change.[5] Considering that it has been over 30 years since the 1990 Act was passed in its original form, is it time to legally reconceive 'the embryo'?

This research was carried out as part of a five-year Wellcome Trust-funded interdisciplinary project entitled 'Confronting the Liminal Spaces of Health Research Regulation'[6] and seeks to explore the ways in which UK law engages with embryonic processes and the scientific processes to which *in vitro* embryos are subject. Embryos created *in vitro* sit at the core of modern reproductive and scientific life. They are uniquely transformative as regulated biological entities, and for that reason, they move between normative delineated legal spaces and beyond them – for example, from creation in the laboratory into the human gestational environment, or from creation in the laboratory to controlled destruction in that same sterile environment. Embryos' processual nature, for this book, lies in their growing, changing, and transforming nature.[7] Embryonic evolution is the most rapidly fluctuating biological process in human life. This complexity is mirrored in legal frameworks that are simultaneously detailed and ambiguous. In the eyes of the law that governs these entities – the 1990 Act (as amended) – embryos are neither subject (in a strict legal sense of being a legal person) nor mere object (in the strict sense of being only a 'thing'),[8] yet, as we will see, the self-same law often supports their treatment as both at the same time.

More granularly, in this book it is argued that in regulating this processual, *liminal* entity, law is regulating for uncertainty. The analysis in this book assesses the extent to which law incorporates and makes use

---

[5] S. Taylor-Alexander and others, 'Confronting the Liminal Spaces of Health Research Regulation: Beyond Regulatory Compression' (2016), *Law, Innovation and Technology*, 8(2), 149–176.

[6] Award No: WT103360MA.

[7] S. Gilbert, 'An Introduction to Early Developmental Processes' in S. Gilbert *Developmental Biology* (6th ed., Sinauer Associates, 2000).

[8] M. Fox, 'Pre-persons, Commodities or Cyborgs: The Legal Construction and Representation of the Embryo' (2000), *Health Care Analysis*, 8(2), 171–188.

of embryonic ontological boundaries. In Part I, this work calls particular attention to the legal boundedness of embryos *in vitro*, which, it is argued, are in contrast to the processes it leads embryos through. To explain, 'legal boundedness' here refers to law's tendency to put the objects of its regulation in 'silos', which can result in 'largely disconnected ecosystems'.[9] It is argued that this has contributed to a 'legal gap' between the conceptual basis of the 1990 Act (as amended) and the 'pathways' it has made available to the embryo.

Further, the analysis in this book claims that embryo regulation, as it stands, is ill equipped to deal with the multifaceted, relational[10] nature between embryos *in vitro* and the variable contexts and processes that the law takes the embryo *into, through*, and *out* of. This work thus calls for, and considers, the basis for a more coherent and robust intellectual defence of the ways in which we justify the different manners in which law treats different types of embryos created purposively towards different ends. The main questions that this book seeks to answer are the following: overall, does law reflect and embody processual regulation, if so, what does this look like? And if not, what form could it take if reform were thought to be desirable?

I.2 Analytical Framework

In order to answer the aforementioned question, a socio-legal analysis is employed that draws on the above-mentioned anthropological concept of 'liminality'. The term, coined by anthropologist Arnold Van Gennep,[11] may be described as being concerned with the spaces *in between* distinct stages of human experience, or with the *process* of transition between such stages. It is often utilised to understand, and examine, those who occupy and often transgress delineated spaces; it is inherently concerned with better comprehension of the processual nature of *becoming*. This analysis, which seeks to understand these processes, thus employs the concept of liminality in order to explore how we can apprehend legal process and legal regulation more deeply with respect to embryos that are created to become particular types of

---

[9] G. Laurie, 'Liminality and the Limits of Law in Health Research Regulation: What Are We Missing in the Spaces In-between?' (2017), *Medical Law Review*, 25(1), 47–72, 50.

[10] Relational to persons who create, use, and gestate them. Discussed further in Chapters 6 and 7.

[11] A. van Gennep, *The Rites of Passage* (University of Chicago Press, 1960).

entity, that is, a possible future person, or object of research, or possibly other ends.

To explain further, even though law has made considerable effort to clarify bio-ontological categories of being (e.g. distinguishing between gamete and embryo), these lines are still blurred. This blurring is demonstrated by ongoing debates, for example, concerning the nature, scope, and limits of embryo research, time limits on abortion, and indeed in UK and European Court of Human Rights (ECHR) case law about whether, when, and how protections might be given to the 'unborn'. A liminal lens emphasises the processual nature of biological growth in early human life – that is, a continuous process from conception to birth and beyond. Part of the problem for this analysis is, therefore, that there is a mismatch between present and evolving scientific and social understanding and legal approaches, when considered along ontological lines. This has significant moral and social implications, and thus begs a question about how well regulation in this area operates and whether it can, or should, be improved. Further, the tripartite liminal process (*into, through,* and *out*)[12] mirrors the process embryos go through under the 1990 Act (as amended). For example, embryos are led *into, through,* and *out* of research, the processes of which (especially 'through') may be prolonged by activities such as embryo freezing (see Figure 6.1).[13]

Overall, this lens enables thinking to move beyond purist legalistic approaches in a field that is especially non-legal. It implies that law requires more than legal reasoning to adequately reflect that which it regulates, especially when it comes to embryos. It also enables the analysis in this book to move *between* and *beyond* delineated legal spaces.

While liminality is central to this work, it is also argued that, as a lens, it does not wholly allow us to assess the *nature of,* and the *reasons for,* the 'legal gap' (identified in Part I). Building on the works of others,[14] it is argued that embryos *in vitro* fit well within a framing that has emerged in response to postmodern categorisations of the 'Other': principally, the

---

[12] Ibid, p. 21. Also see Chapter 6 of this book.

[13] See Figure 1, Chapter 6 of this book.

[14] Namely works by Mary Ford and Isabel Karpin. See M. Ford, 'Nothing and Not Nothing: Law's Ambivalent Response to Transformation and Transgression at the Beginning of Life' in S. Smith and R. Deazley (eds.), *The Legal, Medical and Cultural Regulation of the Body: Transformation and Transgression* (Routledge, 2009); I. Karpin, 'The Uncanny Embryos: Legal Limits to the Human and Reproduction without Women' (2006), *Sydney Law Review*, 28(4), 599–623.

'gothic'.[15] As a response to the 'Othering' of those who do not fall into law's liberalist norms (a sovereign, self-sufficient subject, or an object), a 'gothic' framing helps us to understand, more deeply, the embryo's uncertain nature, and law's responses to it therein.

I.3   Book Structure

This book has been divided into three parts: (1) *Into* Liminality, (2) *Through* Liminality, and (3) *Out* of Liminality. This division emphasises the embryonic processes that law begins, regulates, and ends, and further reflects the tripartite stages of van Gennep's processual understanding of human liminal experience.[16] The structure of this book, and each part, is briefly summarised next.

Part I

In Part I, 'Into Liminality', this work argues that the law governing embryo research and IVF has led the embryo *in vitro*, and itself (the law), *into* a form of (what this book diagnoses as) 'legal stasis'. It is important to note that this book begins with the premise of the embryo as a processual entity, rapidly transforming from one biological state to another. In other words, it is quintessentially *liminal*[17] (the meaning of which is discussed in Chapter 5). It is law's reflection of these processes, within its framework, that this book is interested in. It begins by asking: to what extent does law, in fact, reflect these processes?

Chapter 1 provides a doctrinal tracing of law's engagement with the embryo from its early construction in law to the modern day. It does so with a view to demonstrating law's evolution alongside scientific and societal understandings of the embryo. Notable from this legal history is the law's persistent efforts to engage with the uncertain, processual nature of the embryo. This chapter situates the embryo within its legal context by tracing the inception of 'the embryo' in law and the evolution of its regulation. It aims to show that throughout its relatively short legal

---

[15] See Chapter 4 of this book. Also see, for example: K. Hurley, *Gothic Body* (Cambridge University Press, 1996); V. Sage and A. L. Smith (eds.), *Modern Gothic* (Manchester University Press, 1996); F. Botting, *Gothic* (Routledge, 1996).

[16] See van Gennep, *Rites of Passage*.

[17] This framing of embryos has already been used in a different context, see S. Squier, *Liminal Lives: Imagining the Human at the Frontiers of Biomedicine* (Duke University Press, 2004).

history, the regulation of the early stages of human life has attempted (to one extent or another) to engage with the processual and uncertain nature of the early stages of human life. To this end, the chapter provides a doctrinal and analytical history of 'the embryo' in UK law. This analysis is important here, in order to show that process, in this context, matters for law-making. This framing also sets up Chapter 2's discussion of the contemporary context in which we regulate the embryo *in vitro* and serves as a stark counterpoint because, as will be shown in Chapters 2 and 3, the processual seems to be lost or overlooked today. The analysis in Chapter 2 also adopts a doctrinal approach to look at the embryo-in-law in the present day, the basis of which was set by the Warnock Report[18] and the 1990 Act (as amended). One of the primary ways in which the law has engaged with the embryo is through affording it an ethico-legal 'special status'.[19] The analysis in this chapter assesses current laws in relation to this, particularly regarding the law's engagement with embryonic processes. It finds that despite regulating a multiplicity of embryonic processes and pathways through the law (e.g. a 'research pathway', or a 'reproductive pathway'), all embryos are (at least per the intellectual basis of the 1990 Act) regulated under this singular 'special status'.

In Chapter 3 it is then argued, building upon critical literature on the regulated embryo, that in the context of the present day, the law is inadequately engaging with the embryo's uncertain, processual nature. More granularly, it explores the embryo *in vitro*'s fade from social and legal discourse. This has only intensified the confusion surrounding the 'special' legal status of the embryo, a status unclear in nature, source, and extent. Moreover, the analysis offered in this chapter highlights the temporally limited nature of law's boundary work[20] in this field. It is at this stage that this work makes a marked move from referring to 'the embryo' to referring to 'embryos' in order to reflect this multiplicity. Overall, the ossification of legal development in this area is diagnosed as a 'legal stasis'. It is argued that this is problematic because of what this book calls a 'legal gap' between the intellectual set-up of the 1990 Act and the processes that it regulates. The chapter finishes by asking two questions: (1) 'why might this be?' and (2) 'how might we move law past this stasis, assuming it is desirable to do so?'

---

[18] Report of the Committee of Inquiry into Human Fertilisation and Embryology (Cmnd 9314, 1984) (The Warnock Report).

[19] Ibid. 11.18.

[20] See Taylor-Alexander and others, 'Beyond Compression', 171.

Overall, the analysis from Part I reveals a clear juxtaposition between law, as an institution that creates clear-cut boundaries, and the embryo, as a processual, changing, and rapidly evolving liminal entity. This is not to say that the law is not processual to some extent, which in fact, as this part's analysis shows, it always has been. If process has always been central to law-making in this field, however, as the end of Chapter 3 argues, there is room for its further incorporation into our legal framework, again, assuming it is desirable to do so.

Part II

Part II, 'Through Liminality', explores a hitherto underexplored connection between a response to the postmodern that has emerged – namely, 'the gothic' – and the anthropological lens used in this book, that is, liminality. It builds upon previous analysis regarding the static nature of the regulation of the embryo *in vitro*. Chapters 4 and 5 aim to understand legal responses to embryos, and processual regulation therein, more thoroughly. This part's overarching question is thus: 'how can we understand legal process and legal regulation more deeply?'

With a view to better understanding the above-mentioned 'legal gap', characterised by uncertainty and caution, the analysis in Chapter 4 explores parallels that may be drawn between embryos and a concept that has evolved as a response to the 'Othering' of certain sectors of society: the 'gothic self'. This concept is closely linked to the 'monstrous' and explores the ways in which we respond to persons (and entities) that are not self-sovereign (something that law arguably presupposes). In exploring this framing, this analysis draws on the work of Mary Ford[21] and Isabel Karpin[22] and frames the regulated embryo *in vitro* as paradigmatic of 'the gothic', and emphasises the utility, for law, in recognising the parallels between this concept and embryos. It is argued that framing embryos *in vitro* as 'gothic' is undoubtedly useful for understanding the nature of, and the reasons for, our current regulatory framework more deeply. Nonetheless, it is also argued that, as a frame of analysis, 'the gothic' alone does not address the 'legal gap' fully. This is because it does not directly deal with understanding the dynamics of process in a deeper sense, which, as Part I shows, is required in order to answer its second question: (2) how might we move law past this 'stasis',

---

[21] See Ford, 'Nothing and Not-Nothing'.
[22] See Karpin, 'Uncanny Embryos'.

assuming it is desirable to do so? Chapter 4 thus leaves the question: how might we regulate embryos more processually?

In Chapter 5 the anthropological concept of liminality[23] is introduced and discussed, which – as already noted – is concerned with the dynamics of processes and states of in-betweenness. After Van Gennep developed liminality in the context of tribal societies, others, including Victor Turner,[24] have since built on this concept to encompass several dimensions within modern societies.[25] For this analysis, then, liminality can be used as a tool to help show us how law, along with the embryo, can emerge out of the regulatory purgatory they are in today. Indeed, current law may arguably be described as reflecting many of the major symptoms of 'permanent liminality',[26] a modern theory of liminality concerned with that which does not emerge out of the 'other side' of processes/change. It is argued that both embryos *in vitro* and the law that governs them have features of 'permanent liminality'. Finally, this analysis will draw on lessons from Chapter 4 in order to consider what 'the gothic' and liminality, combined, might tell us about how we can close the previously discussed 'legal gap'.

By the end of Part II, it is shown that there are ways that law can better (in terms of processuality) navigate and capture the contexts that it is leading the embryo *through*. Yet how can law better reflect the uncertain nature of embryonic processes and the technologies that create them? The answer to this is addressed in Part III.

Part III

In Part III, 'Out of Liminality', this research explores how lessons learned from a gothic analysis and a liminal lens (per Part II) may be taken from *conceptualisation to realisation*. It is argued that if the law were to take process seriously (as it has done in the past), and that if liminality teaches us about the permanent liminality of law in this area, then it is perhaps time for the law to explicitly recognise the separate contexts that it is leading the embryo *into, through,* and *out* of.

---

[23] See van Gennep, 'Rites of Passage'.

[24] V. Turner, *The Forest of Symbols: Aspects of Ndembu Ritual* (Cornell University Press, 1967).

[25] For example, see Squier, 'Liminal Lives'.

[26] Á. Szakolczai, 'Permanent (Trickster) Liminality: The Reasons of the Heart and of the Mind' (2017), *Theory and Psychology*, 27, 231–248.

Chapter 6 offers an exploration of what processual regulation *could* look like, as a framework for governing the use and production of embryos *in vitro*. Given that liminality, as a lens, enables us to understand more deeply the multiplicity of contexts in which embryos are used and created, it shall be argued that if law wants to continue accounting for process, as it has done in the past, then it might consider what this book calls a 'context-based approach'. This approach, which explicitly attempts to recognise the separate contexts that law is leading embryos *into, through,* and *out* of, is not prescribed per se but rather offered as a way of legally embracing a processual approach (if that is indeed what we want for law).

Finally, in Chapter 7, the broader implications that a context-based approach might have for three contemporary discussions surrounding recent advancements in science and technology are considered: *in vitro* gametogenesis (IVG), the fourteen-day rule, and partial ectogenesis via artificial womb technologies (AWTs). Importantly, the analysis offered in this chapter is not assessing what we *should* do, but what law *could* possibly do via this approach. It emphasises that the analysis of this book can *add* to legal, ethical, and social discussions about embryos *in vitro*.

I.4   Key Terms

'Embryo'

First, it is important to acknowledge the undecidable, unknowable nature of 'the embryo' (or 'embryos') in definitional terms. There is undoubtedly some disparity within scientific communities themselves, as well as between natural sciences and the social sciences, with regard to their definition.[27] Navigating the biological definition, or purporting to define the embryo in general, is not the aim of this book.

Second, this analysis is primarily concerned with embryos *in vitro*. It does not extend as far as to discuss the research upon and/or use of fetal or abortus tissue. Nonetheless, due to the nature of tracing the legal history of governing this early stage of human life, Chapter 2 does not exclusively focus on embryos (of which there was very little mention until the twentieth century) and thus uses embryo/fetus interchangeably until a concrete *legal* distinction emerges in the chronology.

---

[27] See M. Jacob and B. Prainsack, 'Embryonic Hopes: Controversy, Alliance, and Reproductive Entities in Law and the Social Sciences' (2010). *Social Legal Studies*, 19(4), 497–517.

Third, it is clear that 'the embryo', however defined in law, has no objective definition (like many things), nor shall one be provided here. Rather, law's navigation of actual/possible/multiple definitions are explored, as they have changed throughout history, and as they are used today. It is argued that this navigation is important for the future of human health, as it is greatly affected by the governance of the use of embryos for reproduction and research. As stated, this work will focus on the embryo *in vitro* as a cornerstone to the regulation of reproduction and research under the 1990 Act (as amended). Thus, for the purpose of references to the entity within this book, when referring to embryos *in vitro*, it is referring to entities created within the rubric of the 1990 Act (as amended), in line with the legal definition of embryo given in the legislation under s. 1.

This definition has been used because it is used in the primary legislation with which this research is concerned. By taking this definition, this work is not necessarily supporting its use within law. The above describes what the 1990 Act (as amended) calls 'permitted embryo' (i.e. a 'human' embryo) is human and anything else is not, but it is nonetheless unclear on what 'human' entails. How we should define embryos, or indeed 'human' embryos, is a matter beyond the ambit of this work, the reasoning for which is discussed briefly next, and further in Chapter 7. It was nonetheless important to clarify this here and in advance of the discussion which follows.

In sum, herein when 'the embryo' is referred to here, it is primarily referring to the embryo-in-law (as opposed to 'the embryo' in other contexts). Notably, at the end of Chapter 3, this analysis makes a marked shift from referring to 'the embryo' to 'embryos' in order to reflect the findings of Part I (the multiple 'embryos' governed under the 1990 Act's singular 'special status'). Exceptions are made to this when discussing the works of others.

The Embryo's 'Moral Status' and 'Legal Status'

'Moral status' and 'legal status' are referred to throughout this text in reference to embryos and occasionally fetuses. Here, 'moral status' is primarily taken to mean the moral standing of embryos within society.[28] While the 'moral status' of the embryo is mentioned throughout, it is not the focus of this work per se. Nonetheless, this analysis

---

[28] See A. Jaworska, and J. Tannenbaum, 'The Grounds of Moral Status' (*The Stanford Encyclopedia of Philosophy*, 10 January 2018),www.plato.stanford.edu/entries/grounds-moral-status/.

recognises that neither the embryo's moral status[29] nor value[30] is either fixed or unfixed; there is no objective truth in this regard. 'Legal status' is used to refer to the status afforded to embryos *in vitro* in law, by the 1990 Act (as amended), and underpinned reflection of the Warnock Report's recommendations, a 'special status'. Notably, the meaning of, or contours of, this 'special status' is not described within the Warnock Report. Legal status is of course inherently moralistic, and the key focus for this work is law's interpretation and reflection of this. What the moral status of the embryo is, or should be, is a separate debate. No particular stance is taken in this regard because it is not necessary to do so for the purposes of this book. In addition to the aforementioned, it is also important to acknowledge that there is a crucial legal difference between the 'legal status' of the embryo for IVF and research, and the legal status of the embryo in an abortion context. This difference in moral status was not set out in law (albeit not explicitly articulated) until the 1990 Act.

Overall, the primary point of interrogation of the argument offered in this book is the way in which law navigates embryonic moral status – as focused upon in the Warnock Report – rather than the embryo's intrinsic moral value (which is more difficult for law to capture).

'Process'

As mentioned earlier, this book starts with the premise that 'the embryo' is a processual entity. This subsection explains what is meant by 'process' for the purposes of this work.

There is not one definitive way in which we can talk about process, generally speaking. For the purposes of this book, process is a focal point for two reasons: the inherently (perhaps undeniably) processual, transformational, and rapidly changing nature of embryos *in vitro*; and the regulation of multiple scientific processes (e.g. implantation, research, or cloning) under the framework of the 1990 Act (as amended).

The *Oxford English Dictionary* defines 'process' as 'going on, continuous action, proceeding', and philosophically as 'the course of becoming as opposed to static being'.[31] The term 'process' is employed here in line with these definitions, and the term is relied upon in order to highlight

---

[29] Ibid.
[30] See M. Schroeder, 'Value Theory' (*The Stanford Encyclopedia of Philosophy*, Fall 2016 Edition), Edward Zalta (ed.), www.plato.stanford.edu/archives/fall2016/entries/value-theory/.
[31] 'process, n.', (*OED Online*. June 2020).

the importance of the different steps taken in achieving (potential) embryonic ends. As mentioned earlier, process is an integral part of the liminality literature. Arnold van Gennep used it to highlight the transitional aspects of tribal rites of passage, and much later, Susan Squier discussed the cultural impact(s) of relatively new processes of becoming that embryos (among other entities, e.g. fetuses) can go through as a result of the transformation of medicine.[32] Integral parts of these (liminal) processes are thus a sense of transition, transformation, and becoming, from one state to another. This is what is referred to in this book when the phrase 'processuality of law' is used, whether by reconsidering it, considerably evolving it, or moving boundaries.

I.5   Dimensions of the Enquiry

This section draws out the contours of this book by, first, delineating what it is *not* about and, second, emphasising the key dimensions of this enquiry.

This Book is Not About . . .

How we *ought* to treat embryos, legally or otherwise. As Emily Jackson concludes in *Regulating Reproduction,* 'law is not capable of divining any absolute truths about the moral status of the embryo'.[33] While law cannot distil any objective truths, it arguably still needs to divine some sort of 'right' based on social consensus, and if it is to do so – as it has done – it has to go forth in a legally appropriate[34] manner. It should therefore be noted that what the embryo's moral status *should* be is not directly discussed, but rather the aspects of its regulation that liminality (and the gothic) calls into question. This helps us to critique the law *as it is*. It is suggested that if the law is not well justified, then it becomes problematic for society and for those affected by it. Neither a gothic framing nor liminality necessarily provides a concrete answer to this contentious issue. Nonetheless, it is contended that, as an analytical framework, they can enable us to think about more justifiable ways to regulate embryos in their various states of *becoming.*

---

[32] Particularly, as they are affected (and 'reconfigured') by the relationship between biomedicine and science fiction. See Squier, 'Liminal Lives'.

[33] E. Jackson, *Regulating Reproduction* (Hart, 2001), p. 229.

[34] By 'legally appropriate', I mean appropriate for the pathways or processes it enables persons to put embryos through.

Thus, this analysis is primarily interested in how law deals with the reality of a plurality of entities – embryos – created with different purposes in mind. It is concerned with law's creation of possible pathways and with how it regulates those entities in question as they proceed along the respective pathways. The offering in this book is thus a forensic analysis of law's role in challenging and acknowledging these pathways and providing appropriate structure around them ('appropriate' here meaning that it is suitable for that pathway, and the end to which each pathway leads).

This Book is About . . .

With all of the above in mind, the following delineates the key areas of enquiry for this book, broken up into three parts:

- Part I: In what ways does UK law engage with embryonic processes, if at all?
- Part II: How can we understand legal process and legal regulation more deeply?
- Part III: How can law better reflect the uncertain nature of embryonic processes and the technologies that create them?

Overall, this book asks: does law reflect and embody processual regulation? If so, what does this look like? And if not, what form could it take if reform were thought to be desirable?

Now, to Part I of this book, which begins by exploring the ways in which law has engaged with the embryo as a biological entity of unclear and changing parameters.

PART I

Into Liminality

Part I of this book asks: how consistently does, and can, law treat the embryo? The answer, in short, is that law has treated the embryo inconsistently, and this is due to law changing relatively regularly, historically speaking, to reflect changing knowledge and perceptions of the early stages of human life. In other words, process has been central to law-making. With a view to demonstrating this, the analysis in Chapter 1 provides a historical account of law's engagement with embryonic (and fetal) processes. Building on this, the focus of Chapters 2 and 3 is development of law since the advent of *in vitro* fertilisation (IVF) and the regulatory framework imposed by legislation such as the 1990 Act (as amended). The point is made that while we persist in talking about 'the embryo' in lay and legal circles, law has in fact created a multiplicity of embryos, as, for example, future persons and as research 'artefacts',[1] to name just two. Part I ends with the following conclusions: (1) process is important for law-making in this field and, relatedly, (2) there is a 'legal gap' between the intellectual basis and practical 'realities' of the present framework. This 'problem' then becomes the basis for consideration of alternative conceptualisations explored in Part II.

---

[1] J. K. Mason, *Human Life and Medical Practice* (Edinburgh University Press, 1988), p. 94.

1

The Evolution of 'the Embryo' in Law

A Matter of Process?

1.1 Introduction

Reproductive law in the United Kingdom has developed against a background of competing and changing interests. These interests include a morass of moral and religious values, and, further, the perceived interests of the embryo, the mother, and medical professionals. As time has passed and our biological understandings of the early stages of human life have evolved, the law has attempted to recalibrate the balance of these interests in one way or another. Although reproductive technologies and embryo research have only been available for a handful of decades, legal protection of the embryo (and the fetus) dates back several hundred years. This chapter offers a brief historical tracing of the presence of the embryo in statute and case law (or lack thereof) in the United Kingdom. It has been written as a precursor to a central contribution of this book: if the law wants to continue to reflect the processual nature of the embryo, then we require a frame of legal analysis that captures the embryo's uncertain, processual nature that can inform policy responses to its existence and use. This frame of analysis, a liminal lens, shall be discussed in Part II.

This chapter chronologically traces past legal engagement with the human embryo, from the thirteenth century to the end of the twentieth century. It does so with a view to demonstrating that a historical perspective is required to understand that process is a key facet of lawmaking in this area. Notable from this legal history is the law's persistent efforts to engage with the embryo's uncertain, processual nature. We cannot fully understand our present legal position without understanding the social, moral, and legal contexts from which it was born. By looking at the past 'legal embryo', we can see how the law has reached today's 'legal embryo'. Before this tracing begins, however, some points of clarification should be noted.

First, while the following account focuses on legal history in reference to governance of the early stages of human life, there are other aspects of this history that, for example, direct us to consider the gendering effects of law on women's lives, and it is thus important to note that there are different ways in which history can be told.[2] This book tells history from the perspective of law's engagement with the embryo, with a view to exploring the origins of the legal embryo (i.e. the embryo in law), as an entity distinct from the legal fetus – the beginnings of which are intertwined with evolving understandings of the early stages of human life at the time.

Second, it is important to be clear, at this stage, that the legal demarcation of 'stages' of human life might be seen as categorical, and thus antiprocessual. This is not untrue. Nonetheless, a key point about the development of these 'categories', for this book, is that it (eventually) moved law towards increasingly recognising the transformative nature of gestation and embryonic growth. Another key point, for this chapter, is that to some extent the processual nature of the embryo (*in vivo*) has historically been central to law and legal development. As the next section shall discuss, the origins of legal demarcation between different 'stages' of development go as far back as the thirteenth century in the United Kingdom.

Third, 'the embryo', as an entity, was relatively rarely mentioned in law until the inception of the 1990 Act, although prior laws did govern what we would now call 'the embryonic stages of life'. For these reasons, the following section looks at law's navigation of changing scientific and social perceptions of what we might term 'embryos' and 'fetuses' today, until a legal distinction between these two entities emerged. While this book recognises that 'embryos' and 'fetuses' are commonly considered different biological[3] entities, legally, socially, and scientifically, the demarcation lines between the two remain somewhat blurred, particularly historically. Thus, with the absence of a historical distinction between the two – where both were often referred to as 'the child' – in this first section these terms are used interchangeably where a historical legal distinction has not been made and where such fluid terminology was also used. Relatedly, it is important to note that the embryo *in utero* is relevant for the purposes of this chapter in order to provide a holistic

[2] To echo S. McGuinness and M. Thompson, 'Medicine and Abortion Law: Complicating the Reforming Profession' (2015), *Medical Law Review*, 23(2), 177–199.
[3] This may be considered as different from whether or not one considers embryos and fetuses to be *morally* distinct entities.

overview of the frameworks from which our present one was born. Nonetheless, as the analysis offered here is primarily concerned with the embryo *in vitro* and the regulation of the earliest stages of human life, in later sections the working definition of 'embryo' (at least in terms of demarcating it from a fetus) shall be the early stages of human life as regulated by the 1990 Act.[4]

Fourth, while 'process' and the development of regulatory frameworks are discussed here, the use of the word 'process' should not be taken to imply that these developments were a form of progress, or indeed, 'progressive'. As the following discussion shall show, many legal developments throughout history may be described by some as anti-progressive, particularly for the reproductive rights of women.

Overall, this chapter will show that

- looking purely at contemporary debates on the regulation of embryos *in vitro* would give an incomplete picture of processual regulation, and
- we need a historical perspective to understand that process matters for the regulation of the early stages of human life.

Before we turn to the chronological tracing, the next subsection provides a brief background on 'quickening', a key biological moment for law from the thirteenth to late nineteenth centuries.

1.2 Background

The basis of English and Scots laws governing the early stages of human life, in both civil and criminal contexts, may be found in a concept used in early Christian religious philosophy: 'quickening'. To explain, the term 'quickening', per its use in law, was derived from the ecclesiastical distinction between an *embryo formatus* and an *embryo informatus*[5] – based on the belief that there is a difference between embryos that had 'animated' (began to move within the womb), and thus had a 'soul' (and could therefore be baptised), and those that had not. 'Quickening', a term still used today, refers to the point in pregnancy at which the fetus

---

[4] It is important to note that the purpose of this is not to imply that a clear differentiation should be made between the two stages of growth, but to provide some descriptive clarity for the reader. Biologically, there may be some crossover with current definitions of the fetus, but as there is no clear legal distinction between the two entities, it would not be useful for this book to attempt to make one at this juncture.

[5] B. Dickens, *Abortion and the Law* (MacGibbon and Kee, 1996); G. Williams, *The Sanctity of Life and the Criminal Law* (Knopf, 1957).

becomes 'animated'; in other words, when the woman first feels the fetus's movements in her womb. Throughout much of history, this stage of pregnancy has been of huge philosophical and practical importance to pregnant women; in the days before pregnancy test kits, quickening was often the first (and only) sure sign of pregnancy. For centuries, quickening remained as a legal and moral dividing line when interference (resulting in termination) may (or may not) occur. The law thus started off, in reference to the embryo/fetus, by treating pregnancy in two stages.[6] This is mirrored in Bracton's distinction between a 'formed' fetus and a 'quickened' fetus, in Section 1.3.

It is worth noting that at a similar time to the development and use of 'quickening' in UK law, 'preformation', a theory of the beginnings of human life, was commonly touted by scientists, particularly in the eighteenth century. The theory of preformation, in its original form, held that a 'homunculus' (pre-formed person) was 'planted' in the woman during sexual intercourse, which then grew in size over nine months in her womb.[7] For preformationists, biological growth was thus a matter of physical growth, not biological process. This contrasts with epigenesis:

> For Aristotle, the causes lie internal to the combined fluids rather than outside. An individual life begins when the male and female semen are brought together. This is an external action and it starts the individual developmental process in motion. From that point on, the process is internal and driven by internal causes. The process then leads to development of form of the individual's type.[8]

Thus, to contrast the theories: in one the woman is essentially an incubator, whereas the other recognises (at least more so) the essential role of the woman in embryonic process, with '[p]reformation, stability, and predictability stood on one side, with epigenesis, dynamic process, and change on the other'.[9] While this theory is not referenced in Hansard at any point in parliamentary discussions on the embryo, it is highly

---

[6] For clarificatory purposes: considering that mothers usually cannot feel movement until the 16–20 week stage, in the following sections reference to 'quickening' refers to a stage which we, today, would call the early stage life in the mother's womb a 'fetus' and not an 'embryo'.

[7] A. Baxter, 'Edmund B. Wilson as a Preformationist: Some Reasons for His Acceptance of the Chromosome Theory' (1976), *Journal of the History of Biology*, 9(1), 29–57, 30.

[8] J. Maienschein, 'Epigenesis and Preformationism' (*The Stanford Encyclopedia of Philosophy*, first published 11 October 2015), www.plato.stanford.edu/archives/spr2017/entries/epigenesis/.

[9] Ibid.

possible that the rise and fall of preformation theory had a direct effect on the law. As we shall see later, the return of epigenesis in the nineteenth century coincided with the removal of the quickening distinction; in its place came a more processual legal approach.

It was not until the late eighteenth century that doctors started to learn more about the nature of the embryo/fetus pre-quickening, and eventually the embryo's cellular processes became clearer in the nineteenth century with advances in microscopy. Interestingly, Aristotle is also credited with the theory of epigenesis (the theory that an embryo evolves from cell differentiation), the cellular theory commonly held today (albeit in a different form than Aristotle's). Thus, preformation and epigenesis stood in stark contrast until the latter was proven biologically accurate through experiments in the nineteenth century.[10] Until then, the law addressed scientific (and perhaps moral) uncertainty surrounding how we should treat embryos by providing no sanction against interference at this stage.

1.3   Pre-nineteenth Century

Henry of Bracton[11] made one of the earliest recorded references to the relationship between early human life and the law in the United Kingdom. Writing in the thirteenth century, he posited that where a fetus had formed or quickened, terminating it while *en ventre sa mere* (in the mother's womb) was murder:[12]

> If one strikes a pregnant woman or gives her poison in order to procure an abortion, if the fetus is already formed or quickened, especially if it is quickened, he commits homicide.[13]

It seems that for Bracton, causing the miscarriage of a fetus that had began moving was more morally and legally criminal than terminating a fetus that had only formed, which occurs several weeks before quickening (around week 8).[14] Here lies one of the first instances of an attempt

---

[10] Baxter, 'Edmund B. Wilson as a Preformationist', 30.

[11] Also known as Henry Bretton, Henry Bratton, and Henry de Bracton.

[12] S. Thorne (trans.), *Bracton on the Laws and Customs of England*, vol. II (Belknap, 1968); A. Grubb, 'Abortion Law in England: The Medicalization of a Crime' (1990), *Journal of Law and Medical Ethics*, 18(1–2), 146–161, 147.

[13] Thorne, *Bracton*, p. 341.

[14] 'Your Pregnancy Week by Week' (*NHS*, 17 July 2017), www.nhs.uk/conditions/pregnancy-and-baby/pages/pregnancy-weeks-4–5–6–7–8.aspx?tabname=pregnancy.

to account for process in law. While this was of course not explicit, one can infer from the use of quickening as a legal 'marker' that there was some degree of recognition of rapid growth and development of the early stages of life *in utero*. Critics might argue that this was a matter of legal utility rather than an attempt to recognise process; as discussed earlier, it would have been difficult to know at this time whether or not a woman was pregnant before quickening. Nonetheless, it is argued here that 'processual law'[15] – described later – does not have to be intended or created with the purpose of being processual. Nor was it always entirely processual. Notably, it is the importance of the process of development for making and amending law that this offering wishes to highlight.

In 1641, Sir Edward Coke wrote that while the abortion of a fetus was a 'great misprision', it was 'no murder'.[16] He did, however, consider abortion worthy of criminal punishment:

> If a woman be quick with childe, and by a potion or otherwise killeth it in her wombe, or if a man beat her, whereby the child dyeth in her body, and she is delivered of a dead childe, this is great misprision, and no murder; but if he childe be born alive and dyeth of the potion, battery, or other cause, this is murder: for in law it is accounted a reasonable creature, in *rerum natura*, when it is born alive.[17]

In other words, at this time, terminating an unborn embryo/fetus was not 'murder' in common law yet still a punishable criminal offence. As of yet, 'the embryo' had not emerged as a legally recognised entity. It was not granted legal protection at this stage, nor was it commonly referred to in law. It seems that the legal 'marker' at this time was based on what they 'relied' on as evidence (at least, what they thought they could rely on). It is unclear what was meant here by 'born alive', but from his discussion of the status of the 'child' in the womb in the sentence beforehand, we can glean that Coke was referring to *ex utero*, or 'born' children. This type of approach, to some extent, accounts for the processes that need to take place *in utero* and during birth, before an embryo/fetus can be 'born alive'.

One of the earliest direct legal references to an 'embryo' in the United Kingdom may be found a short time after Coke's writings, but in Scots

---

[15] By this, I mean law that accounts for process in one way or another (although not necessarily 'fully').

[16] E. Coke, *Institutions of the Laws of England Vol. III* (1622), p. 50.

[17] Ibid.

law, in the case of *The Town of Stirling* v. *the Unfreemen in Falkirk and Kilsith* from 1672:[18]

> That there is a great difference to be made between a law that never attained observance, and a law that once was observed, but has long lain in desuetude; the second is, indeed, a law, because it had once a perfect and a consummate being; the first is no better than an embryo, and deserves not the name of a law; and of this kind be the acts founded upon by the pursuers. That the regalities have possessed all these privileges immemorially.[19]

The above phrase 'no better than an embryo' arguably suggests that the advocate for the Town of Stirling (who later became Lord Fountainhall) regarded embryos as less deserving of legal recognition than one that had been 'observed' (i.e. the pregnancy was visible/tangible). Growth *in utero*, to the point of physical visibility, had to have been observed then, for the law to recognise the fetus as deserving of its attention (here, retrospectively). Furthermore, it exemplifies understandings of embryonic/fetal growth's effect on the physical, legal limits of proof at that time, where quickening still applied as both a civil and a criminal law test.[20]

Writing almost a century later, William Blackstone traced the historical evolution of abortion in common law, confirming the writings of those before him. Although his works were predominantly written in relation to civil rights and civil immunities under the heading of the right of security, his commentary provides insight into the legal status of the embryo at that time and the preceding years:

> Life is the immediate gift of God, a right inherent by nature in every individual; and it begins in contemplation of law as soon as an infant is able to stir in the mother's womb. For if a woman is quick with child, and by a potion, or otherwise, killeth it in her womb; or if any one beat her, whereby the child dieth in her body, and she is delivered of a dead child; this, though not murder, was by the antient law homicide or manslaughter. But at present it is not looked upon in quite so atrocious a light, though it remains a very heinous misdemeanour. An infant in *ventre sa mere*, or in the mother's womb, is supposed in law to be born for many purposes. It is capable of having a legacy, or a surrender of a copyhold estate made to it. It may have a guardian assigned to it; and it is enabled to have an estate limited to its use, and to take afterwards by such limitation,

---

[18] (1672) 2 Bro Sup 642.
[19] Ibid., at 644.
[20] See *Nurse* v. *Yerworth* (1674) 3 Swanston 608, 620.

as if it were then actually born. And in this point the civil law agrees with ours.[21]

Stages in growth process, however demarcated, were thus important for criminal purposes. At this time (1765), and in contrast to earlier years, while the abortion of a quickened fetus was a criminal offence, it was not murder.

Moreover, quickening evolved as a bright moral *and* legal line for other areas of criminal sanction, too. A few years later, in 1770, Blackstone wrote:

> Life begins in contemplation of law as soon as an infant is able to stir in the mother's womb . . . [t]o be saved from the gallows a woman must be quick with child – for barely with child, unless he be alive in the womb, is not sufficient.[22]

The firm sanctions provided by criminal law thus intertwined with civil law to depict the physically apparent, quickened fetus as if it were 'born' for many legal purposes.[23] Indeed, before the invention of ultrasound technology (in the twentieth century, discussed later) it would be hard to know that an embryo was there, and in order to be guilty of procuring or attempting to procure an abortion, *mens rea* was necessary.[24] Similarly, intent to leave inheritance could not be presumed at that time where quickening had not occurred. In fact, in this era law was more commonly concerned with the unborn 'child' as a potential inheritor, than as a potential 'victim'; the majority of case law on unborn children at this time fell within the civil realm.[25] The underlying presence of the criminal law remained nonetheless. Although Blackstone noted that abortion was no longer a very serious offence, the common law continued to take it as a lesser criminal yet still 'heinous'[26] criminal offence. It seems that at this time, before early-stage pregnancy was

---

[21] W. Blackstone, 'Amendment IX, Document I', in *Commentaries on the Laws of England* (Chicago University Press, 1765), p. 388.

[22] W. Blackstone, *Blackstone's Commentaries*, 4th ed. (Clarendon Press, 1770) p. 129; quoted in D. Madden, *Medicine, Ethics and the Law in Ireland*, 2nd ed. (Bloomsbury Professional, 2011) p. 206.

[23] For example, the law of inheritance, or the criminal offence of causing an abortion.

[24] While the presence of *mens rea* as a requirement in law has been variable throughout English legal history, it can be traced back to Bracton's time. See E. Chesney, 'Concept of *Mens Rea* in the Criminal Law' (1939), *Journal of Criminal Law and Criminology*, 29(5), 627–644.

[25] Based upon searches via Westlaw, and other online case law resources.

[26] Blackstone, *Commentaries*, p. 388.

ascertainable by medicine, law's way of dealing with uncertainty with regard to the embryo/fetus was not to attach any criminal offence. Only when the fetus's presence was certain could an offence have occurred.

To summarise the above, the origins of legal protection of the early stages of human life in the United Kingdom date back as far as the thirteenth century, with 'quickening' acting as a bright legal and moral boundary. For centuries afterwards, this distinction stood fast and became crystallised in our legal system through common law, and then through statutes. This crystallisation may be attributed to the low technical and physical visibility of the embryo/fetus during these times. The distinction between pre- and post-quickening was evidently a demarcation that remained important for law in the United Kingdom during the seventeenth and eighteenth centuries. Although *partus formatus* was less commonly referred to at this time, pre-quickening and pre-*partus formatus* were thought to occur at a similar time, when the 'whole body' of the fetus has formed, usually in the third month. But how do these boundaries interact with processes? As explored in Chapters 2–3, legal boundaries, based on understandings of embryonic/fetal processes, were tallied with law's requirement for some sort of certainty with regard to what we can and cannot do (in both criminal and civil law).

1.4   The Nineteenth Century

The early 1800s saw the introduction of stricter criminal sentences against those who interfered with embryos/fetuses *in vivo*. It also witnessed the introduction of statutory frameworks on the matter, which provided more legal detail than previously. The legal sanctions attached to the pre- and post-quickening distinction of the seventeenth and early eighteenth centuries were reinstated by one of the first Acts of English law which gave status to what we would now refer to as the fetus (then 'child'), Lord Ellenborough's Act 1803 (the 1803 Act).[27] While causing the termination of a pregnancy did not constitute murder in and of itself under the statute, it rendered an *intended* act of causing or performing an abortion one that was punishable by death.[28] Under s. 1, the death penalty was prescribed where an abortion was attempted or performed

---

[27] Also known as the 'Malicious Shooting or Stabbing Act 1803'.
[28] A similar Act was also enacted in Scotland around this time – see Malicious Wounding, etc. (Scotland Act) 1825.

post-quickening. Otherwise, s. 2 prescribed 'transportation'[29] for four-teen years. In other words, the 1803 Act differentiated between procure-ment, or attempts to procure an abortion, *before* and *after* 'quickening'.

The Offences Against the Person Act 1828 (OAP Act 1828)[30] repealed the 1803 Act in its consolidation of offences against the person, and once again, prescribed the death penalty for post-quickening abortions[31] (pre-quickening abortions were deemed a lesser offence). While s. 2 of the 1803 Act only punished abortions carried out via the use of instruments or tools, the OAP Act 1828 extended this prohibition on post-quickening abortion to include efforts carried out by *any* means. Sir Robert Peel, who steered the OAP Act 1828 through the House of Commons, declared that the purpose of the Bill was to clarify and simplify the frameworks and that its contents were considered desirable by 'persons whose knowledge of the subject and experience entitled their opinions to credit and respect'.[32] Thus, as (relatively) modern medicine grew as a discipline, law increas-ingly drew its attention to it.[33]

Capital punishment for attempting to procure or causing post-quickening abortions was not repealed until the Offences Against the Person Act 1837 (OAP Act 1837). The objective of the OAP Act 1837 was to render the law relating to offences against the person more lenient, thereby facilitating enforcement.[34] Interestingly, this Act also revoked the enduring distinction between pre- and post-quickening abortions. Section 6 of the OAP Act 1837 replaced this section of the OAP Act 1828 and abolished the death penalty for abortions 'post-quickening'. While an offence under the new Act no longer prescribed capital punishment, the penalties remained harsh. Section 8 of the OAP Act 1828 prescribed hard labour and solitary confinement as punishments. Now, 'causing miscar-riage' at any stage of pregnancy was a punishable offence. Thus, as techno-logical perceptions of the fetus became clearer (visibly and physically),

---

[29] A common alternative to the death penalty in the eighteenth and part of the nineteenth centuries, where convicted criminals were transported to one of the colonies to serve their sentences.

[30] Also known as 'Lord Lansdowne's Act'. This Act only applied in England and Wales.

[31] OAP Act 1828, s. 13.

[32] (1828) 19 Pad Deb HC, 350.

[33] As an aside, alongside its incorporation of medical opinion, the law was undoubtedly also affected by changing variables in society, religion, economy, and political agendas (for example). Thus, these other factors of course also affected the level and series of punish-ments attached.

[34] J. Keown, *Abortion, Doctors and the Law: Some Aspects of the Legal Regulation of Abortion in England from 1803 to 1982* (Cambridge University Press, 2002).

quickening was gradually replaced as a legal marker by other earlier stages of pregnancy. For example, the stethoscope was invented a few years before the OAP Act 1828 by Laennec and became widely adopted by physicians; it was used to perceive movement and the heartbeat of the fetus within the mother's womb.[35] In the dissolution of the pre- and post-quickening distinction, it seems that legal protection had been extended to all stages of pregnancy, including what we would call 'the embryo' today. Thus, the early stages of human life *in vivo* were protected in law from the moment of conception (as long as it could be proven that the woman was pregnant).[36] Apparently the reasoning behind this change was the subjectivity of the criterion for 'quickening',[37] which, as aforementioned, is based on the woman's first perception of fetal movement.

As pregnancy became a more medicalised process[38] (and less of a religious 'event') – which seemingly resulted in the medicalisation of abortion law – quickening dissolved as a bright moral and legal limit, and the law began to move towards the (relatively) more gradualist approach we have today. The medicalisation of pregnancy coincided with increased visual knowledge of early stages of human life (e.g. post-mortem experimentation in 1723 revealed that male and female embryos do not develop at different rates).[39] Nonetheless, as we have seen, while the harshness of sanctions against the termination of pregnancy declined with the rise of medicine, the law became increasingly restrictive at the same time. The disappearance of 'quickening' from the OAP Act 1837 suggests that the appeals of obstetricians and doctors at the time did not go unnoticed.[40] Remarkably, a survey revealed that there was no consensus that quickening marked the start of fetal life in the areas of medical jurisprudence and obstetrics.[41] As far back as 1794, there have been recorded medical claims

---

[35] J. Heilbron, *The Oxford Companion to the History of Modern Science* (Oxford University Press, 2003).

[36] *Rex v. Scudder* (1828) 1 Mood CC 216.

[37] 'Correspondence between his Majesty's Principal Secretary of State for the Home Department and the Commissioners Appointed to Inquire into the State of the Criminal Law' (1837) HC XXXI 43.

[38] To quote Marie Fox: 'I share Sheldon's understanding of "medicalization" as a process whereby medical discourses become dominant to the extent that other understandings and knowledges are marginalized', in M. Fox, 'Pre-persons, Commodities or Cyborgs', 185; S. Sheldon, '"Who is the Mother to Make the Judgment?": The Constructions of Woman in English Abortion Law' (1993), *Feminist Legal Studies*, 1(1), 3–22.

[39] J. Needham, *A History of Embryology*, 2nd ed. (Cambridge University Press, 2015), p. 76.

[40] Keown, 'Abortion, Doctors and the Law', p. 33.

[41] Based largely on the Index-Catalogue of the Library of the Office of the Surgeon-General (Washington, DC); see Keown, 'Abortion, Doctors and the Law', p. 31.

that there is no difference between a/the pre- and post-quickening 'child', aside from its growing size.[42] Medical opinion at that – and earlier – time thus undermined the significance which law (and lay opinion) ascribed to quickening.[43] Nonetheless, as shown here, the law eventually caught up with this approach.

Several years later, the Offences Against the Person Act 1861 (OAP Act 1861) wholly repealed the OAP Act 1837. Until the OAP Act 1861, it was unclear whether it constituted an offence for a woman to commit self-abortion. The new Act confirmed the tripartite features of the ruling in *R v. Goodhall* (1846):[44] (1) that pregnancy was not necessary for an offence to have occurred where committed by a third party; (2) the prohibition of self-abortion; and (3) the offence of obtaining or supplying means commonly known as intended to procure a miscarriage.[45] The law had thus gradually developed in a manner that increased its restriction on abortion through the medium of criminal law, following the incorporation of predominant medical consensus of the time.[46] While punishments were relatively less 'extreme', the breadth of sanctions and possible perpetrators (including the woman herself) broadened.

The development of the medical profession and its professional interests have significantly shaped the landscape of abortion law in England, Wales, and Scotland.[47] The medicalisation of pregnancy[48] thus became consolidated through the criminal law. But was the advance of the medical profession the most prevalent drive for legislative changes over the years? And what does this have to do with processual law, if anything? Do the development of medicine and processual law go hand in hand? This is not necessarily the case; medicine (to some degree) furthers our understanding of process. Whether these understandings are correct – or further, interpreted in a progressive fashion in law – is another issue. One might say that as the boundaries of proof in this area have changed, so too have our attitudes toward the fetus and embryo. Or, are these changes

---

[42] T. Denman, *An Introduction to the Practice of Midwifery*, vol. 1 (J Johnson, 1794), p. 26. Also see J. Burns, *The Anatomy of the Gravid Uterus* (Glasgow University Press, 1799), p. 115.

[43] J. Herring, *Medical Law and Ethics* (Oxford University Press, 2016) p. 334.

[44] *R v. Goodhall* (1846) 1Den C 187.

[45] Ibid.

[46] Grubb, 'Abortion Law in England', 147.

[47] McGuinness and Thompson, 'Medicine and Abortion Law', 178.

[48] See R. Johanson and others, 'Has the Medicalisation of Childbirth Gone Too Far?' (2002), *British Medical Journal*, 324(7432), 892–895 ; B. Rothman, 'Pregnancy, Birth and Risk: An Introduction' (2014), *Health, Risk and Society*, 16(1), 1–6.

singularly associated with advances in medical understandings and practice? Perhaps, but considering the apparent lack of medical consensus in
the late 1700s and the early 1800s on whether quickening was the defining moment in which a woman became 'with child', it must be questioned
whether there is more to this than first meets the eye. Whilst the embryo/
fetus was set against the hard sanction that the criminal law represented,
the criminal law – whether attempts to consolidate and clarify (like
Ellenborough and Lansdowne), facilitate prosecution (1837), or consolidate and confirm the common law (1861) – increased levels of punishment (albeit while removing capital punishment) against intent to
procure, or successfully procure abortion.

   While the years preceding the twentieth century gradually extended
laws governing the embryo/fetus and attached the criminal law to the
regulation of the early stages of human life, it arguably laid a path for legal
process and made way for the incorporation of social considerations into
the law. We have seen evidence that law began to leave behind the
question of 'when does life begin to matter?' and started to think about
the broader network of actors in early life processes (albeit not in a way
that reflects the interests of women). It is of particular significance to
reiterate that process and progress are not synonymous. Indeed, the
increasingly severe range of punishments for termination of pregnancy
was not necessarily progressive.[49] While it may be described as such in
one sense – in that capital punishment was removed as a sanction – the
growth of criminal law (and thus range of crimes and possible perpetrators) in this area may not necessarily be seen as 'progress'. Process and
progress thus do make easy bedfellows. Nonetheless, a move away from
one legal boundary with quickening towards legally encompassing all
stages of pregnancy is, in and of itself, processual. On the other hand, one
boundary was just replaced with another; legally binding the early stages
of human life to rules seems to have been the predominant legal response
to embryonic processes from the outset. While this might sound coun-
terintuitive per a 'processual' approach, delineating stages of growth
undoubtedly recognises development.

   As mentioned earlier, towards the end of the nineteenth century,
preformationism was abandoned in favour of epigenesis, given the
rapid advances in microscopy that occurred at that time. While the law
had not yet reached the 'gradualist' approach of the amended Abortion

---

[49] Depending on one's definition of progress, notably for someone who has a more conservative position on abortion, this might be viewed as progressive.

Act 1967 and the 1990 Act (as amended) today, the removal of the quickening distinction arguably reflected increased awareness that pregnancy and embryonic/fetal growth were a process, not sudden (and perhaps not even divine) 'events'. New modes of visibility beyond fetal movements drove law to react to new understandings of embryonic/fetal processes. Overall, it seems that law began to change rapidly with the explosion of experimental science and new technologies in the late nineteenth and (as we shall see next) twentieth centuries. Until then 'quickening' and preformation (and other theories of conception/growth that we do not rely on today, such as formation)[50] stood as moral, legal, and scientific navigators of the uncertainty that went with conception and embryonic/fetal growth. The use of experimental techniques and the advances in microscopy (and the increased knowledge of embryonic/fetal development that came with that) in the nineteenth century were arguably mirrored in law with amendments to the way that stages of the process of embryonic and fetal growth were depicted in law.

1.5   The Twentieth Century

As we have seen, the common law's insistence upon only extending protection to a 'reasonable creature in being'[51] limited the old criminal law's protection of the fetus/embryo.[52] Up until the late twentieth century, Parliament added to the common law through a patchwork of statutory provisions, and in doing so provided 'some semblance of protection for the fetus at various stages in development'.[53]

With the advancement of science, 'quickening' was gradually used less and less in civil and criminal legal rhetoric and was replaced by other markers such as viability – the 'moments' of which have become far more 'visible'. Under the Infant Life (Preservation) Act 1929 (ILP Act),[54] procuring or attempting to procure an abortion was no longer a criminal offence, as long as it was carried out (a) for the purpose of preserving the life of the mother and (b) in good faith. Nonetheless, it was deemed illegal in all other circumstances to terminate a viable fetus

---

[50] For example: Thorne, 'Bracton on the Laws and Customs of England', p. 279; Grubb, 'Abortion Law in England', 147.

[51] Coke, 'Institutions', p. 50

[52] G. Cole and S. Frankowski, *Abortion and Protection of the Human Fetus: Legal Problems in a Cross-cultural Perspective* (Martinus Nijhoff, 1987), p. 9 5.

[53] Ibid.

[54] This Act did not apply in Scotland.

'capable of being born alive'. Viability[55] as a legal boundary was thus enshrined in the ILP Act at twenty-eight weeks, four weeks later than previous law (as advances had been made in science at the time, meaning the fetus was presumed viable at a later stage).[56]

In 1939, the landmark case of *R* v. *Bourne*[57] paved the way for the later Abortion Act 1967 (1967 Act). For the purposes of this analysis, this historical legal development does not say anything about embryo *in vitro* (thus far), but, importantly, it informs us about the nature of law's evolution with regard to incorporating the processes of the early stages of human life. Here it was held that a doctor might lawfully perform an abortion, despite s. 58 of the then OAP Act 1861.[58] In *R* v. *Bourne*, a young girl was raped and became pregnant. Her doctor, Bourne, performed an abortion on her and then turned himself in to the police. In the trial, Macnaughten J upheld Bourne's defence that the indictment for abortion should be altered to include the word 'unlawful', so that the Crown would have to establish that the defendant's use of an 'instrument' was 'unlawful'. In his summary, Macnaughten J distinguished between a skilful surgeon performing openly and 'charitably', and the private termination of pregnancy for 'gain' by an 'unskilled operator'.[59] He also rejected the view that there was a clear line between health and danger to one's life – that life could be greatly hindered by one's health.[60] The law at the time has been described as lying between those who wanted women to be able to have abortions and religious views that it should never be performed, to which end it was only allowed in order to preserve the mother's life. Here we can see an incorporation of (relative) social justice aims into a judgment. It should be noted that although *Bourne* is widely regarded as having carved the legal landscape in this area, there is disagreement amongst legal commentary on the extent to which *Bourne* can be read as a momentous liberalisation on the law on abortion.[61] It has thus not been lauded by all as a victory for social

---

[55] The time at which a fetus may be 'born alive' if it were to be *ex utero*.

[56] See HL Deb, 06 December 1928, vol 72, cols 425–429, col 425.

[57] [1939] 1 KB 687.

[58] L. Bibbings, 'Legal Commentary – R v Bourne: A Historical Context' in Stephen Smith and others (eds.), *Ethical Judgments: Re-Writing Medical Law* (Bloomsbury, 2017), p. 158.

[59] *R* v. *Bourne*, paras. 689–690.

[60] Ibid.

[61] See McGuinness and Thompson 'Medicine and Abortion Law'; S. Sheldon, *Beyond control: Medical Power and abortion control* (Pluto, 1997), p. 18, who describes it as having 'carried the law far beyond the intention and letter of the statutes'; Keown, 'Abortion, Doctors and the Law', pp. 52–57 who argued that 'This view is based on the

considerations, per the perceived interests of the woman.[62] While an explicit provision for 'therapeutic abortion' may have been absent from the OAP Act 1861, in reality, this procedure was nonetheless regularly performed on women at the time, and precedent for this gradually extended in case law up until the legal cementation in the *Bourne* case. While *Bourne* was more about context than process itself, shortly after the case a gradated approach to criminal sanctions at early stages of human life was introduced, gradating the process of embryonic/fetal evolution *in utero* – its relative moral/legal value directly tied to the well-being of the woman.

After *Bourne*, the scope of therapeutic abortion was extended further in *R v. Bergmann and Ferguson*[63] and *R v. Newton and Stungo*[64] to respectively include the honesty of a doctor's belief as a defence and considerations of the woman's physical and mental health. Nonetheless, the effect of these cases and the ILP Act was that the termination of an embryo/fetus was a criminal offence, save in certain circumstances where the life or health of the mother was at stake. The strongest legal protection was given to a viable fetus under the ILP Act, the termination of which was a criminal offence in any circumstance. Physiological visibility was eventually replaced as an important biological and legal 'moment' by technical visibility when engineer Tom Brown and obstetrician Ian Donald developed the first ultrasound machine, first used in Glasgow, Scotland, in 1956. Further advances in molecular biology were made in the 1950s when the DNA helical structure was discovered. This led to the emergence of developmental biology, which studies the correlations between genetics and the embryo's morphological development.

Some years later, the 1967 Act cemented the *Bourne*, *Bergmann*, and *Newton* cases, as the first statute relating to the early stages of human life to have territorial extent over Scotland, in addition to England and Wales. The grounds for abortion are set out, to this day, in ss. 1(1) and (2) of the 1967 Act. Similar to before, no explicit reference was made to the 'embryo' in this statute, which clearly maintained that the

---

belief that the prohibition on abortion by s.58 was absolute and was so regarded by the courts until 1938. This belief is, however, inconsistent with certain judicial and extra judicial pronouncements ... the case appears not so much as an example of radical judicial legislation as of conservative exposition of the law.'

[62] For an alternative judgment that considers this more, see, for example, S. McGuinness 'Judgment 1- R v Bourne [1939] 1 KB 687', in Stephen Smith and others (eds.), *Ethical Judgments: Re-Writing Medical Law* (Bloomsbury, 2017), pp. 146–150.

[63] *R v. Bergmann and Ferguson* [1948] 1 BMJ 1008.

[64] *R v. Newton and Stungo* [1958] CrimLR 469.

termination of pregnancy at any stage was illegal, save in certain prescribed circumstances.[65] It is worth noting that while the 1967 Act has
clearly been shaped by evolving medical opinion, the extent to which the
1967 Act, even in its updated form, acts as a permissive piece of social
legislation has been questioned by some. For example, Sheldon argues
that the primary purpose and consequence of the 1967 Act was not to
promote the reproductive autonomy of women but instead to found
a more severe yet subtle system of medical control over the fertility of
women.[66]

At this time, a link still existed between this Act and the ILP Act, and
from twenty-eight weeks, the fetus was legally protected in almost all
circumstances.[67] It is worth noting that in terms of the Congenital
Disabilities (Civil Liability) Act 1976,[68] the law provided a degree of
retrospective protection to the embryo *in vivo*, but only if it was born
alive.[69] As we will see in Chapter 2, this has parallels with the Human
Fertilisation and Embryology Act 1990, which, in effect, protects some
embryos because of their status as a future person. Under the Congenital
Disabilities (Civil Liability) Act 1976, damages could be awarded as
a result of injury to the embryo/fetus *in utero* caused by the negligent
actions of third party (although 'embryo' was not explicitly mentioned in
this Act either). This was part of a network of frameworks at play, a facet
of the law that remains today with the co-existence of frameworks like the
1967 Act and the 1990 Act, notwithstanding the case law.

1.6   Conclusions

Historically speaking, process has been a central facet of regulating the
embryo in the United Kingdom. It is nonetheless worth noting that the
scientific, visual experiences of the embryo that were relayed to society
shaped the law throughout medico-legal history. It is important to
consider that visibility (i.e. the relative visibility of its developmental
processes) will not have been the only factor in legal change here.
Religion and politics, amongst other things, are likely to have played

---

[65] Where continuance of pregnancy would have risked the life or health of the woman or
existing children/family, or where there was a risk that the child would be born with
a serious physical or mental handicap. See Abortion Act 1967, s5(2).

[66] Sheldon, 'Beyond Control', p. 30.

[67] Abortion Act 1967, s5(1).

[68] England and Wales only.

[69] For more on this, see Chapter 7, section 4.

a significant role. These, however, do not necessarily detract from the fundamental role of the embryo's scientific visibility in shaping all of this.

From the above we can see that the processual nature of law lay in the fact that regulation commenced by asking 'when does life begin?' and then 'when does life begin to matter?' Throughout history, the goal posts marking out legal boundaries on these questions have shifted in accordance with scientific, religious, and social changes. However, the issue for this work is not what caused these shifts, but more where these limits shifted to. Law became processual, relative to the social, scientific, and religious limits at the time, having made judgment on what 'matters' based on what was known at the time; that is, they believed that at the 'quickening' stage of the process, a mother can feel fetal movement and/ or the pregnancy is physically visible.

Up until the end of the twentieth century the term 'embryo' had little mention in law. Despite this, it was protected for much of history, particularly after the quickening distinction was dissolved in the nineteenth century. Quickening thus acted as a legal limit before this point, which reflected knowledge of the time around the way in which embryos/ fetuses *in utero* evolve. With the rise of science and technical visibility, the legal boundary of quickening was removed. No longer did the law only protect the fetus after the woman first felt its movements; instead, the whole process of pregnancy fell within the ambit of law's protection.[70] The above frameworks should not be hailed as progressive advances in the law (process does not always mean progress), but rather as a step back that further criminalised women and gave protection to the very early stages of human life in the womb. Therefore, a key aspect of the relation between law and process that this change in law articulates, for the purpose of this analysis, is the turbulent relationship between process and progress. Nonetheless, the changes beyond the original framework for 'quickening' were certainly advancement towards what we have now.

Quickening was replaced as a legal 'line in the sand' by fetal viability, which was enshrined in law by the ILP Act 1929, at twenty-eight weeks (later reduced to twenty-four weeks in the 1990 Act's amendments to the 1967 Act). By the 1950s science had advanced even further; ultrasound had been invented and the helical structure of DNA had been discovered. With these advances, the processual nature of the early stages of human life was more visible than ever. For the first time, we could see images of

---

[70] While the relation between law and process shall be explored more fully in Chapter 4 of this book, as argued earlier, process and progress do not always go hand in hand.

the embryo/fetus growing within the mother's womb. Shortly after these advances came the 1967 Act, which, despite its serious flaws, was a socially progressive piece of legislation relative to the laws of its kind that had come before it. While this Act did not explicitly recognise 'the embryo' (at this stage in time, there was probably little need to), as a then progressive piece of legislation, it was more processual than those that had come before it. Here, the relative moral value of the fetus was reflected in law as a factor directly intertwined with the physical and/or mental health of the woman (or the fetus's hypothetical future health). To explain, the law's processual nature lay in the fact that it made persistent efforts to account for the processual nature of embryos/fetuses, although, as we have seen, this has not necessarily always resulted in 'progressive' law.

Overall, such a tracing of the history of the laws that govern(ed) the early stages of human life has demonstrated how much the embryo's 'visibility'[71] has affected what it 'is' over time (socially and legally). Visibility has been a key link to social and biological understanding of process, and the law has evolved at relatively regular intervals in history to reflect this. While the very early stages of human life are not visible to the human eye, modern science has allowed us to see and understand early life more than ever. Medical professional, legal, and social attitudes have thus changed. The law has evolved from protection of the embryo/fetus at a later stage, to protecting the embryo/fetus throughout gestation, to protecting embryos and fetuses with exceptions based upon 'social considerations', to the present legal governance and protection of the embryo that starts where an egg is in the process of fertilisation (albeit only *in vitro*). This reveals an interesting feature of embryo governance: with the emergence of technological 'visibility' of the embryo, the criminal limits to proving pregnancy changed, and eventually ebbed away. There is something curious about the concurrent relative increase in legal protections for the early stages of life, and the increasing incorporation of 'social considerations' into the same laws. The criminal and civil laws in this area have thus been relative to our understanding: that is, to some extent, a relative reflection of our knowledge of biological process.

To summarise the findings and arguments within this first chapter, brief analyses of historical legal developments in this field reveal deeper

---

[71] As technology has advanced, humans have been able to see – literally – what the early stages of life actually look like, for example through ultrasound and microscopes.

understandings of law and society's relationship with embryos *in vitro*, namely:

- Process has been historically important for law, regarding the regula-tion of embryos/foetuses. Historically doing something of course does not always mean we should continue doing it, but *if* one sees it as a positive facet of lawmaking in this area, and as a facet that enables the symbiotic relationship between law, science, and society, then law ought to reflect this appreciation of processes.

As revealed by further analysis in the next chapter, key elements can be distilled from law's evolution in this area that appear in the framework we have now. This history was arguably an important precursor to the 1990 regime, particularly with regard to law's boundaries and 'boundary work'[72] (see Chapter 3) surrounding the early stages of human life.

---

[72] For a more detailed discussion on this, see Taylor-Alexander and others, 'Beyond Compression', 171.

'The Embryo' in Law Today

The Human Fertilisation and Embryology Act 1990 and Beyond

2.1 Introduction

As Chapter 1 has shown, law-making surrounding the early stages of human life evolved hand in hand with social, religious, and scientific accounts of *process*. The analysis offered in this chapter continues from the last and presents two further claims:

- Like its historical counterparts in the regulation of the early stages of human life, the 1990 Act (as amended) has processual aspects. There is not necessarily a disjunction between the 1990 Act (as amended) and the historical development of the early stages of human life but with the history of process in law in mind;
- The intellectual basis of the law currently treats embryos singularly as 'the embryo' by virtue of according it one 'special status'. In reality, the 1990 Act (as amended) creates multiple processes for, and categories of, embryos *in vitro* with seemingly multiple implicit 'statuses'. There are thus ways in which law could *better* embrace biological, social, and other forms of process.

To build the case for these claims, this analysis traces the history of the 1990 Act (as amended) and summarises the present regulatory framework governing the embryo *in vitro* with reference to its legal 'special status'. It briefly summarises some of the key arguments put forward in the Warnock Report relating to the moral and legal status of the embryo *in vitro* and the enactment of these arguments in law, including subsequent amendments of the framework. The chapter finds that, like its historical counterparts,[1] embryonic, moral, scientific, and other forms of *process* were important considerations for the Warnock Report, which provided the intellectual basis for the 1990 Act.

---

[1] Counterparts in the sense that they also regulated the early stages of human life.

2.2   The Warnock Report (1984)

In 1984, the Warnock Committee published the Report of the Committee of Inquiry into Human Fertilisation and Embryology, also known as the Warnock Report (hereafter 'the Report'). The following subsections summarise the key issues tackled by the Committee in relation to the embryo's legal status. This has been done here with a view to demonstrating the ethical and legal deliberation that took place as a precursor to regulating the embryo *in vitro* through the 1990 Act. This deliberative process, though not necessarily without flaw,[2] was an essential part of law-making in this area. It brought legal and scientific practice out of uncertainty (i.e. due to the lack of a statutory framework for *in vitro* fertilisation (IVF) pre-1990) to a new state of being where embryos can legally be created, used, and stored for reproductive and research purposes under certain prescribed circumstances. The following gives a detailed account of key statements and arguments in the Committee's deliberative process.

2.2.1   Regulating for the Future

In the late 1970s, the embryo was thrust into legal, ethical, and public debate when Louise Brown became the first child born from IVF. For the first time in history, scientists could closely observe some of the earliest stages of human life entirely outside of the human body. Human embryos, newly visible in a physical and scientific sense, also became clearly perceptible as existing at the margins of what we commonly conceive to be 'human life'. As a result, new horizons in the fields of reproductive medicine and research were revealed, and diverse perspectives took shape around these possibilities. Embryos *in vitro* thus embodied different hopes and fears for people.[3] While embryo research created new realms of possibility for some (e.g. those who would now benefit from this new fertility treatment), this advancement came coupled with concerns over the rapid advance of science and the 'slippery slope' to morally undesirable practices.[4] Scepticism about the moral acceptability of assisted conception and, in particular, research on

---

[2] Some critiques of the Warnock Report are discussed later.

[3] M. Mulkay, 'Frankenstein and the Debate over Embryo Research' (1996), *Science, Technology and Human Values*, 21(2), 157–176; M. Fox and T. Murphy, 'Can Law Facilitate Embryonic Hopes?' (2010), *Social and Legal Studies*, 19, 498–505.

[4] Jackson, *Regulating Reproduction*, p. 182.

embryos (necessarily involving the creation and destruction of embryos for such purposes) led to several attempts at barring embryo disposal.[5]

In 1982, against this backdrop of public emotion and uncertainty, the UK government established the Committee of Inquiry into Human Fertilisation and Embryology (the Warnock Committee). Baroness Mary Warnock, a philosopher, headed the Warnock Committee, which consisted of academics, legal, and medical professionals. They were assigned by the government to consider

> [r]ecent and potential developments in medicine and science related to human fertilisation and embryology; to consider what policies and safeguards should be applied, including consideration of the social, ethical, and legal implications of these developments; and to make recommendations.[6]

This Committee was the first of its kind to consider the ethical implications of scientific developments in human fertilisation and embryology. Its remit was to consider the permissibility of using embryos in IVF and research, as well as the nature of the embryo itself. To provide some background, the Report's foreword begins with the following:

> Our Inquiry was set up to examine, among other things, the ethical implications of new developments in the field. In common usage, the word 'ethical' is not absolutely unambiguous. It is often used in the context, for example, of medical or legal ethics, to refer to professionally acceptable practice. We were obliged to interpret the concept of ethics in a less restricted way. We had to direct our attention not only to future practice and possible legislation, but also to the principles on which such practices and such legislation would rest.[7]

Here the Warnock Committee gave a clear nod to the potential for future change in the uses of embryos *in vitro* and the regulation of those practices in this area. Interestingly, the Committee made clear here that they aimed to set up the fundamental pillars that would endure throughout these scientific and legal changes, without reference to potential change in 'ethics' (in their reference to the principles on which future legislation would rest). Whether this was intentional is unclear. The foreword refers to the social consensus at the time, which was that the law requires governance by 'some principles or other'[8] and that some lines should be drawn in this field which must not be crossed.

---

[5] See Section 2.2.3.
[6] 'Warnock Report', para. 1.2.
[7] Ibid., para. 1.
[8] Ibid., para. 2.

Despite concerns about 'slippery slopes', the Report emphasised the importance of 'keeping the temporal perspective short, and reliance on imagination to a minimum':[9]

> The pace of scientific discovery is unpredictable. Indeed, a number of major developments have taken place during the lifetime of the Inquiry. The changes, which take place in society itself, are also difficult to predict. The impact of scientific discoveries on the society of the future is therefore doubly hard to predict. We took the pragmatic view that we could react only to what we knew, and what we could realistically foresee. This meant that we must react to the ways in which people now see childlessness and the process of family formation, taking into account the range of views encompassed by our pluralistic society, the nature and value of clinical and scientific advances and the benefits of research.[10]

Here we see a recognition that this type of law (one that governs a rapidly changing scientific field) is temporally limited, given the manner in which science, family, and society's views of embryos (and thus their hopes for law in relation to them) can evolve relatively rapidly. Perhaps even the Committee itself would not have intended for all of its recommendations to stand the test of time in the way that they have. As discussed later, durability is not necessarily a productive 'hope' for law in this field,[11] where rapid scientific and social changes take place. The Committee also emphasised the societal sentiment at the time: that there should be limits to these practices, as without them we would be 'society without moral scruples'.[12] As Baroness Warnock herself stated at a 2016 Progress Educational Trust event:

> People generally want some principles or other to govern the development and use of the new techniques. There must be some barriers that are not to be crossed, some limits fixed, beyond which people must not be allowed to go.[13]

In order to alleviate concerns surrounding where such techniques may lead in the future, the Committee recommended that a licensing body be

---

[9] M. Mulkay, *The Embryo Research Debate: Science and the Politics of Reproduction* (Cambridge University Press, 1997), p. 129.

[10] 'Warnock Report', para. 1.5.

[11] See M. A. Jacob and B. Prainsack, 'Embryonic Hopes: Controversy, Alliance, and Reproductive Entities in Law and the Social Sciences' (2010), *Social and Legal Studies*, 19(4), 497–517.

[12] Ibid.

[13] M. Warnock, 'The Warnock Report and the 14-Day Rule' (*Rethinking the Ethics of Embryo Research: Genome Editing, 13 Days and beyond*, London, 7 December 2016).

established to monitor embryo research. In answer to this, the Human Fertilisation and Embryology Authority (HFEA) – an independent regulator of the use of gametes for reproduction and embryos for treatment and research[14] – was established under the 1990 Act. This body ensures that those they have licensed[15] store and use embryos in a manner that is consistent with the 1990 Act.[16] While it has the authority and discretion to make these licensing decisions, it does not have the power to license any practice clearly outwith their remit – as provided by the same Act. Today, the HFEA represents the longest established regulator of human embryo research in the world.[17]

2.2.2   A 'Special Status'

The Report was evidently written with an absence of moral consensus in mind, as the Committee was careful to emphasise early on that consensus was near impossible to reach. Nonetheless, they also recognised the importance of legislation as a benchmark for societal moral standards. To quote extensively from the Report's foreword:

> In recognising that there should be limits, people are bearing witness to the existence of a moral ideal of society. But in our pluralistic society it is not to be expected that any one set of principles can be enunciated to be completely accepted by everyone. This is not to say that the enunciating of principles is arbitrary, or that there is no shared morality whatever. *The law itself, binding on everyone in society, whatever their beliefs, is the embodiment of a common moral position. It sets out a broad framework for what is morally acceptable within society.* Another philosopher put it thus: 'The reasons that lead a reflective man to prefer one . . . legal system to another must be moral reasons: that is he must find his reasons in some order of priority of interests and activities, in the kind of life that he praises and admires'. In recommending legislation, then, we are recommending a kind of society that we can, all of us: praise and admire, even if, in detail, we may individually wish that it were different. Within the broad limits of legislation there is room for different, and perhaps much more

---

[14] Human Fertilisation and Embryology Authority, 'How We Regulate', *HFEA*, www .hfea.gov.uk/about-us/how-we-regulate.

[15] It is a criminal offence to store or use embryos without a licence from the HFEA, see 1990 Act (as amended).

[16] For a detailed account and discussion of the HFEA, and its regulatory role(s), see A. Alghrani, *Regulating Assisted Reproductive Technologies: New Horizons* (Cambridge University Press, 2019), pp. 34–60.

[17] S. Devaney, *Stem Cell Research and the Collaborative Regulation of Innovation* (Routledge, 2013), p. 62.

stringent, moral rules. What is legally permissible may be thought of as the minimum requirement for a tolerable society. Individuals or communities may voluntarily adopt standards that are more exacting. It has been our business, however, to recommend how the broad framework should be established, within our particular area of concern.[18]

There is no untruth to this; the law sets out a broad framework for what is morally acceptable in society,[19] and it did so with the 1990 Act – the result of this Report. Yet how, legally speaking, is it practical to continue with a legal framework centred around a singular 'special status' for the embryo, when it implicitly morally demarcates types of embryos, namely those used for reproduction and those used for research? As discussed in Parts 2 and 3 of this book, a case can be made for legally harnessing the processual nature of embryo regulation and the multiple, not unitary, processes the Act regulates. This is not to critique the approach of the report at the time; the text specifically recognises the unpredictability of future science.[20] Indeed, with recent developments[21] perhaps it is time for *another* Warnock-esque Report that would consider the intellectual underpinnings of laws and regulation governing the production, use, and storage of embryos *in vitro*.

Notably, before the 1990 Act came into force, the human embryo had no legal status per se.[22] It did not have legal personhood, nor did it have a right to life. Nonetheless, as we have seen in Chapter 1, certain laws were in place, such as the Abortion Act 1967, which accorded the embryo/fetus *in utero* certain protections. The Report noted this and suggested that while they did not recommend that embryos be afforded the same status as children or adults:

> 11.17 ... The status of the embryo is a matter of fundamental principle which should be enshrined in legislation. *We recommend that the embryo of the human species should be afforded some protection in law ....*
>
> 11.18 That protection should exist does not entail that this protection may not be waived in certain specific circumstances. Having examined the evidence presented to us about the types of research which might be carried out on human embryos produced *in vitro*, the majority of us hold that such research should not be totally prohibited. We do not want to see a situation in which human embryos are frivolously or unnecessarily used in research but we are bound to take account of the fact that the advances in the

---

[18] 'Warnock Report', paras. 2–3. Emphasis added.

[19] The role of law in society is of course debatable and much more complex than this. For more on this, see, e.g., the works of Thomas Hobbes, John Locke, and Immanuel Kant.

[20] 'Warnock Report', para. 1.5.

[21] See Chapter 7 of this book.

[22] 'Warnock Report', para. 11.16.

treatment of infertility, which we have discussed in the earlier part of this report, could not have taken place without such research; and that continued research is essential, if advances in treatment and medical knowledge are to continue. A majority of us therefore agreed that research on human embryos should continue. *Nevertheless, because of the special status that we accord to the human embryo, such research must be subject to stringent controls and monitoring.*[23]

The Report did not explain, however, what this 'special status' entails, nor did it signify its philosophical source.[24] This is not to say that this 'status' was not justified then, on some level, as a kind of 'comfort blanket' in the sociopolitical climate of the time. The status was seemingly put forward as a safeguard upon the slippage of that research into 'frivolous'[25] territories. The Committee referred to this in the next section of their report, where they emphasise that a precise time limit of the development of an embryo *in vitro* was required 'in order to allay public anxiety'.[26]

In order to do so, the Committee suggested what is now a keystone of legal frameworks worldwide: a fourteen-day time limit on research carried out on embryos *in vitro*. The primitive streak, which marks the beginning of gastrulation (the process of forming a multilayered structure called 'gastrula'), appears around day fourteen of development in humans. For the Committee, this stage was the best marker in development to place a time limit as it 'marks the beginning of individual development of the embryo'.[27] Interestingly, on the creation of embryos for research, some members felt that there was a 'clear moral distinction between the research use of embryos available by chance . . . and embryos brought into being for the purposes of research alone and where there is no question of their being transferred into a woman'.[28] The Committee nonetheless recommended that, as this should be controlled by legislation, an embryo *in vitro* may be the subject of research 'whatever its provenance', up to the fourteen days after fertilisation took place.[29] At the time, most authorities put the development of the streak at about fifteen days after fertilisation.[30] The Committee also noted that they were

---

[23] Ibid., paras. 11.17–8. Emphasis added.
[24] Ford, 'Nothing and Not-Nothing'.
[25] M. Warnock, *A Question of Life: The Warnock Report on Human Fertilisation and Embryology* (Blackwell, 1985), p. 64.
[26] 'Warnock Report', para. 11.19.
[27] Ibid., para. 11.22.
[28] Ibid., para. 11.25.
[29] Ibid., para. 11.30.
[30] Ibid.

satisfied that 'spare' embryos 'may be used as subjects for research', as long as informed consent was gained from the couple for whom the embryo was generated.[31] Here, we see the introduction of a new boundary, joining the other boundaries attributed to the embryo/fetus in law up to this time.[32] In some ways, the 'primitive streak' is the Committee's own version of 'quickening'. After all, law has replaced one boundary with another to reflect changing consensuses (medical, ethical, social, etc.) regarding the early stages of human life. Perhaps unwittingly, this seems to follow previous legal trends toward delineating stages in the growth process with bright legal lines.

In the end, the Report took, broadly speaking, a utilitarian approach to its recommendations and deliberations.[33] Baroness Warnock later spoke of this approach in 2007, when she observed:

> At the centre of the moral thinking behind the 1990 Act was broad utilitarianism . . . .. As legislators, parliamentarians have to be utilitarian in the broadest possible sense . . . . On the committee, we thought that utilitarianism in this broad sense was the philosophy that must lie behind any legislation – weighing up harms against benefits.[34]

The Report did not explicitly answer the question of 'when does life begin to matter morally?', (see below) – to which there is no objective answer – but rather considered the viewpoints submitted and 'provide[d] the human embryo with a special status without actually defining that moral status'.[35] Nonetheless, the Committee can be understood as *implicitly* having answered the latter question, by allowing research up to a certain stage in development.[36] In other words, they prescribed that 'as the embryo develops, it should receive greater legal protection due to its increasing moral value and potential'.[37] This policy, known as the 'gradualist approach', is somewhat in line with the Abortion Act 1967, which affords more protection to the fetus as it reaches later stages in development[38] (although in other ways these laws do not align at all).

---

[31] Ibid., para. 11.24.

[32] Discussed in Chapter 5 of this book. Also see G. Laurie, 'Liminality and the Limits of Law' (2017), *Medical Law Review*, 25(1), 49.

[33] N. Hammond-Browning, 'Ethics, Embryos and Evidence: A Look Back at Warnock' (2015), *Medical Law Review*, 23(4), 588–619.

[34] Mary Warnock, HL Deb 19 November 2007, vol. 696, col. 721.

[35] Hammond-Browning, 'Ethics, Embryos and Evidence', 605.

[36] Ibid., 606.

[37] Ibid.

[38] See Abortion Act 1967, s. 1.

A gradualist approach in and of itself may be described as recognising the processual (but not necessarily progressively so). It seems that it was important for the Committee that such an approach continue. This was not mentioned explicitly but is implicit in the Committee's efforts to replicate a somewhat gradualist approach that recognises embryonic development (and any 'significant' markers within it).

The Report was quite explicit in that it was not going to tackle questions of the meaning of human 'life' or 'personhood'. Instead, it articulated its remit as 'how it is right to treat the human embryo'.[39] The Report examined the arguments for and against the use of human embryos for research. Here the Committee noted the plethora of views on the embryo's status, evidenced by the above-mentioned submissions received prior to the Report.[40] They discussed each position in turn, before concluding that while the embryo deserves some protection in law, this protection should not be absolute.[41] Notably, the source of this protection is not entirely clear in the Report. It cited the state of law at the time, which afforded some protection to the embryo, but not absolute protection.[42] Nonetheless, one can glean from their recommendations that this protection is sourced (at least in part) by virtue of the embryo being a member of the human species.[43] Further, any recognition of the embryo as morally recognisable from the moment of creation would have been a huge step back from the recognition of the bodily integrity and autonomy of women with regard to reproduction, brought about in law (at least relatively speaking) by the 1967 Act.[44]

That being said, it is evident that an issue for the Committee was how to regulate such a controversial field, where a plurality of views exists on the matter. The Committee thus reviewed a wide range of evidence from a variety of groups, bodies, and persons. In her 2015 article, Natasha Hammond-Browning explored and discussed this evidence upon which the Committee's recommendations (and thus subsequent law) were based.[45] From her examination of the evidence submitted,[46] she found

---

[39] 'Warnock Report', para. 11.9.
[40] Ibid.
[41] Ibid.
[42] Ibid., para. 11.16.
[43] Ibid., para. 84.
[44] Hammond-Browning, 'Ethics, Embryos and Evidence', 608.
[45] Ibid., 588.
[46] Gathered during a week-long visit to the Houses of Parliament. Ninety-seven pieces of evidence relevant to the debate were found, as well as 101 submissions made post-

that two central ethical questions emerged: 'When does life begin to matter morally?' and 'Should we permit research upon human embryos?'[47] While the Committee purposely did not answer the former, evidence gathered on both questions fed into their central query: how should we regulate embryos? Noting that there was little consensus in the submissions, and notwithstanding that a consensus is unlikely to ever be reached on this matter, Hammond-Browning divided the evidence in favour of or in opposition to embryo research into nine different headings (each of which she discussed in turn).[48] On this basis, she found that the diversity of views on the matter contained in the submitted evidence made reaching consensus a serious challenge for the Committee.

To take stock, so far we have seen that as the process of pregnancy became more 'medical' and less of a religious event, the law has responded to these new understandings of the early stages of human life. Throughout this evolution in understanding from the thirteenth to the twentieth centuries, the key question in law (framed in one way or another) seemed to be the same as that tackled by the Committee: how should law treat the early stages of human life? Considering the relative 'boom' in new understandings that occurred in the late twentieth century, culminating in the use of IVF and birth of Louise Brown, a considerable new amount of knowledge (and public concern) needed to be navigated in law. While the remit and deliberative process of the Committee was the first of its kind, the key question for them was almost the same as that for policymakers of the past: how should we treat the embryo legally? The Report discussed the question of *when*, in the embryonic process, the state should delineate legal limits (as law had always done in the past), by recommending a 'limit' on research based on the development of the primitive streak at fourteen days. This was arguably a reflection of process, by delineating a stage in the biological process that had been determined as important by those charged with law-making or informing law-making. That process remained important for the Committee, as we have seen through the previous summation of their deliberations. Notably, the Report did not refer to previous iterations of legal–moral lines, neither quickening nor viability (presumably because these were much later stages in the process and thus not relevant

---

publication of the Report. Hammond-Browning also found submissions from 300 organisations and 695 submissions from the public. See Hammond-Browning, 'Ethics, Embryos and Evidence', 591–592.

[47] Ibid.

[48] Ibid., 593.

to them). Yet there are similarities between the Committee's approach and previous iterations of laws governing the early stages of human life. The Committee, tasked with deliberating on how the United Kingdom ought to treat the embryo in law, dealt with moral uncertainty by providing boundaries at a stage in the process deemed 'appropriate' in accordance with the socio-medical climate of the time. While they met the task by providing a 'compromise', the societal response to the resulting bill still reflected the moral uncertainty navigated in their report.

The language of the Report itself was also mindful of the process and progress of science (i.e. that it would undoubtedly evolve beyond their remit). Further, with its consideration of laws governing the very early stages of human life and their underpinning principles, the Report, brought a relatively new entity, the embryo *in vitro* (and its scientific uses), out of the uncertainty it had previously been shrouded in during the 1970s. Now, over thirty years since the Warnock Report was published, its influence remains strong within our legislative framework on human fertilisation and embryology.[49] As the offering in the rest of this chapter shows, notwithstanding the importance of biological, scientific, and social process for the Report, the 1990 Act and laws before then, the processuality of law – whether by reconsidering it, considerably evolving it, or moving boundaries – has slowly halted, particularly after the 2008 amendments.[50]

Six years after the Report was published, the government enacted legislation closely based upon its recommendations: the Human Fertilisation and Embryology Act 1990. This Act provided boundaries and parameters on reproductive and research practices concerning the embryo. Yet in these six years, the enactment of this legislation was delayed by a political 'tug of war' between pro-research and pro-life groups.[51]

2.3 The Embryo Post-Warnock: 1984–1990

Themes of Frankenstein and the 'mad scientist' permeated public debates and media coverage during and after the Committee's deliberations. These parallels were drawn as part of some rather vociferous objection to assisted conception and embryo research from the pro-life movement,

---

[49] Ibid., 589.
[50] With the exception of the Human Fertilisation and Embryology (Mitochondrial Donation) Regulations 2015.
[51] Mulkay, 'The Embryo Research Debate'.

particularly groups such as Life and the Society for the Protection of the Unborn Child. These groups were active in the organisation and briefing of MPs and Peers opposed to the proposals for regulation laid out in the Warnock Report; at the time, these organisations appeared to have both parliamentary and public opinion on their side.[52] As Mulkay notes, this conservative lobby was 'well organised, virtually unopposed and in control of a large section of parliamentary opinion'.[53] In 1985, their efforts nearly succeeded with Enoch Powell's Unborn Children (Protection) Bill 1985 (UCP Bill),[54] which passed at first reading. It only failed to go any further because 'an alliance of scientists and Members of Parliament succeeded in talking it out of time'.[55] The UCP Bill did not explicitly purport to ban embryo research, but instead proposed the banning of embryo disposal, which would have rendered research impossible. Embryo research, however, is a crucial antecedent to infertility treatment. As Baroness Warnock stated at the Progress Educational Trust's 2016 conference: ' . . . if we are to have IVF, we need research. The two very much go hand in hand.'[56]

Between 1984 and 1990, the scientific and medical community continued to campaign and eventually swayed parliamentary and public opinion, chiefly by emphasising the potential benefits of embryo research to human health.[57] For example, the Progress Educational Trust (established in November 1985) arranged for families affected by genetic disease to visit members of the House of Lords prior to the debates on the Human Fertilisation and Embryology Bill.[58] The public were consulted through a Green Paper[59] and a White Paper,[60] which showed general support for embryo research and assisted reproduction within ethical limits. Despite general support from the public and scientific spheres, uncertainty surrounding how we should morally and legally treat embryos and what this law might lead to in the future permeated debates throughout the 1990 Act's inception and beyond. From this we

---

[52] Ibid., p. 183.
[53] Mulkay, 'Frankenstein', 19.
[54] This bill prescribed that embryos should only be created if they were going to be implanted into a woman. This would have prevented most IVF treatment and all forms of embryo research.
[55] Jackson, 'Regulating Reproduction', p. 183.
[56] Warnock, 'The Warnock Report and the 14-Day Rule'.
[57] Jackson, 'Regulating Reproduction', p. 183.
[58] Ibid.
[59] Legislation of Human Infertility Services and Embryo Research (1986) (Cm 46).
[60] Human Fertilisation and Embryology: A framework for Legislation (1987) (Cm 259).

can see that the only certainty when it comes to the embryo is that its status was (and still is) heavily contested. Regular reference to fictional genre in the news media expressed widespread fears about the advance of technology and science. As Mulkay concludes, while those against research predominantly used this science-fiction imagery, it paradoxically ended up weakening their campaign because of its fictional connotations.[61] There was thus an imaginative thread throughout the debate;[62] an 'extended temporal perspective'[63] into the unknown future, and these gaps were thus filled with premonitions of possibility. It 'created interpretive space in which to exercise their critical imagination'.[64] Indeed, the unregulated embryo of the 1970s and 1980s may be described as what liminal scholars would call a 'condition of possibility',[65] typical of a space 'in between' that the embryo of the time certainly occupied, that is, between a space of scientific and public consciousness and legal regulation. Notably, between 1985 and 1991 ARTs were regulated in a similar way to other fields of medicine, for example the GMC.[66]

As briefly highlighted earlier, in discussing the embryo and its potential legal status, the Report and the resulting 1990 Act arguably brought the embryo out of this particular liminal condition (the un(der)regulated possibilities of which caused great concern), into a new, bounded condition where these concerns were allayed. Law's response to public uncertainty and the unknown was to enact boundaries based on the Warnock's reflection of embryonic processes. Despite the prevalent concerns surrounding 'slippery slopes' and 'mad scientists', the Bill passed and the 1990 Act came into force on 1st November 1990.

2.4   The Human Fertilisation and Embryology Act 1990 (as Amended)

The 1990 Act was one of the first statutes of its kind in the world and has since been used throughout the world as a template for similar

---

[61]   Mulkay, 'Frankenstein', 173.
[62]   From both sides, some supporters of research were also cited by Mulkay as looking to the future.
[63]   Mulkay, 'Frankenstein', 170.
[64]   Ibid., 171.
[65]   For example, see T. Stanley, 'Three Parent Babies: unethical, scary and wrong' (*Telegraph*, 03 February 2015), www.telegraph.co.uk/news/health/11380784/Three-parent-babies-unethical-scary-and-wrong.html
[66]   See Alghrani, 'Regulating Assisted Reproductive Technologies', pp. 24–25.

frameworks for assisted reproduction and research using human embryos. This section summarises some of the key features of the *original* 1990 Act for the purposes of this book – with a particular focus on the definition of 'embryos' and the ways in which their 'special status' has been reflected in the statute.

The 1990 Act was introduced to regulate IVF and embryo research, and provide a statutory basis for the HFEA. As mentioned earlier, it also acted to expand the permitted circumstances for abortion under the 1967 Act, and thus (for many, but not all)[67] solidified abortion for reasons other than risk to life in law.[68] There are several sections of the original 1990 Act that are worth noting for the purposes of this analysis. First, in s.1, the 1990 Act defined the embryo as follows:

1. **Meaning of 'embryo', 'gamete', and associated expressions**
(1) In this Act, except where otherwise stated –
   (a) embryo means a live human embryo where fertilisation is complete, and
   (b) references to an embryo include an egg in the process of fertilisation, and, for this purpose, fertilisation is not complete until the appearance of a two cell zygote.
(2) This Act, so far as it governs bringing about the creation of an embryo, applies only to bringing about the creation of an embryo outside the human body; and in this Act –
   (a) references to embryos the creation of which was brought about *in vitro* (in their application to those where fertilisation is complete) are to those where fertilisation began outside the human body whether or not it was completed there, and
   (b) references to embryos taken from a woman do not include embryos whose creation was brought about *in vitro*.
(3) This Act, so far as it governs the keeping or use of an embryo, applies only to keeping or using an embryo outside the human body.

Here, in a somewhat revolutionary swoop, for the first time in legal history, the 1990 Act provided a statutory definition of the 'embryo'. Interestingly, for the purposes of this book, is that it made use of the word

---

[67] See Sheldon, 'Who is the mother to make the judgment?'
[68] In addition to amending s1 of the 1967 Abortion Act, subsections (4) and (5) of section 37 of the 1990 Act also amended the wording of s5(1) and (2) of the Infant Life (Preservation) Act 1921.

'process', and in some ways, it might be argued as having recognised the processual quality of the embryo. For example, s. (b) seemingly accounted for the fact that fertilisation is not a 'moment' but a transition from one state (two separate gametes) to another (a two-cell zygote). Yet it is also worth noting that these legal provisions were (and still are) simultaneously anti-processual.[69] The law-makers took the word 'process' and then entirely contradicted what the ordinary meaning of this word arguably entails by including multiple cellular, zygotic, and embryonic stages under one heading (for the purposes of the 1990 Act): 'embryo'. This, in and of itself, is not necessarily problematic; it was a legal tool used to capture all embryonic processes *in vitro*. This definition was later proven incomplete by the *Quintavalle*[70] case, discussed later. Under the 1990 Act, a 'human' cellular entity was thus an 'embryo' as soon as fertilisation is complete, which the Act defined as being marked by the presence of a two-cell zygote. This stage happens as a result of mitosis.[71] When an embryo is fertilised *in vivo*, both of these latter stages occur before implantation into the uterine wall. Section 2(3) of the 1990 Act prescribed that a woman is not 'pregnant' until implantation has taken place.

The 1990 Act is thus governed (and still governs) the embryo before pregnancy takes *in utero*. This was in stark contrast to the pre-twentieth-century laws which did not protect early human life until well after the stage that implantation takes place (at least sixteen weeks). A further contrast to the laws that came before the 1990 Act is that this framework allows for a multiplicity of technological processes to create and use the embryos it regulates. In the past, embryos could only ever exist *in vivo/in utero*, and thus the only outcomes possible were either termination or birth. These outcomes have not changed under the 1990 Act, but the processes by which they reach these ends have multiplied. Under this new framework, for example, embryos could be led through implantation, frozen, or used for research. Even when on a reproductive 'pathway' through the law,[72] many embryos still end up being destroyed as part of the IVF process, as often more are created than needed for implantation. Further, there is no complete programme of embryo donation to other women. Surplus frozen embryos are therefore often destroyed – particularly if stored close to their

---

[69] See the Introduction to this book, section 4.3, and Chapter 5.
[70] [2003] UKHL 13.
[71] Mitosis is a type of cell division that results in two 'daughter' cells. These 'daughter' cells then each divide to produce to more, and their 'daughter' cells divide, and so on.
[72] See Chapter 6 of this book.

time limit – and a degree of surplus embryos are donated for research. Many of the processes legislated within the framework of the 1990 Act thus result in termination of the embryo.

In s.3, the original Act specified certain prohibitions in connection with embryos:

3. Prohibitions in connection with embryos

(3) A licence cannot authorise –

(a) keeping or using an embryo after the appearance of the primitive streak,

(b) placing an embryo in any animal,

(c) keeping or using an embryo in any circumstances in which regulations prohibit its keeping or use, or

(d) replacing a nucleus of a cell of an embryo with a nucleus taken from a cell of any person, embryo or subsequent development of an embryo.

(4) For the purposes of subsection (3)(a) above, the primitive streak is to be taken to have appeared in an embryo not later than the end of the period of 14 days beginning with the day when the gametes are mixed, not counting any time during which the embryo is stored.

This section of the 1990 Act also introduced the subsection that famously embodies the Warnock Report's 'compromise position': the fourteen-day rule. Thus, for the first time it was legal to carry out scientific research on human embryos, but within a limit of fourteen days.[73] While the 1990 Act enacted most of the proposals put forward by the Warnock Report, it remained silent on the key issue of 'respect' for the embryo.[74] The fourteen-day rule's embodiment in this Act was essentially an operationalisation of the 'respect' called for by the Warnock Committee, as were other limits on the use and storage of embryos, such as prohibiting their placement into an animal. From this we can see that only one particular embryonic context was truly *protected* by law, with regards to where it may be placed and who may place it *in utero*, amongst other things.

The provision of the fourteen-day rule aimed to provide a compromise between the competing aims of research and those of 'pro-life' groups by providing a cut-off for research at the point in embryonic development

---

[73] Section 3(4) 1990 Act (as amended).

[74] Fox and Murphy, 'Embryonic Hopes', 498–499.

where it begins to develop the structure that will eventually become the spinal cord. There are, however, calls for this rule to be revised after recent studies published in the scientific journals *Nature*[75] and *Nature Cell Biology*[76] have revealed that, for the first time, the embryo has been kept *in vitro* for as long as thirteen days. Shortly after, the Nuffield Council on Bioethics announced plans to explore a review of the fourteen-day time limit.[77] This shall be explored further in Chapter 7.

In s. 3(3)(d) we can see one of the pre-emptive rules of the 1990 Act,[78] which explicitly outlawed human cloning (which had not been developed at the time but was later inserted by the 2008 Act), for any purpose, as per the Warnock Recommendations. However, generally in a research context the placement of the resulting embryo *in utero* is strictly forbidden. There are good reasons for this. For example, research embryos do not necessarily have to be entirely biologically 'human'.[79] A new research process was thus legislated for under the 1990 Act, albeit in a very unclear way (the limits surrounding human–animal hybrids were later clarified in the 2008 amendments). As with any other 'research' embryo, on this pathway through the law, there is only one available end to the process (at the moment): termination. The 1990 Act did not explicitly mention what is meant by 'human embryo', except what can be inferred by its explicit ban on keeping an animal egg fertilised by human sperm – in order to test the sperm's fertility or normality – beyond the two-cell stage.[80] Arguably, from the 1990 Act's conception, the law has inexplicitly demarcated between 'types' of embryos, namely reproductive embryos and research/therapeutic embryos. 'Research embryos' must always, and ultimately, be disposed of; thus to say they are as 'protected' as reproductive embryos, or more so embryos *in utero*, would arguably be logically incoherent.

---

[75] A. Deglincerti and others, 'Self-organization of the Attached Human Embryo' (2016), *Nature*, 533(7602), 251–254.

[76] M. Shahbazi and others, 'Self-organization of the Human Embryo in the Absence of Maternal Tissues' (2016), *Nature Cell Biology*, 18(6), 700–708.

[77] See 'Council to consider "14 day rule" in embryo research' (*Nuffield Council on Bioethics*, 5 May 2016), www.nuffieldbioethics.org/news/2016/council-14-day-rule-embryo-research/.

[78] The 2008 amendments inserted a pre-emptive provision on mitochondrial replacement (see Human Fertilisation and Embryology Act 2008 ss1(5), 3(5) and 26). This, of course, was changed in the Human Fertilisation and Embryology (Mitochondrial donation) Regulations 2015.

[79] See Human Fertilisation and Embryology Act 1990, Schedule 2, s3(5).

[80] See 1990 Act. Schedule 2, s1(f).

What should we make of this in light of a processual analysis? It seems that quickening was removed as a stark legal–moral boundary, only to be replaced by others (the fourteen-day rule being a good example of this). As our understandings of developmental processes have changed, so have the legal boundaries that attempt to reflect those processes: first, quickening; then, viability in the early twentieth century; and now, for certain embryos, the fourteen-day rule. Each process, in its own way, has become 'the new quickening', that is a new ethico-legal line in the sand. It thus seems that law's boundaries have fluctuated, historically, in accordance with what we believe we know (to a degree). This, therefore, is the element of law that partly reflects process. Another example of processuality here, yet relating to embryos (and fetuses) *in utero*, is s.37 of the 1990 Act, which significantly amended s.1 of the 1967 Act and extended the permitted circumstances under which a woman may terminate her pregnancy.[81] While it did not explicitly differentiate between the different 'stages' of pregnancy, the 1990 Act's amendments broke the connection between the 1967 Act and the ILP Act by inserting the twenty-four-week time limit in s.1(1)(a). With these amendments, the law included more facets of (perceived) women's interests, in addition to those included under the original version of the 1967 Act. Under this new amended version, abortions may be carried out after twenty-four weeks/'viability' if the woman meets certain criteria. Notably, at the time, the insertion of the twenty-four-week limit was of practical insignificance, as very few abortions were then carried out after this stage, as at this point the fetus was presumed 'viable.'[82] Nonetheless, while the medicalisation of abortion law (i.e. medical knowledge shaping the substance of law) has muted the anti-abortion lobby,[83] it may still have unanticipated consequences. By the 1990s, with advances in medicine, the timeline of fetal viability shortened from twenty-eight weeks per the ILP Act to twenty-four weeks. When discussed in the House of Commons, it was noted that advances in science since the ILP Act mean that fetal viability could begin as early as twenty-four weeks.[84] Although fetal viability may make sense as a biological/legal boundary for many, scientific progress in this area is progressively reducing the age at which a premature baby can survive (although there are biological limits to this without ectogenesis,

[81] See Abortion Act 1967 (as amended) s1(1)(a)-(d).
[82] See Sheldon, 'Beyond Control', Chapter 6.
[83] Jackson, 'Regulating Reproduction', p. 83.
[84] See HC Deb 24 April 1990, vol 171, cols 166–304, 173.

i.e. artificial wombs outside of the woman's body).[85] This begs questions about how these lines will be drawn if prospective technologies such as ectogenesis become feasible.[86] There has already been academic debate on the drawing of somewhat 'arbitrary' lines in this area of regulation. For example, the twenty-four-week limit sits in juxtaposition to embryo research laws, as we see later, where a line of 'respect' is drawn at fourteen days.[87] These challenges to the 1990 and 1967 Acts are discussed further in Chapter 7 of this book.

Between 1990 and 2000, the 1990 Act remained steadfast.[88] One of law's main roles is to provide certainty to its subjects and arguably the 1990 Act did just that by dictating what we can and cannot do with regards to *in vitro* reproduction and research, thus bringing law relating to the early stages of human life out of the uncertainty of the 1970s and early 1980s. As we have seen, this uncertainty did not just stem from uncertainty surrounding what the law actually *is*, but also from societal disagreement regarding how we ought to treat embryos. The latter did not disappear with the 1990 Act, of course, but by providing a framework with a 'compromise', it did navigate this second kind of uncertainty in some sense. This uncertainty arguably returned, however, when the soundness of the 1990 Act was brought into question after concerns were raised about the 'slippery slope' to human reproductive cloning[89] several years after the first successfully cloned mammal was born in 1997 – Dolly the sheep.[90] Further, in 2000 legislation was passed to extend the purposes for which embryos may be used for research,

---

[85] G. Winter 'The Future of Artificial Wombs' (2017), *British Journal of Midwifery*, 25 (7), 416.

[86] See Z. Istvan, 'Artificial wombs are coming and the controversy is already here' (*Motherboard*, 4 August 2014), www.motherboard.vice.com/read/artificial-wombs-are-coming-and-the-controversys-already-here

[87] For more on this, see Jackson, 'Regulating reproduction', chapter 3.

[88] One of the few amendments to this Act worth noting in this context occurred in s156 of the 1994 Criminal Justice and Public Order Act, which amended s3 to include s3A (prohibition in connection with germ cells), which was coupled with a criminal sanction (as outlined above).

[89] Notably those in opposition to the practice often appealed to the dignity of the embryo. For discussion surrounding this see for example: D. Beyleveld, *Human Dignity in Bioethics and Biolaw* (Oxford University Press, 2001); R. Brownsword, 'Stem Cells and Cloning: Where the Regulatory Consensus Fails' (2004), *New England Law Review*, 39(3), 535–571.

[90] For summaries of the issues see, for example: J. Harris '"Goodbye Dolly?" The Ethics of Human Cloning' (1997), *Journal of Medical Ethics*, 23(6), 353–360; L. Hellsten, 'Dolly: Scientific Breakthrough or Frankenstein's Monster? Journalistic and Scientific Metaphors of Cloning' (2000), *Metaphor and Symbol*, 15(4), 213–221.

including increasing knowledge about serious disease and developing treatments for such disease.[91] The foundations of the 1990 Act were called into question in 2001 when the legality of a new form of cloning (cell nuclear replacement) was called into question. This case and the reactionary laws pushed through after it provide prime example of how advances in scientific processes may require a change in law to reflect those processes.

2.5   Quintavalle (2001–2003)

2.5.1   The Facts

In *Quintavalle*,[92] the issue before the Courts was whether embryos created by cell nuclear replacement (CNR), a cloning process, fell under the 1990 Act. CNR is the procedure through which the 'nucleus of an oocyte [is replaced with] with a nucleus taken from a somatic cell of another person'.[93] While the 1990 Act had a pre-emptive cloning clause in s.3(d), at the time, the 1990 Act defined an embryo as 'a live human embryo where *fertilisation is complete*'.[94] CNR, however, does not involve fertilisation. The court's navigation of this issue proved important for the 1990 Act, the landscape of which changed following this series of judgments. Because of *Quintavalle*, the 1990 Act was later amended to include 'any process capable of resulting in an embryo', and thus the legislative debacle over cloned embryos was effectively drawn to a close.

The case was first brought to the High Court, where it was held that a CNR embryo did not fall under the 1990 Act, as it was not 'an embryo where fertilisation is complete.'[95] Although the Secretary of State argued that a purposive approach should be taken in this case, the judge decided that such an approach would 'involve an impermissible rewriting and extension of the definition'.[96] In response to Crane J's judgment in the first instance of this case, the UK government rapidly produced 'knee-jerk' legislation that criminalised placing of an embryo that has been created by any method other than fertilisation in the

---

[91] Human Fertilisation and Embryology (Research Purposes) Regulations 2001.

[92] *R (Quintavalle)* v. *Secretary of State for Health* [2001] All ER 1013.

[93] T. Callus, 'Omnis definitio periculosa est: on the Definition of the Term "Embryo" in the Human Fertilisation & Embryology Act 1990' (2003), *Medical Law International*, 6 (1), 1–11.

[94] 1990 Act, s1(1)(a). Emphasis added.

[95] 1990 Act, s1(a).

[96] *Quintavalle* [2001], at 62.

womb of a woman:[97] the Human Reproductive Cloning Act 2001 (HRC Act). However, the statute left a legislative gap with regard to therapeutic cloning (i.e. cloning for research purposes) until the House of Lords authoritative decision in 2003, where the distinction for legal purposes was reintroduced

In 2002, the case was taken to the Court of Appeal,[98] where the appeal was upheld. The Court held that an embryo created by CNR and embryos created by IVF were 'morphologically and functionally indistinguishable'.[99] The Court's decision was made on the basis that both entities had the capacity to develop into a human being, and, further, that the policy of the 1990 Act was intended to cover all embryos created outside of the body.[100] This judgment thus confirmed the HFEA's capacity to license the creation of cloned organisms.[101]

Finally, the case was appealed to the House of Lords, who, in a rather strongly worded ruling that effectively shut down the debate on cloning at the time, unanimously sustained the decision of the Court of Appeal.[102] The Court held, dismissing the appeal, that s.1(1) of the 1990 Act should be given a purposive construction[103] (where the court considers the original purpose of the statute) and that it should be interpreted in the context of the 1990 Act as a whole, rather than based on specific wording.[104] As the 1990 Act was created to regulate live human embryos created outside of the human body, it was held that no activity in this field was intended to be left outwith its ambit.[105] It was also held that since Parliament could not have envisaged the creation of an embryo by any method other than fertilisation at the time of enactment,[106] the 1990 Act could not have intended to distinguish between an embryo created in this way and one produced by fertilisation. Furthermore, it was held that embryos created by CNR and those created by IVF are 'similar organisms', and thus 'fell within the same genus of

---

[97] D. Morgan and M. Ford, 'Cell Phoney: Human Cloning after Quintavalle' (2004), *Journal of Medical Ethics*, 30(6) 524.

[98] *R (Quintavalle) v. Secretary of State for Health* [2002] All EWCA Civ 29.

[99] Ibid., at 639.

[100] Morgan and Ford, 'Cell Phoney', 524.

[101] Callus, 'Omnis definitio periculosa est', 1–2.

[102] *Regina (on the application of Quintavalle) v. Secretary of State for Health* [2003] UKHL 13.

[103] *Royal College of Nursing v. Department of Health and Social Security* [1981] AC 800.

[104] *Quintavalle* [2003], at 8.

[105] Ibid., at 14.

[106] Ibid., at 7.

facts' as those whereby the policy of the 1990 Act was formulated by Parliament.[107] The court also held that CNR did not fall within s.3(3)(d) of the 1990 Act. The manner in which the embryos were created was not the main issue at hand, according to the House of Lords, but rather the fact that Parliament had intended to cover all embryos created outside the human body with the 1990 Act.[108] As *Quintavalle* and the resulting legislation demonstrated, CNR was a huge scientific advancement that the 1990 Act had failed to anticipate, even though it was mentioned in the Warnock Report.

Why did the House of Lords make this decision? As aforementioned, perhaps disallowing CNR to fall under the section may have opened a 'can of worms'. By distinguishing between the creation of cloned embryos for reproductive purposes and research purposes, the courts drew yet another 'line in the sand'. Yet, how useful is the implicit regulatory distinction between therapeutic and reproductive cloning? Martin Johnson argues that the current law captures embryonic process to some extent with the introduction of the reproductive/therapeutic distinction, by distinguishing between two 'classes' of embryo. Nonetheless, he also argues that it could also do more: 'What is being proposed here is a generalizing extension of this concept to reproductive and therapeutic "processes in general" and to reproductive and therapeutic "embryos" in particular.'[109] Nonetheless, these types of demarcations were discarded as a regulatory solution by the 2005 House of Commons Science and Technology Committee (HCSTC) report[110] (see section 2.5.2 below).

Arguably, *Quintavalle*[111] has demonstrated that we *can* alter the embryo's explicit, legal definition under certain circumstances. Further, the case inexplicitly widened the reproductive/therapeutic distinction. It is not unforeseeable that a similar amendment to those made in 2008 may recur if required. Nonetheless, while important, none of the policy discussions during, or indeed after, *Quintavalle* have addressed the nature and extent of the embryo's legal status. Notably, when definition and status are addressed holistically, it becomes clear that they are not

---

[107] Ibid., at 15.

[108] D. Solter and others, *Embryo Research in Pluralistic Europe*, vol. 21 (Springer Science & Business Media, 2003), p. 122.

[109] M. Johnson, 'Escaping the Tyranny of the Embryo? A New Approach to ART Regulation Based on UK and Australian Experiences' (2006), *Human Reproduction*, 21(11), 2756–2765, 2761.

[110] House of Commons Science and Technology Committee, 'Human Reproductive Technologies and the Law: Report of the Fifth Session 2004-5' (2005).

[111] *Quintavalle* [2003].

entirely distinct; a change in one has implications for the other. For example, by introducing clarification regarding the definition of the embryo, as noted earlier, the 2008 amendments consolidated the (inexplicit) legal distinction in status between reproductive and therapeutic cloning. After all, the legislative response to uncertainty here, as we have seen, was initially a knee-jerk ban on reproductive cloning, but even this law did not cover all forms of cloning; it left a gap regarding therapeutic cloning, which the courts eventually filled on appeal. This case arguably cemented different 'types' of embryo in law. Thus, as the legal wedge between 'reproductive' and 'therapeutic' embryos grew, as a correlative, the types of processes and the network of pathways available for embryos under law also grew.

Now, licences for treatment cannot be legally awarded where cloned embryos have a reproductive end and a distinction between therapeutic and reproductive cloning has been introduced into the law. *Quintavalle* thus raised important questions about the function of the judiciary in statutory interpretation in reference to the status of the embryo in law today. While the court's role in making (and unmaking) law is not the direct subject of this book, it is important to note the part it has played in the law we have today. The *Quintavalle* case and the resulting 2008 amendments to the 1990 Act also brought the embryo out of legal uncertainty, if not out of a 'dangerous' moral and legal space. In this space, certain research practices were unregulated and/or research practices had been left open to legal challenges through a gap in the law. In this way, we were brought out of legal uncertainty regarding how we can treat embryos under law (i.e. what was and was not legal), and we saw this again in *Quintavalle* with regards to cloning for research purposes.

On the subject of case law it is worth noting, briefly, the (non) role of the European Court of Human Rights (ECtHR) on UK law governing the embryo/fetus. Generally speaking, the ECtHR has avoided ruling definitively on the legal status of the embryo/fetus, but has considered whether they have a right to life under Article 2 of the Convention,[112] holding that this point falls under countries' margin of appreciation.[113] It has recognised that the health and interests of the mother implicitly limit the embryo's/fetus's rights.[114] These cases nonetheless have arguably had

---

[112] See, for example *Vo v. France* (2005) 40 EHRR 12; *Evans v. UK* (2008) 46 EHRR 34.

[113] See *Brüggemann and Scheuten v. Federal Republic of Germany* [1977] EHRR 113 on state interference with reproduction and margin of appreciation per Article 8; and *Vo v. France* at 82 regarding margin of appreciation per Article 2.

[114] See *Paton v. UK* (1980) EHRR 408 at 415; and *Vo v. France* at 80.

little (if any) effect on the UK's governance of the embryo *in vitro*. It is also worth noting that in *Brüstle*,[115] a patent case, the European Court of Justice (ECJ) laid down a legal definition of 'embryo'.[116] These examples are all connected through the different ways in which courts will/will not intervene to define/protect the embryo. Yet at the same time, it is also important to acknowledge that there are very different policy consider-ations at play. In the UK, the focus has been on the research/'therapeutic' use of embryos and their use for reproduction; ECHR case law has focused more on access to abortion services and the legal status (person-hood) of the embryo/fetus therein; and finally, the ECJ has engaged in this debate to an extent, regarding acceptable commercial practices, monopolies, and patents. Nonetheless, underlying all of this, for the UK there is a floating, vague notion of the 'special status' of the embryo and the extent to which it should be recognised and taken into account in law. Despite evolving distinctions within our framework as amendments (and decisions) are made, the singular 'special status' has remained.

2.5.2   The Aftermath: Defining 'The Embryo'? (2005–2008)

In 2005, the HCSTC produced their fifth annual report. Post-*Quintavalle*, one of the main issues at hand was how to define the human embryo under the 1990 Act. Citing the House of Lords' judgment in *Quintavalle*, the report stated that:

> This purposive approach to the definition of an embryo could be seen as resolving the definition of the embryo. Nonetheless, in its evidence, the HFEA suggests that the definition contained in the HFE Act is unsatisfac-tory and proposes that 'An amended definition of "embryo" and "gam-etes" might clarify that the remit of the Act also extends to embryos that have been created by other means than "fertilisation" (CNR, partheno-genesis), and to artificially created gametes'.[117]

The HCSTC report then went on to describe *three* ways in which 'the perceived problem of the definition of an embryo can be addressed', notably with specific reference to the issues that arose from cloning, based on evidence put forward by academics and professionals. They concluded that defining the embryo would not be suitable. As Chapter 3

[115] *Brüstle* v. *Greenpeace* (C-34/10) [2012] All ER EC 809.

[116] Ibid., at 12: 'An embryo is a fertilised human ovum capable of development, from the time of karyogamy . . .'

[117] House of Commons Science and Technology Committee, 'Human Reproductive Technologies and the Law: Report of the Fifth Session 2004-5' (HC, 2005), 51.

discusses, while the HCSTC was rather dismissive of (re)defining the embryo, academics later called for new definition(s) in order to provide more clarity to this murky legal landscape. First, the HCSTC report discussed redefining 'embryo' on the basis of how it was created:

a) By redefining an embryo, at least defining those types of embryo that fall under legislation, according to the way in which they were *created*. This has the advantage of clarity but it fails to embrace any future technique that might be developed. For example, it might become possible to reprogramme an adult cell to behave like an embryo. Vivian Nathanson from the BMA says: 'The question, really, is whether it is possible to find a simple definition that would capture not only all current scientific possibilities but the ones that people speculate might happen within the next 10–15 years [...] but if one cannot find an acceptable phrase for that then we would still commend putting in the concept of cell nuclear replacement because it is so important'. If this approach were to be adopted, the legislation would need to be sufficiently flexible to allow new forms of embryo to be included. An alternative approach would be to distinguish between fertilised embryos and what Professor Kenyon Mason of Edinburgh Law School termed 'laboratory artefacts'. Dr Veronica van Heyningen, a geneticist who contributed to our online consultation, also made this distinction: 'I would not [...] think that laboratory experiments where you transplant a nucleus for entirely laboratory purposes into an oocyte [egg [...]]] is an embryo'. By making this distinction, as the Human Reproductive Cloning Act 2001 does, it would be possible to provide that only embryos for which fertilisation had taken place could be implanted. The disadvantage of this would be that some of these 'laboratory artefacts' may have benefits, both for infertility treatment and avoiding genetic diseases.[118]

Interestingly, while the HCSTC report emphasised that attempts to define the embryo based on mode of creation or its capabilities should not be made, the 1990 Act later developed to demarcate and define embryos in a manner which arguably derives precisely from the manner of their creation by clarifying the rules surrounding admixed embryos. Recent advancements such as *in vitro* gametogenesis (which the HCSTC allude to in the above excerpt where they say it 'might become possible to reprogramme an adult cell to behave like an embryo') prove the HCSTC's

---

[118] Ibid., p.26. Emphasis added.

hypothesis that this mode of definition would not capture all. Had the 1990 Act been changed to do so, it seems very likely that another *Quintavalle* scenario would have arisen.

The HCSTC report next considered how we might define embryos based on their 'capabilities':

b) By *defining an embryo by its capabilities*. For example, it could embrace any diploid cell (two sets of chromosomes) with the potential to differentiate. However, Professor Lee M Silver from Princeton University describes a broader definition: 'There's a word biologists use to describe a cell, or group of cells, that by itself can develop into a whole animal or person: That word is "embryo". Each random bunch of eight to 10 human ES [embryonic stem] cells is nothing more or less than a "naked" human embryo – that is, an embryo without its pre-placental "coat"'. This comment illustrates the danger that embryonic stem cells might be swept up by such a definition. This problem might be solved by including the provision that the cell(s) must have the potential to develop in the womb in order to be defined as an embryo. However, the cells' potential might be open to debate and subject to technological advances. The Scottish Council on Human Bioethics cites German legislation in which any totipotent cell (capable of developing into a complete organism or differentiating into any of its cells or tissues), which has been extracted from an embryo which may divide and develop into an individual human being once the necessary further conditions are provided, is considered to be an embryo.[119]

Paragraph 52(b) is not necessarily illogical; unforeseen entities (such as pluripotent stem cells) may be caught up in definitions based on capabilities. While this book does not necessarily propose that the embryo should be terminologically defined, critiques such as this are arguably symptomatic of the embryo's 'legal status' (and definition's) opacity. As discussed briefly below and further in Chapter 6, the law cannot be expected to withstand *all* technological advances; it is thus important to revisit it. Some might believe that where there are new technologies, law has to be absolutely 'bullet proof' or even 'future proof'. On the contrary, if the law is too 'bullet proof', and thus rigid, it cannot revisit and/or be flexible in light of scientific or social changes.

---

[119] Ibid., p.26–7. Emphasis added.

Having decided that embryos should not be defined by their mode of creation *or* their capabilities, the HCSTC suggested:

c) A final option would be to *avoid any definition*, as is the case in the 2001 Human Reproductive Cloning Act. Using this approach, the term 'embryo' would cover the normal usage of the word. We understand that this approach has been taken by the French in recent legislation.[120]

It is certainly questionable whether we can define something so complicated in statute, but if the law were to be reconsidered, is there anything to be said for a definition based upon creation or capabilities (paras 52(a)-(b) above)? Further, is there anything to be said for an approach that combines both? Interestingly, Paragraph 53, below, also refers to 'other forms of embryo' and their regulation 'insofar as they are created and used for research purposes':

> 53. We are concerned that any legal *definitions* of the embryo based on the way it was *created* or its *capabilities* would either be open to legal challenge or fail to withstand technological advance. The attempt to define an embryo in the HFE Act has proved counter-productive, and we recommend that any future legislation should resist the temptation to redefine it. We consider that a better approach would be to define the forms of embryo that can be implanted and under what circumstances. Using this approach, only those forms of embryo specified by the legislation, such as those created by fertilisation, could be implanted in the womb and thereby used for reproductive purposes. Other forms of embryo would be regulated insofar as they are created and used for research purposes.[121]

Here, the HCSTC contended that defining the embryo would be counterproductive. Defining the forms of embryo that can be implanted, and banning all others, might be logically and practically appealing. It ensures that anything that might be generally held as morally undesirable cannot be implanted (at least not without first having public/legal consultation and subsequent legal change). Nonetheless, legal loopholes cannot be completely avoided, as *Quintavalle* has shown. This approach thus comes with its own problems. Writing in the same year as the HCSTC (2005), Catherine Stanton and John Harris argued that: ' ... the need for clarification of terms such as "embryo" is important, not solely in the ethical debate, but also to ensure clarity in areas of

---

[120] Ibid., p.28. Emphasis added.
[121] Ibid. Emphasis added.

regulation'.[122] Some, however, argue that such clarification can render law 'rigid and inflexible',[123] and consequently that law should just outline what is to be illegal.[124] Stanton and Harris argue that while this might sound appealing, it would not work for two reasons. First, it is impossible to predict what advances we will have and therefore whether we should outlaw them. Secondly, they pointed out that avoiding definitions like 'human embryo' leaves uncertainty, as it did with CNR in 2005[125] (until the 1990 Act was changed in 2008). They argued that in a post-Dolly era, the status of embryos created by CNR, and the difficulties caused by advances in science, means we need to alter our terminology: ' . . . drafting less prescriptive legislation in areas of technological development may not be the panacea it initially appears. Particularly in cases where the criminal law is at issue, legislation should err on the side of clarity, putting present-day certainty ahead of possible future uncertainty.'[126] Of course, shortly after this was written the law did alter its terminology, but science has continued to advance since the 2008 amendments, and while this was a step in the right direction, arguably it did not go far enough (for some).[127] Even post-2008 amendments, some confusion still remains has to how new embryos (e.g. those created by *in vitro* gametogenesis, see Chapter 7) should fall under the current framework.

Presumably the legal challenge that many supporters of embryo research fear might be something similar to the above *Quintavalle* scenario. Nonetheless, paragraph 53 of the HCSTC report did not note the arguably positive legal solution that came from the evolution of the 1990 Act (positive in terms of enabling the aims of the 1990 Act, which the HCSTC support). Further, it is arguable that, looking at the wording in (c) and 53, we can see a focus on end-point in the reproductive or research process. It is essentially saying, 'here are the processes we allow and thus here are the end points we allow' (to be born you have to be genetically 'human' and not cloned). It allowed cloning, but only

---

[122] C. Stanton and J. Harris, 'The Moral Status of the Embryo Post-Dolly' (2005), *Journal of Medical Ethics*, 31(4), 221–225, 223.

[123] B. Gogarty, 'What Exactly is an Exact Copy? And Why it Matters When Trying to Ban Human Reproductive Cloning in Australia' (2003), *Journal of Medical Ethics*, 29(2), 84–89, 84.

[124] Ibid.

[125] Stanton and Harris, 'The Moral Status of the Embryo', 224.

[126] Ibid.

[127] See M. Fox, 'The Human Fertilisation and Embryology Act 2008: Tinkering at the Margins' (2009), *Feminist Legal Studies*, 17(3), 333–344.

based on one particular end-point (disposal). For this book, an integral feature of taking a processual approach is that one needs to know what that process is leading to (see Chapter 5). The HCSTC thus seem to have engaged with process, but only to some extent; because they did not account for the features of embryonic transformation and evolution (although perhaps they did not want to, given the post-*Quintavalle* climate of the time).

A year after the HCSTC report, the 2006 Department of Health published a White Paper on the review of the 1990 Act continued in similar vein and concluded that the legal *status quo* regarding human embryos should remain:

> The Government has concluded that the foundations of the current law remain sound, and provide an effective and appropriate model of regula-tion for the development and use of human reproductive technologies. This echoes the findings of the recent inquiry by the House of Commons Science and Technology Committee, which similarly concluded that the approach taken to the status of the human embryo remained appropriate.[128]

It is unclear what 'foundations of the current law' meant, although it seems likely that it referred to the philosophical basis of the framework – i.e. a 'special status' – taken from the recommendations of the Warnock Report. Although the approach advocated by both reports has resulted in somewhat desirable legal and technological outcomes (for those who support IVF and research, regulated through a 'compromise position'), its adequacy after having stood as a pillar of the 1990 Act (as amended) for thirty years nonetheless needs to be subjected to on-going scrutiny. As the *Quintavalle* saga has shown and the critiques of the law that have surfaced in recent years (for example the fourteen-day rule) confirm, opening up the embryo debate runs risk of research being 'shut down', which is undesirable to those who support it.

From what we have seen so far, from the original Act, to *Quintavalle*, to the HCSTC White Paper, law needs to be adaptive. What happened, post-*Quintavalle*, however, was the creation of multiple rules for embryos in law and a deepening of the reproductive/therapeutic distinc-tion, and that in doing so has not accounted for the multiplicity of embryonic processes the 1990 Act leads embryos through (and indeed the ends it leads them towards) as identified earlier. That is, the current

---

[128] Department of Health, 'Review of the Human Fertilisation and Embryology Act' (White Paper, Cm6989, 2006), 1.8.

legal framework, under the rubric of a 'special status', is masking these processes. We thus arguably need to consider the way in which we can manage this in a more transparent and coherent manner.[129]

It is important to note that the context-based approach proposed later in this book does not intend to counter this perspective. It is clear, from cases such as *Quintavalle* and the benefit of hindsight, that clarifying the meaning of 'embryo' by either definition or capability alone would not sufficiently capture some of the advancements that have happened since 2005. Nonetheless, as discussed further in Chapter 6, a context-based approach does advocate a reconsideration of the embryo's legal onto-logical constitution(s) with processuality (as central to law-making here) in mind.

2.6 The Human Fertilisation and Embryology Act 2008 and Beyond (2008–2020)

This section briefly explores the 1990 Act (as amended), as it stands today, before going on to engage with the critical literature surrounding the evolution and status of the embryo under the 1990 Act (as amended) in the next chapter.

The recommendations in the 2006 White Paper eventually became the Human Fertilisation and Embryology Bill, after scrutiny by a Joint Committee of both houses. This Bill received Royal Assent in November 2008 and became the 2008 Act. Some of the key amendments it made to the 1990 Act (some of which have already been discussed) included:[130]

- *The meaning of 'embryo' changed.* It is no longer defined as one 'where fertilisation is complete'. Instead, it is still a 'live human embryo', which can include an egg in the process of fertilisation, but it may also include an egg 'undergoing any other process capable of resulting in an embryo'.[131] This section also explicitly excludes human admixed embryos from the meaning of 'embryo'.[132] This is a nod to human cloning, another technique of creating an embryo not foreseen in the

---

[129] Parts 2 and 3 of this book consider this.

[130] Some other notable changes made include; change for need for a father, prohibition on sex selection, changes to parenthood and consent. See Alghrani, *Regulating Assisted Reproductive Technologies*, p. 30.

[131] 2008 Act, s1(2).

[132] Ibid.

original 1990 Act. Interestingly, the HFEA website refers to this as 'ensuring that the creation and use of all human embryos outside the body – whatever the process used in their creation – are subject to regulation',[133] rather than the introduction of governance of CNR techniques to the 1990 Act.

- *The 2008 Act inserts s. 3ZA*, which details permitted embryos, gametes, and so on for placement in a woman.[134] This section explicitly excludes embryos where nuclear or mitochondrial DNA have been altered being placed in a woman. Nonetheless, s. 26 of the 2008 Act also inserts s. 35A, which provides that modifications may be made in respect of the latter, which indeed later took place in 2015.[135] The amendment also explicitly excludes embryos created by cloning techniques being placed in a woman; and

- *The 2008 Act also inserts s. 4A*, which allows for the licensed keeping and use of human admixed embryos for up to fourteen days, as long as they are not placed in a woman.[136] Here the legal construct of 'the embryo' has changed within the confines of the 1990 Act, as driven by advances in science. This change arguably brought the embryo out of a condition of uncontrolled flux (highlighted by the *Quintavalle* case) and into the boundedness of the law. Nonetheless, in making this change Parliament was careful not to revisit the embryo's 'special status'.

Regarding the first bullet point, it is worth noting that this amendment moved us to the stage where law to some extent recognises processes needed for an embryo to be eventually born (as we have seen). Today, because of technology, the law also recognises new processes that can result in embryos. Further, the amendments specifically forbid that certain embryos appear in certain contexts, e.g. implantation in a woman's womb.[137] The legal response to the many transformative possibilities of embryos has been to prohibit them at the earliest stage, including human cloning, human chimeras, and 'enhanced' humans. As Karpin argues:

---

[133] 'Human Fertilisation and Embryology Act 2008' (*Department of Health*, 26 July 2010), www .webarchive.nationalarchives.gov.uk/+/http://www.dh.gov.uk/en/Publicationsandstatistics/ Legislation/Actsandbills/DH_080211

[134] 2008 Act, s3(5).

[135] Human Fertilisation and Embryology (Mitochondrial Donation) Regulations 2015.

[136] 2008 Act, s4(2).

[137] Karpin argues that by articulating the particular contexts in which the embryo cannot appear, the law creates new possibilities for the embryo. See Karpin, 'Uncanny embryos', 602.

> It is through the enactment of prohibitory legislation that (legislative) life
> is given to entities that are yet to be made. In so doing, the law gives reality
> to the fantasy of the very beings that it seeks to deny. Law through both
> regulation and prohibition carries us forward in the imaginary leap that is
> necessary to take us from the embryonic being to the *post-human*
> being.[138]

In this way, lawmakers could consider possibilities and possible teleologies or futures for embryos that we do not want. Yet, it arguably provides a way of thinking about it in a more processual way. Whether we want these embryos, is, of course, another question.

Despite the remaining underlying 'special status' of the embryo in the 1990 Act (as amended), the word 'status', or any other of similar meaning, does not appear once in the 1990 Act (as amended) in reference to the embryo. It is clear, however, that the recommendations of the Warnock Report, made in light of its proposal for a 'special status', are reflected here, operationalised through provisions such as the fourteen-day rule and s4A. The 1990 Act adopted the precise time limit recommended in the aforementioned report and also criminalised many of the activities in alignment with the report's recommendations. Admixed embryos, CNR, and mitochondrial donations, three of the biggest changes to the original 1990 Act, were all referred to in Chapter 12 (Possible Future Developments in Research) of the Warnock Report. Cloning was mentioned, but not advised for or against, as it was not technically possible at the time.[139] Admixed embryos were discussed in more depth in the Report, as the technique was available at the time. The Warnock Committee took the view that this was justified and should be subject to licensing and termination at the two-cell stage.[140] This was enacted within Schedule 2 of the original Act, and clarified further in the 2008 amendments. The Warnock Committee also noted the potential for the prevention of genetic defects and the insertion of 'a replacement gene which will remedy the defect'.[141] On this, they believed that developments in this field would be precluded by the controls they recommended, but also envisaged that the guidance on this may be reviewed in the future to 'take account of both changes in scientific knowledge and changes in public attitudes'.[142]

---

[138] Ibid.
[139] 'Warnock Report', para. 12.11 and para. 12.14.
[140] Ibid., para.12.2-12.3.
[141] Ibid., para. 12.15.
[142] Ibid., 12.16.

Notably, since the 2008 amendments, the 1990 Act has been further by incremental regulations, for example, to allow lic(treatment using mitochondrial replacement therapy under th Fertilisation and Embryology (Mitochondrial Donation) R(2015. Aside from regulations such as these, however, no significant amendments have taken place, especially not any that address or affect the 'special' status of the embryo under the Act. While the 1990 Act has been subsequently amended, these amendments do not stray from the Report's original recommendations with respect to any future possible technique that they strongly recommended should be precluded by law.[143] Indeed, Chapter 12 of the Warnock Report addressed several 'possible future developments in research', some of which are indeed now possible today: trans-species fertilisation, ectogenesis, cloning, nucleus substitution, and the gestation of human embryos in other species.[144] For some, the Committee merely described what the technique might involve, whilst for others (especially the gestation of human embryos in other species), the Committee emphatically recommended that they should be a criminal offence. Overall, then, law has not strayed far (if at all) from the Report's recommendations published in 1984. Nonetheless, it has arguably evolved from 1990 to 2008 to 2015 beyond the Warnock Committee's original vision.

2.7 Conclusions

Historically, law and regulation has developed to reflect the changing boundaries of what is 'certain' and 'uncertain'. New uncertainties arise[145] and some old ones remained.[146] We have moved, in some ways, from one type of uncertainty to another when it comes to embryo regulation, and this is because the embryo is an inherently processual entity; that in and of itself has not changed. This is not necessarily a 'bad' thing for law, for uncertainty can be used positively. Nonetheless, as discussed further in the next chapter, ineffectively capturing that uncertainty can be problematic. This book is not advocating that we create absolute certainty in

---

[143] See Warnock Report, 70–74.
[144] Ibid.
[145] I.e. Should research and reproductive embryos be treated the same? Should the 14-day rule be extended? What can we find out about time between 14 and 28 days? Etcetera.
[146] I.e. The question of how we should treat embryos is, of course, is never certain because there is no objective answer; in recognition of moral pluralism it is very much a subjective matter.

the law, nor absolute processuality (arguably neither of which are possible), but rather that we navigate the uncertain, processual nature of the embryo and that the law that governs it does so in a way that enables us to navigate that liminality and emerge out of the other side where deemed appropriate.

Indeed, the human embryo hovers, legally, between several cultural and moral categories, in addition to biological categories, too. While it clearly does not have a legally articulated 'status' under the 1990 Act, it occupies a legal (and for some, moral) threshold between all of these aforementioned categories. Thus, while there is no explicit legal status of the embryo, what we have, legally, is still *something*. By virtue of giving the embryo *in vitro* legal recognition, with attached allowances and limits, it arguably has a status of sorts. Furthermore, bearing in mind that the law adopted most of the Warnock Report's recommendations, its status may indeed be described as 'special', as the Report prescribed. It is 'not nothing',[147] yet not a 'person'. From what we have seen, its status remains 'special', the meaning of which is unclear except that it is afforded 'respect' of sorts. Beyond that, we can glean little regarding what is the extent or nature of this status from domestic law. It does not have an explicit legal status, but, as some argue, it may have one implicitly.[148]

The Warnock Committee, tasked with navigating moral uncertainty with regards to how we ought to treat embryos-in-law, met this uncertainty by proposing a 'compromise' (whether or not it was a compromise is another matter). This compromise was met by affording all embryos *in vitro* a 'special status', recognising embryos' unquestionably human origins, and the (perceived) value we thus afford them (to whatever extent). The above has also taught us that this 'special status' is singular, all encompassing, for all embryos. But as we have seen, the 1990 Act has multiple embryos, and multiple processes, arguably further entrenched by the 2008 amendments. As an interim conclusion, therefore: there is an intellectual gap between the intellectual basis of the 1990 Act (a singular, all-encompassing, and vague status) and the practical realities of the multiplicity of pathways (and ends) embryos are led through under this framework. The dimensions of this gap shall be discussed further in the next chapter.

---

[147] *St George's Healthcare NHS Trust* v. *S* [1998] All ER 673, [1998] 3 WLR 936, 952.
[148] Hammond-Browning, 'Ethics, Embryos and Evidence', 606.

3

From Process to Purgatory

Moving Beyond Legal Stasis

3.1 Introduction

Since the 1990 Act's inception, and especially after its subsequent amendment in 2008, the legal status of the embryo has been subject to a considerable amount of academic discussion. While there has been substantial support for the Warnock Committee's steadfast approach, calls are increasingly being made to revisit the 1990 Act (as amended) in the light of recent advances in technology and changes in societal perception of these techniques. Notably, while these critiques of the 1990 Act (as amended) and the embryo's 'special status' are varied, efforts within academic literature to provide alternatives for embryo regulation are rare compared to critiques of the regulatory structure itself. The analysis offered in this book has found that while some writers do provide suggestions for alternative regimes, these are only starting points upon which future regulation could build. While appealing, as points of consideration for any revision of the legislative framework, they therefore tend to leave analytical gaps.

We have seen thus far that the intellectual underpinning of the 1990 Act (as amended) – the embryo's rather vague 'special status' – has not changed since the Act's inception. Moreover, we have seen that any attempts to change the intellectual basis of the Act, for example the 2008 Act, have been cautious at best. Thus, as a way of mapping the landscape to date, and also of clearing a path towards novel approaches to regulating the embryo, this chapter undertakes two important tasks: (1) an academic analysis of the caution mentioned earlier – a fade from discourse – which has only intensified the confusion surrounding the 'special' legal status of the embryo; and (2) an assessment of some of the ways in which the unclear nature, source, and extent of the legal status of the embryo could be clarified by exploring two key normative legal tools that are often employed to provide certainty – binding objects within a regulatory space and drawing boundaries. Ultimately, this chapter posits that the root of the vague nature of the embryo's 'special status' is a prevailing *uncertainty* regarding how we ought to treat embryos *in vitro*, because, by its very nature, it does not easily fit into normative social, moral, or legal categories.

3.2   Towards Legal Stasis?

With the advent of new technologies, particularly with the incorporation of regulated stem cell research (SCR) into the 1990 Act in 2000, the embryo's apparently singular and unchanging 'special status' has become increasingly problematic as a legal mechanism and, indeed, as a legal reality. This is not due to the indefensibility of this mechanism at the time it was made but rather because of the legal stasis and unreflexive (re)iteration of the embryo's 'special status' that the 1990 Act and its subsequent amendments perpetuate. It is important to recognise that while not all commentaries analysed below cite process explicitly, it is nonetheless the case that important lessons can be drawn from them for the purposes of this book because of law's failure to reflect the embryo's processual and enduringly *uncertain* nature.

3.2.1   Fade from Discourse

The contested nature of the status of the embryo has generally faded from both policy and public spheres of discussion in recent years.[1] For some, this is surprising given that the legislation (and the Warnock Report) 'failed to resolve the fundamental issue of the juridical status of the embryo'.[2] However, according to Fox, this juridical status is of both practical and theoretical importance considering the number of embryos that exist 'in a cryopreserved state and legal limbo in laboratories around the world'.[3] As briefly discussed in Chapter 2, the courts have done little to address this, and, in fact, the embryo's presence in judicial commentary is markedly decreasing. This is not to say that the courts can or

---

[1] Although discussions surrounding the status of embryos came to the fore very briefly when, in 2016, questions were raised over extending the fourteen-day time limit on research. See Chapter 7 of this book.

[2] M. Fox, 'Pre-persons, Commodities or Cyborgs: The Legal Construction and Representation of the Embryo' (2000), *Health Care Analysis*, 8(2), 171.

[3] Ibid., 172.

should do anything to address this; on the contrary, there are clear limitations on judicial action that would prevent any court from doing this. Moreover, for a purposive approach to be adopted again towards the interpretation of the meaning of 'embryo' in law (as it was in *Quintavalle*) in any new case, the original purpose or intention of the 1990 Act (as amended) would have to remain unchanged by scientific and/or social progress. Yet this is clearly not the case today, particularly as social, political, and scientific understandings of embryos, assisted reproduction, and embryo research have changed considerably over time. In sum, the hands of the courts are tied unless and until a new case is brought to them that challenges the status of the embryo and raises significant legal questions about the fitness for purpose of the underlying legislation.

A further compounding factor is that the policy reasons behind this fade from discourse are, to an extent, quite clear. As Baroness Mary Warnock has iterated in the past, and reiterated at the 2016 Progress Educational Trust Conference, *in vitro* fertilisation (IVF) and embryo research came very close to being blocked by Enoch Powell's Bill.[4] While the risk of losing the benefits of IVF and embryo research entirely is one which some might intuitively not wish to take, one cannot ignore the relatively progressive evolution in society and social views on these matters since 1985. There are those who believe that public and policy debate may not necessarily lead to the demise of the 1990 Act. For example, Callus argues that the decision in *Quintavalle*[5] 'stifled democratic debate' on the development of cloning techniques. She maintains that cases such as this demonstrate how the law has become servile to science and to scientific criteria, which in turn subdues full democratic debate.[6] For Callus, such debate would not 'smother' promising research such as this; rather, it would enable a balance between respect for the embryo and respect for those who benefit from these types of research.[7]

---

[4] See M. Warnock, 'The Warnock Report and the 14-day Rule' (*Rethinking the Ethics of Embryo Research: Genome Editing, 13 Days and beyond*, London, 7 December 2016). She also iterated that she believes that those who oppose embryo research are still there in the sidelines, 'rallying ... forces'. She added that every time there have been amendments to the 1990 Act, we have seen the same forces have come together and made it extremely precarious as to whether the law would go through. From this, it may be understandable as to why legislators might not want to bring the embryo's status to the forefront again.

[5] See *Quintavalle* [2003].

[6] T. Callus, 'Omnis definitio periculosa est: On the Definition of the Term "Embryo" in the Human Fertilisation & Embryology Act 1990' (2003), *Medical Law International*, 6 (1), 1–11.

[7] Ibid., p. 8.

Perhaps the answer to this is as Mason concludes: that in order to satisfy the pro-life lobby, any reform in the law should recognise that 'no-one can deny that the embryo represents a form of human life deserving, as the Warnock Committee had it, some sort of protection and respect in law'.[8]

Jackson describes the 1990 Act (as amended), based on the Warnock Report's recommendations, as having 'stood the test of time rather well'.[9] Sarah Franklin, in praise of the Report, goes further. She writes:

> In spite of the many criticisms of the Warnock Report for its failure to address the supposedly crucial issue of 'the moral status of the human embryo' (criticisms Warnock fully anticipated and skilfully answered in the original Preface to her report) . . . we can see in retrospect why she was wise to do so . . . embryos exist as a plurality. It is not possible to give them an 'absolute' status – legally or ethically any more than socially or politically.[10]

Arguing that 'when some legislation is preferable to none, the absolute must give way to the acceptable', Franklin contrasts the United Kingdom to the United States, where the dominance of particular religious views over public and political debate has (at least in the past) resulted in a legal stalemate and, as a result, there is little regulation in this area.[11] She thus posits that, if we are to learn from this, the law cannot be absolutist but must prescribe what is acceptable as a minimum (as the Warnock Committee did). Similar to Franklin, Natasha Hammond-Browning argues that while the embryo's status in law is equivocal, it was based upon evidence received by the Committee in their attempt to determine a suitable mode of regulation for this field in a pragmatic manner at a time where there was no regulation at all.[12]

Hammond-Browning praises the work of the Committee and its subsequent report, which she describes 'an excellent demonstration of a report that took into account diverse views in order to make recommendations on a number of divisive issues'.[13] Nonetheless, she also

---

[8] J. K. Mason, 'Discord and Disposal of Embryos' (2004), *Edinburgh Law Review*, 8(1), 84–93, 92.

[9] E. Jackson, 'The Human Fertilisation and Embryology Bill' (2008), *Expert Review of Obstetrics and Gynaecology*, 3(4), 429–431, 429.

[10] S. Franklin, 'Response to Marie Fox and Thérèse Murphy' (2010), *Social Legal Studies*, 19, 505–510, 508–509.

[11] Ibid.

[12] N. Hammond-Browning, 'Ethics, Embryos and Evidence: A Look Back at Warnock' (2015), *Medical Law Review*, 23(4), 619.

[13] Ibid.

concludes her paper by calling for another Warnock-esque committee in this 'new era of reproductive technologies and reproductive ethics':[14] 'advances in human fertilisation and embryology treatment and research have progressed far beyond what was envisaged by the Warnock Committee in the early 1980s'.[15] Citing some of the more recent advances in reproductive science, for example mitochondrial replacement therapy, she prescribes

> a new committee that had as its remit the ethical, legal, and social consideration of these new and future uses of reproductive technologies and research would undoubtedly be of much value in regulating this next era of human fertilisation and embryology, in much the same way that Warnock has for the past 30 years.[16]

Indeed, as she points out, there have been some excellent reports produced in this field since Warnock – for example, from bodies such as the Nuffield Council on Bioethics – but none has looked at this field as holistically as the Warnock Report did.[17] Hammond-Browning has not been alone in her analysis. Sarah Franklin comments that an appropriate aspiration for law in this field would be for more legislative initiatives like the Warnock Committee 'that both show respect for diversity, and use discordances as a resource in the effort to create a workable and sustainable compromise'.[18] She points out that we must remember that morality is not only collective but also individual, and in this manner, initiatives such as these are (and should be) led with a spirit not of absolution but of toleration.[19]

It is clear that there has been much praise and support for the Warnock Report over the years. It was thorough in its approach, and its recommendations have certainly withstood numerous technological and scientific advances. Yet there is an important distinction to be made here, between critiquing the 1990 Act (as amended) as it stands today and the extent to which its origins were justified *at the time*.[20] Despite later ruling out revisiting the embryo in law, in 2004, the Department of Health stated that while the 1990 Act (as amended) had performed well and

---

[14] Ibid., 589.
[15] Ibid., 617.
[16] Ibid., 618.
[17] Ibid.
[18] Franklin, 'Response to Marie Fox and Thérèse Murphy', 508.
[19] Ibid.
[20] This is not to say that there are no commentators who believe that the 1990 Act and the recommendations it was built upon are not adequate today.

continued to do so, 'any cutting-edge legislation, no matter how successful, needs at some stage to be reviewed and any necessary readjustments
made to ensure that it continues to be effective'.[21] While the original
Report is to be praised as seminal work in this regulatory minefield, the
societal, legal, and technological advances that have occurred since then
mean that it is time for the matter to be reviewed. What the following
discussion also reveals, however, is that there is more dissensus when it
comes to the ethical desirability of an apparent lack of decision on the
embryo's legal status in both the Report and the subsequent Act. This has
led, in turn, to confusing law.

The Warnock Report, which as we have seen was in and of itself not
entirely un-processual, has stood fast as the intellectual basis for our legislative framework for over thirty years. Notwithstanding, we might ask why,
when we have seen an increasing rhetorical move to disentangle the legal
status of the embryo from other considerations in policy discussions (such
as that of the potential child),[22] have we not seen a similar move within the
regulatory framework? Questions raised by the issue of the embryo's 'special
status' are exemplary of the implications of the law when it remains static in
a fast-moving area. While the pathways and boundaries within the 1990 Act
have shifted with technological advances, deepening the reproductive and
therapeutic distinction, the central 'pillars' that serve the foundation of
lawful dealings with the embryo have not moved at all. Thus, while there
have been considerable scientific developments with respect to what it is
possible to do with (and to) an embryo, there has been no official revisiting of
what is *justifiable* to do to an embryo in terms of how we *ought* to treat
embryos in law. In other words, law has come to a standstill; it has ossified.

When the Department of Health issued the White Paper that led to the
amended 1990 Act in 2008, a question arose regarding whether the 1990
Act should be repealed and replaced altogether.[23] This did not come to
fruition. Furthermore, as already mentioned, the Department of Health
had explicitly ruled out revisiting the embryo's status the previous year
(2006).[24] The policy reasoning behind the stagnancy of the embryo's

---

[21] Science and Technology Committee, 'Science and Technology – Written Evidence' (HC, 2004), Appendix 1, Annex B.

[22] M. Johnson, 'Escaping the Tyranny of the Embryo? A New Approach to ART Regulation Based on UK and Australian Experiences' (2006), *Human Reproduction*, 21(11), 2757.

[23] M. Fox, 'The Human Fertilisation and Embryology Act 2008: Tinkering at the Margins' (2009), *Feminist Legal Studies*, 17(3), 334.

[24] Department of Health, 'Review of the Human Fertilisation and Embryology Act' (White Paper, Cm6989, 2006), para. 1.8.

status is clear. For example, some have suggested that legislative reform was driven by the government's desire, first, to avoid opening the 'cans of worms' that are abortion and the embryo's legal status and, second, to maintain the United Kingdom's position at the forefront of research and technologies in this field.[25] Nonetheless, Fox argues that the eventual amendments to the 1990 Act were a missed opportunity to 're-think the appropriate model of regulation to govern fertility treatment and embryology research in the UK':[26]

> By ruling out any reconsideration of the underpinning principles of the 1990 Act, the government foreclosed the possibility of a radical reappraisal of the ways in which we regulate fertility treatment and embryo research.[27]

She adds that the result of this was an undesirably complex and confusing legislative regime.[28] Fox also agrees with Ford that the 'fundamental status of the embryo continues to be as elusive and ambivalent as ever … ensuring that the legislation would close off even more contentious debates about what it might mean to be human'.[29] She adds that all of this is not necessarily surprising; not only have *in vitro* procedures become normalised, but the reproduction and research business has also become rather lucrative, meaning that successive governments have been keener than ever to maintain Britain's position at the forefront of this field.[30]

As advancements in science came to the fore of public concern, particularly around the turn of the millennium regarding SCR and again a few years later regarding cell nuclear replacement (CNR), debate began to take place regarding clarity of terms used in the 1990 Act (as amended). Several writers contend that the 1990 Act (as amended) is not fit for regulatory purposes today. Not only has it been 'plagued by twists, turns and controversy' throughout its legislative life, but its regulatory agency has repeatedly found itself 'in the eye of the storm'.[31] The original

---

[25] Fox, 'Tinkering at the Margins', 333.

[26] Ibid.

[27] Ibid., 342.

[28] As she points out, while some of the frameworks pay heed to the changing structures in family life, 'they fail to embrace the possibilities offered by repro-technologies to radically re-think the nature of parenthood or family, while the welfare of the child remains a matter to be determined largely by health professionals'. Fox, 'Tinkering at the Margins', 342.

[29] Ibid.

[30] Ibid.

[31] M. Fox and T. Murphy, 'Response to Sarah Franklin' (2010), *Social and Legal Studies*, 19 (4), 510–513, 511.

1990 Act and its amended version from 2008 have suffered from a multitude of criticism, including in the media,[32] ranging from the alleged failure of these pieces of legislation to prevent the exploitation of women[33] under their 'excessive bureaucracy'.[34] One of these criticisms, particularly amongst academics, has been the nature and source of the embryo's ethico-legal status within the 1990 Act (as amended).

As discussed in Parts I and III of this book, the answer to this problem is not necessarily to change the embryo's legal status but rather to reconsider the status as a legal tool for regulating a morally relative entity, especially if there is potential for the furtherance of social justice aims through law (such as reproductive autonomy). Yet before this is explored, the rest of this section posits that a common thread may be drawn: law's response to the uncertain nature of the embryo *in vitro* is no longer intellectually defensible. This book argues that this is attributable in large part to a growing facet of the 1990 Act (as amended), namely the embryo's 'legal stasis'. This ossification of legal development has not gone unnoticed, as the previous discussion shows. Other critiques of the embryo's status are often made in parallel with this point, while some go even further to claim that the basis of the 1990 Act was flawed from inception (rather than arguing that the current framework simply needs revisiting). The following section summarises some of the reasons put forward by socio-legal literature as to *why* this stagnancy is problematic, namely that the special status itself is unclear.

While legislative initiatives such as the Warnock Committee are undoubtedly productive and can justifiably encompass the spirit of moral pluralism much needed in a contentious field such as this, any such basis must nevertheless constantly be revisited to ensure that it remains sound as technology advances; moreover, if an alternative legal initiative is to be contemplated, then the soundness of the original starting point must first be challenged robustly because it has long served responsible regulation in the field. To this end, many starting points for any revision of our current framework, although not necessarily

---

[32] It has previously had, generally speaking, pro-life tendencies. See M. Mulkay, *The Embryo Research Debate: Science and the Politics of Reproduction* (Cambridge University Press, 1997).

[33] A. Jha, 'Winston: IVF Clinics Corrupt and Greedy', *The Guardian* (21 May 2007).

[34] J. Meikle, 'Axe IVF Watchdog, Says Fertility Expert', *The Guardian* (11 December 2014); I. Sample, 'Clone Research Hampered by Red Tape Says Fertility Expert', *The Guardian* (2 March 2007). More recent critiques include P. Saunders and G. Watts, 'Should MPs Sanction Three-Parent Babies?', *The Guardian* (12 June 2012); and S. Connor, 'Inside the Black Box of Human Development', *The Guardian* (5 June 2016).

discussed in the context of a 'new Warnock', have been provided by socio-legal academics. These are explored in the following section.

3.2.2 A Status Unclear in Nature, Source, and Extent

Writing in 2010, Fox and Murphy argue that the precise legal status of the embryo 'remains undecided, or perhaps undecidable',[35] and further that the 2008 Act 'remained silent on this key issue'.[36] They quote Stephanie Hennette-Vauchez, who describes the failure to offer clear legal definition of the embryo as 'the socio-legal (non)construction of the embryo'.[37] They iterate that 'law seems to reject the judgment of social theorists that embryos are "elusive" . . . or "unruly"'.[38] Yet contrary to law's rejection, the unruly nature of embryos should be embraced, as it has done so historically. To explain, as the analysis in Chapter 2 has shown, regulation of the early stages of human life has fluctuated relatively regularly in line with new social and scientific understandings of the former. If this history has shown today's law anything, it is that embryos are indeed 'elusive' and 'unruly', especially in the context of regulation. This notion thus requires further exploration

Ford has also argued that the embryo's 'special status' 'contains one of the most arresting examples of an ambivalent response to the embryo/ foetus.'[39] Her exploration of the embryo's 'special status' included potentiality, interests, relationships, and notions of human dignity, and concluded that all of these are problematic, if not meaningless, as a basis for 'special status'. For example, Ford has suggested that if those who wish to ascribe 'special status' also support legal access to termination of pregnancy and the right of a woman to refuse medical treatment, then the rhetoric becomes unsustainable.[40] Notwithstanding the contradictory

---

[35] M. Fox and T. Murphy, 'Can Law Facilitate Embryonic Hopes?' (2010), *Social and Legal Studies*, 19, 498.

[36] Ibid., 499.

[37] Ibid., in S. Hennette-Vauchez, 'Words Count – How Interest in Stem Cells Has Made the Embryo Available: A Look at the French Law of Bioethics' (2009), *Medical Law Review*, 17 (1), 52–75, 54.

[38] Referring to G. Becker, *The Elusive Embryo: How Women and Men Approach New Reproductive Technologies* (University of California Press, 2000); and B. Latour, *We Have Never Been Modern* (Harvard University Press, 1993).

[39] M. Ford, 'Nothing and Not Nothing: Law's Ambivalent Response to Transformation and Transgression at the Beginning of Life' in S. Smith and R. Deazley (eds.), *The Legal, Medical and Cultural Regulation of the Body: Transformation and Transgression* (Routledge, 2009), 22.

[40] Ibid., 31.

provisions of the 1967 Act and the 1990 Act (as amended), she points out that it is difficult to 'value' an embryo in practice if we allow it to be destroyed. This reflects Mason's point:

> Either the *in vitro* embryo of Homo sapiens is a human being with rights that are absolute in themselves, and which only become comparative when they are in conflict with those human beings in a more developed state, or it is an artefact to be regarded in the same light as any other product of the laboratory.[41]

To put Mason's argument even more starkly, either we use embryos for research (and thus destroy them) or we do not. On this matter, Ford asks: even if the 'special' status has a justifiable source, how can we 'value' it in practice except by avoiding harming and/or destroying it? If those who want to accord the embryo this status but not make termination of pregnancy illegal, then 'special respect' seems meaningless in practical terms.[42] It is difficult to enable a 'middle position'; we either allow embryos to be destroyed or do not. For Ford, the embryo's 'special status' is thus purely rhetorical or symbolic, as it does not oblige us to 'act or refrain in any way'.[43] Yet this is not the case, as time is an essential component of the clear legal boundaries put in place by the 1990 Act (as amended). Research can only be carried out on embryos for up to fourteen days, no longer. To not refrain from doing so would be a clear breach of the Act. The concept of the 'special status' is still very powerful and has acted as a heuristic to 'stop us in our tracks' with regard to research on embryos, or at least to act as a strong moral brake on our actions. Seen in this way, it is a precautionary position that reflects the fact that we, as a society, afford a degree of value to embryos, and thus the special status caveat requires us to proceed cautiously, to reflect, to justify fully, to revisit, to revise, and to continue to monitor as we progress scientifically. If we did not value the embryo at all, then we would have carte blanche to treat it howsoever we wished. If that were the case, research at 30 or 60 or 180 days would not present a problem. Therefore, the embryo's special status need not be an all-or-nothing brake on research, nor a restriction-free green light position. It thus means *something* in a legal sense, however admittedly meaningless it might be in other senses, be these ethical or religious. The 'special status' in law, then, is not a 'compromise' in the sense that it still allows for

---

[41] J. K. Mason, *Human Life and Medical Practice* (Edinburgh University Press, 1988), p. 94.
[42] Ford, 'Nothing and Not-Nothing', 31.
[43] Ibid., 43.

research on (and ultimately the destruction of) embryos, but rather it can be considered as a legal and ethical 'comfort blanket'. Nonetheless, it cannot be denied that ultimately underlying the initial ideal of the singular 'special' is a kind of dualism: 'reproductive' embryos on one side (who only ever are on the receiving end of that status to the extent that they cannot be admixed) and research on the other which, for all intents and purposes, are treated as 'artefacts'. There is thus an intellectual mismatch here. That is, there is an incoherence, or 'gap', between the set-up of the law and the realities of the processes for which the framework legislates. This gap has only been widened by the deepening of the reproductive/therapeutic distinction in *Quintavalle.*

Moreover, as discussed in Chapter 2, the Warnock Report recommended that the human embryo's special status should be a fundamental principle enshrined in law, without explaining '*either* what form it is to take *or* how it is to be justified'.[44] Ford has also pointed out that while the Committee described it as a 'fundamental principle which should be enshrined in law',[45] they also added the caveat that the latter 'does not entail that this protection may not be waived in certain specific circumstances'.[46] Ford thus described the Committee's response as a representation of 'a microcosm of wider cultural uncertainty and ambivalence about how such entities ought to be regarded'.[47]

> In the end, the law is ill-equipped to respond satisfactorily to life before birth. The kind of 'special status' which best befits the 'inchoate' embryo/ foetus, therefore, is one that reflects law's failure to make sense of it, and the reasons for that failure: the status of the postmodern Other. Of course, this kind of status cannot be conferred by law. Whether postmodernist theory will develop in a way that embraces the Otherness of the embryo/ foetus remains to be seen.[48]

The murkiness of the nature, source, and extent of the embryo's status is not an issue in and of itself for this book; its uncertainty is something that is unavoidable. Nonetheless, this unclear status is at the very least symptomatic of law's way of navigating the embryo's uncertain, processual nature. This having been said, uncertainty and ambivalence regarding the embryo, characteristic of a liminal state, are not intrinsically unproductive or

---

[44] See M. Warnock, *A Question of Life: The Warnock Report on Human Fertilisation and Embryology* (Blackwell, 1985).
[45] 'Warnock Report', 11.17.
[46] Ibid., 11.18.
[47] Ford, 'Nothing and Not-Nothing', 23.
[48] Ibid., 44.

undesirable.[49] Indeed, navigating this uncertainty – that is, the uncertainties surrounding how we ought to treat embryos, legally, has been the task for the law (governing the early stages of human life) since the very first attempts to regulate in this field. Moreover, and as discussed further in Part II, evolving out of uncertainty (and thus characteristically towards a degree of certainty) is neither necessarily productive nor progressive. To explain and defend these claims, we must strive further to understand the legal response to this uncertainty or ambivalence; in the coming section the argument is made that key to reflecting the relative 'value' of the embryo is to see the regulatory enterprise with social justice aims in mind, as introduced in Chapter 2.

3.3   Reconceiving the Embryo *In Vitro*: Changing Boundaries to Move Beyond Stasis?

In the 1990 Act's inception, the Warnock Committee and policymakers navigated two types of uncertainty with regard to embryos (and indeed fetuses):

1. Uncertainty regarding how we ought to treat them in law; and
2. Sometimes, uncertainty regarding what the law governing embryos is (i.e. in the 1970s, and early 2000s).

Embryonic uncertainty returns to the fore where the second type of uncertainty (legal uncertainty) arises, as we saw with *Quintavalle*. How can, or should, we navigate that uncertainty when new issues arise? New issues including technologies such as ectogenesis and *in vitro* gametogenesis are (at the time of writing) close to becoming a reality.[50] If one accepts that the status of the embryo has ossified within law, what can, or should, we do, if anything? Any attempts to break this stasis will involve revising the contours of this regulatory space – governing science, research and reproductive technologies – which is filled with bounded objects.[51] Binding objects in a regulatory space *can be* a useful tool, for example in the instance of embryo regulation it is seemingly an attempt to place certainty on such uncertain entities. A core problem for this analysis, however, is that the embryo *in vitro* is inherently bound up with scientific possibility and the constant change to various ontologies

---

[49]   Discussed further in Part Two of this book.
[50]   These will be discussed more fully in Chapter 7.
[51]   See Taylor-Alexander and others, 'Beyond Regulatory Compression'.

relating to embryos that possibility can bring. The way in which the law has bounded embryonic ontologies, therefore, is temporally limited. This section thus separates the following discussion into calls to move beyond two (interrelated) normative legal boundaries: (1) definitions and (2) and legal 'lines in the sand'. These types of boundaries, in the way that they are operationalised under the 1990 Act (as amended), are reflections of the embryo's 'special status' in one way or the other. This section does not argue that we should replace or remove the embryo's 'special status' per se, but rather that we should think about what embryonic definitions fall under that status, and what limits to or *boundaries* within the realm of reproduction and research we want to draw based on that. For this analysis, revisiting the special status of the embryo, and the implications it has for legal boundaries and bounded objects, is key to moving beyond legal stasis.

3.3.1 *Beyond Boundaries: Should We Redefine 'The Embryo'?*

It is self-evident that the legal embryo is very much bounded within law, not only under categorical descriptions (e.g. as 'embryo' or admixed embryo), but further under one broad 'special status'. This certainly does not reflect the multiplicity of continuous processes that take place under the 1990 Act. One might counter-argue – in defence of the 'special status' as a pillar of the framework – that equally an immutable status can always accommodate changing scientific understandings and thus need not change. However, the way in which we define embryos within the framework of the Act and the status of the embryo are interlinked, if not inseparable from one another. To revise one, without at least considering the intellectual underpinnings of the other, is intellectually indefensible because legal tools such as definition and time-limits (or otherwise) *operationalise* that status.

Amongst literature that calls for the law in this field to be updated in accordance with societal and/or scientific advances, there are some who call for the definition of 'embryo' to be revisited. Often, this is to reflect newer, more accurate understandings of 'biological reality'. While these might sound appealing on a scientific level in their reflection of current 'truths', the challenge is that not only is the attempt to legally reflect 'biological reality' nearly impossible, but it is also limited as a sole or principal basis for moving beyond legal stasis.

Johnson argues that early legislative responses to the human embryo in the United Kingdom have exaggerated the protection of the human embryo at the expense of other parties.[52] While he admits that more recent changes, for example the 2008 Act, have 'lessened this embryonic grip', the formulation of law in this area 'distorts legal thinking and is fundamentally in conflict with biological understanding'.[53] Johnson theorises that it is not strictly correct to call the regulated biological entity an 'embryo' until carried inside a placental support system. He posits that if we understand an embryo as a group of cells that can give rise to a fetus and therefore a baby, it cannot do so until it attaches to this system of 'extra-embryonic tissues'. In the United Kingdom, however, the zygotic and embryogenic periods are captured by legal definition.[54] He points out that while the term 'embryo' is used as a categorical description, the embryo's development is a 'continuous process'.[55] Yet, it is a common legal tool to demarcate stages of almost any process, in order to provide clarity, and some suggest that clear definitions of certain categories such as gametes and embryos are required in order to protect early human life from 'abusive destruction'.[56] To address the tensions, however, one option would be to define pre-implantation embryos as a 'zygote' (specifically the period beginning with fertilisation and ending with the achievement of nuclear syngamy),[57] based on 'objective scientific arguments' so that laws may be coherent and easily applicable to the regulation of techniques which lead to embryo destruction, without compromising the rights of infertile patients.[58] But even if this position were adopted, what is particularly complex here is that any demarcation distorts the reality of the rapidly changing, processual nature of development. It is perhaps trite, yet powerfully true, that legally defining the embryo is difficult because it is a definition that biology cannot really provide. For Johnson, however, 'the fact that lawyers ask biologists inappropriate questions is no reason to give unbiological answers'.[59] He adds, however, also that even if there were agreement on the biological definition of the embryo, it would not necessarily last very long: 'discoveries and new technologies challenge concepts and understandings'.[60]

---

[52] Johnson, 'Escaping the Tyranny of the Embryo?', 2756.
[53] Ibid.
[54] 1990 Act, s1.
[55] Johnson, 'Escaping the Tyranny of the Embryo?', 2758.
[56] J. Tesarik and E. Greco, 'A Zygote is Not an Embryo: Ethical and Legal Considerations' (2004), *Reproductive Biomedicine Online*, 9(1), 13–16, 15.
[57] Pronuclear fusion, where the nuclei of the female and male progenitors fuse
[58] Tesarik and Greco, 'A Zygote is Not an Embryo', 16.
[59] Johnson, 'Escaping the Tyranny of the Embryo?', 2759.
[60] Ibid.

Many proposals to update the definition of the embryo under the 1990 Act (as amended), such as those earlier, logically seek to combine law and science. However, there is merit in an approach that accounts for the broader context in which the creation, use, storage and disposal of *in vitro* operates; that is, looking beyond definition towards the broader network of considerations that are in play when producing/using embryos. This having been said, there are theoretical gaps in such an approach (or at least in the manifestations that have been presented to date); these would need to be addressed in order for it to be used as a basis for embedding human development more firmly and with suitable justification. An objective definition of 'embryo' that withstands the test of time is not something science can or should provide. This also partially explains why law has to come up with its own definition based on all contributing factors. In other words, 'biological understandings' are not purely 'biological' and involve a plethora of considerations including social, moral, anthropological, and those that arise from bioethical reflection on what is at stake.

While a definitional approach to embryo regulation undoubtedly has its limits and indeed embryonic categories may be described as fictional and not reflective of science, legal categories are not necessarily the only issue that requires focus. According to Thomas: 'The truth value of the legal fiction is not simply ambiguous or subjective; it is actually quite irrelevant.'[61] The law must provide its own definition(s). Rather than fixating on the rigidity of categories as per Johnson and others,[62] we can instead consider the fluidity and reflexiveness of those boundaries. As we have seen, there is little disagreement that the embryo is fluid, and a common question that flows from this is: how can the law deal with this? Alternatively, however, a more effective question might be: is the law's technique (the use of legal fictions) actually working efficiently? We seemingly cannot avoid the law's need for categorisation, and therefore fictions will be an inevitable outcome. In regulating something like this, law not only creates its own fictions, but also its own 'truths' in the form of a new 'class' of embryo: the 'legal embryo'. Or, more accurately we should talk of 'legal embryos' – the plural here is important because it captures the legal reality that not all embryos are created equal: some are destined for destruction from the start.

---

[61] Y. Thomas, 'Fictio Legis: L'empire de la fiction Romaine et ses limites Medievales' (1995), Droits, 21, 18; M. Jacob and B. Prainsack, 'Unfreezing Embryos?' (2010), *Social and Legal Studies*, 19 (2010), 513–517, 515.
[62] See for example Tesarik and Greco, 'A Zygote is Not an Embryo'.

All research and reproductive practice *in vitro* occur within one particular 'regulatory space',[63] which Laurie describes as the 'metaphysical environment occupied by institutional actors and bounded by law'.[64] He notes that in health research regulation, legal instruments often adopt a 'bounded object' approach, which is typified by the creation of artificial constructs within law. These become the object of dedicated regulators 'who operate within legally defined spheres or "silos"'.[65] A paradigm example of this is the HFEA. However, while embryos have been bounded within the regulatory space that is the 1990 Act (as amended), in practice their creation and use often sits on and crosses various *boundaries*. For science and technology studies (STS) scholars, such as Susan Leigh Star, 'boundary objects' (something that is used in different ways in different communities) are valuable because they have 'interpretative flexibility', which, she points out, is a feature that exists with any 'object'.[66] In explaining this phenomenon, Leigh Star refers to her and Griesemer's example of a road map, which she explains can have different meanings/ uses for different groups such as campers or geologists.[67] Boundary objects thus occupy shared spaces. To use Leigh Star's map example, again: ' . . . such maps may resemble each other, overlap, and even seem indistinguishable to an outsider's eye. Their difference depends on the use and interpretation of the object.'[68] Considering the earlier discussions of embryonic (non)categorisation and the utility of 'bounded objects' for discussions surrounding health research regulation (per Laurie's analysis), perhaps then, embryos *in vitro* are also boundary objects. Phrased interrogatively, is 'the embryo' not a 'boundary object' capable of interpretative flexibility?[69] If so, then what does this flexibility mean in the context of the legal embryo?

---

[63] See Laurie, 'Liminality and the Limits of Law'; also see R. Baldwin and others, *Understanding Regulation: Theory, Strategy, and Practice*, 2nd ed. (Oxford University Press, 2012); F. Vibert, *The New Regulatory Space: Reframing Democratic Governance* (Edward Elgar, 2014).

[64] Laurie, 'Liminality and the Limits of Law', 48.

[65] Ibid., 49.

[66] As do other aspects, see S. L. Star, 'This is Not a Boundary Object: Reflections on the Origin of a Concept' (2010),*Science, Technology, and Human Values* 35(5), 601–617, 602.

[67] See S. L. Star and J. Griesemer, 'Institutional Ecology, Translations and Boundary Objects: Amateurs and Professionals in Berkeley's Museum of Vertebrate Zoology 1907–39' (1989), *Social*, 19(3), 387–420.

[68] Star, 'This is Not a Boundary Object', 602.

[69] For more on embryos as boundary objects per their use for PGD and SCR, see C. Williams and others, 'Human Embryos as Boundary Objects? Some Reflections on the Biomedical Worlds of Embryonic Stem Cells and Pre-implantation Genetic Diagnosis' (2008), *New Genetics and Society*, 27(1), 7–18.

Arguably, it requires us to consider the temporal element of embryo regulation, because the meaning of the legal embryo is inherently bound up with scientific possibility, and this changes over time. Equally, this flexibility is connected to our social understandings of *in vitro* embryos and constantly shifting social values, that is our attitudes towards various types of research.

As Taylor-Alexander and others comment, 'a liminal approach complements this scholarship because it highlights the effects of rigid or static classificatory systems in the fluid contexts of biomedical research and regulation'.[70] Coupling this observation with STS literature, one may posit that embryos as 'boundary objects' are valuable to us precisely because they have interpretive flexibility, which – importantly – draws attention to the networks at play within the 'silo'[71] of embryo regulation. Thus, the 'embryo' takes on particular meaning for the researchers and regulators working within the regulatory space bounded by the operation of the Human Fertilisation and Embryology Act. This perspective sits at odds with any attempt to produce a singular categorisation of 'the embryo' in law. Yet this is not to say that categorisation is entirely impractical here. Jacob and Prainsack, noting that we must also be alive to the potential 'failure' of once-successful law in this area,[72] argue that: 'While law entails an explicit need for actionability, most social scientists would resist the imperative to even temporarily "freeze" meanings and to operationalize them for application to "the real world".'[73] Embryos *in vitro*, however, are inherently tied up with scientific knowledge(s) and possibility; they are thus in a constant state of change. Yet, as Jacob and Prainsack's analysis points out, temporal, physical freezing is required at certain intervals.[74] We have seen that the law requires categorisation here, as it does with almost everything. For Jacob and Prainsack, categorisation in itself is a placeholder for something 'messier'.[75] We cannot expect for our hopes, or indeed fears,[76] for this area of law to remain the same for a quarter of a century. Law-makers must be willing, as has been the case in the past, to move the boundaries of law itself in accordance with new 'understandings' (not purely biological).

[70] Taylor-Alexander and others, 'Beyond Regulatory Compression', 170.
[71] Laurie, 'Liminality and the Limits of Law', 50.
[72] Mulkay, 'Rhetorics of Hope and Fear in the Great Embryo Debate', 721–742.
[73] Jacob and Prainsack, 'Unfreezing Embryos?', 513.
[74] Ibid., 514.
[75] Ibid.
[76] See M. Mulkay, 'Rhetorics of Hope and Fear'.

To quote Fox and Murphy, we must 'ditch durability'[77] in the regulation of this fast-paced field. In this way, we can address concerns surrounding law's reflection of 'biological reality' highlighted by critiques that focus on definition. We can thus unfreeze concepts such as quickening and make them malleable, and then freeze them again at a later point if necessary.[78] We have seen this in the law's use of constructs such as 'viability'. If ontological boundaries (or the boundaries at which embryos sit) are not fixed, as they are not in the case of 'the embryo', then neither should the law be that demarcates them. This is not to say that regular *change* is necessary, but that we must be open (to borrow from Jacob and Prainsack) to 'unfreezing' the law in order to revisit its basic tenets.[79] It is important that scientific possibility, and the fluidity of social values coexist in law-making. If policymakers only concern themselves with the former, then law would be a slave to scientific possibility; this cannot be the sole criterion to create a defensible meaning of the legal embryo.

Overall, the ontological boundaries of embryos in and outwith law, particularly those *in vitro*, are uncertain: law's response to this reality has been instead to legislate 'the embryo'. As argued previously, this has left a 'gap' between the intellectual basis of the 1990 Act and the reality of what it legislates for: there are multiple contexts in which embryos can be *legally* created and instrumentalised. Uncertainty regarding embryonic process does not solely stem from uncertainties regarding biology, but also from uncertainties regarding how we feel about the embryo, and from changes in the network of actors involved in constructing the embryo's processes. To limit a regulatory framework to decisions based on apparently objective science, intent, and illusively definable outcomes (in the manner Johnson has described) contextualised within 'biological understanding' is to miss much about what is actually occurring in the *process* of creating the 'legal embryo', including missing considerations of non-biological understandings (such as the creation of new, non-biological family structures). This is not to say, however, that biological understanding should be discounted from legal (re)considerations; on the contrary, as we have seen in Chapter 2, they have been a key 'motor' for the evolution of law throughout history, and must remain central to any law reform. But what is missing is detail on how law and the dynamics of this processual approach might interact. As Parts II and III

---

[77] Fox and Murphy, 'Response to Sarah Franklin', 510.

[78] Jacob and Prainsack, 'Unfreezing Embryos?', 514.

[79] How this might occur, in reference to the 1990 Act (as amended), is the subject of Parts Two and Three of this book.

of this book discuss, the lens of liminality (itself concerned with revealing the dynamics of process) acts as a key conceptual step between contextualising the embryo, process, and legal processes and regulations.

3.3.2 Beyond Boundaries: Is it Ever Useful to Draw Legal 'Lines in the Sand'?

Law has moved the 'goal posts' of its embryonic/fetal boundaries throughout history.[80] This continued up to the 1990 Act, yet embryos/fetuses have not been comfortably fitted within the boundaries law provides persons and objects. Notwithstanding, and building on the previous discussion of embryos as 'bounded objects', or indeed 'boundary objects', this sub-section considers literature that discusses the ubiquitous binary approach to law and regulation, and demonstrates ways in which we can now think beyond a boundried approach to the regulation of embryos *in vitro*.

Dickenson has noted that law considers those that it regulates to be either a person/subject or a thing/object, but not both.[81] The current discussion builds on this kind of perspective to discuss work that cites the predominance of the subject-object/property-person binary within law. For example, in the context of 'everyday cyborgs' (i.e. persons with integrated technologies/prosthetics), Quigley and Ayihongbe note:

> Broadly speaking, the law is divided into that which relates to persons (assault and battery, personal injury, medical negligence, etc.) and that which relates to things in the external world (land law, personal property, sale of goods, etc.).[82]

It is a central tenet of this analysis that the embryo *in vitro* does not fit neatly into such binary categories. Multiple embryos are created towards diverse ends. Moreover, it is worth noting at this stage that regulation of embryos *in vitro* does not practically regulate the embryos themselves but rather the dealings between persons who come into contact with, use, or produce embryos *in vitro*; that is, those that guide the embryos *into, through,* and *out* of these legal processes in various ways.

---

[80] See Chapter 1 of this book.

[81] D. Dickenson, *Property in the Body: Feminist Perspectives*, 2nd ed. (Cambridge University Press, 2017), p. 5.

[82] M. Quigley and S. Ayihongbe, 'Everyday Cyborgs: On Integrated Persons and Integrated Goods' (2018), *Medical Law Review*, 26(2), 276–308, 288.

So, how can law manage those entities that sit somewhere between the bounds of person and technology? In her 2000 article, Fox examines the 'ways in which the embryo is constructed in bioethical and legal discourse and [explores] the consequences of these constructions for the process of legal regulation'.[83] Fox posits that it would be productive to shift from the property–personhood binary towards locating embryos within a 'biotechnological milieu'.[84] This may be done, she suggests, by using a 'cyborg' metaphor when discussing embryos (or positing the embryo as a 'cyborg'), which would thus contextualise embryos within our responses to other cyborgs.[85] For Fox, the term 'cyborg' involves the coupling of animal and machine (for the embryo, technology that enables its maintenance *in vitro*). As such, it neatly captures 'the quintessentially technological nature of cryo-preserved embryos'.[86] In this regard, Fox cites Sarah Franklin, who has argued that 'in its ability to embody the union of science and nature, the embryo might be described as a cyborg kinship entity'.[87] Thus, Fox posits that 'designating embryo bodies as cyborgs opens up productive new ways of thinking in which we can acknowledge that as a technological life-form they certainly matter, but leave open for debate the question of *how much* they matter'.[88] For Fox, this formulation situates the embryo within a complex matrix of biotechnological entities. It moves us away from a focus on whether or not it matters as an isolated being, and forces us to question how much cryogenically preserved embryos matter in relation to other creatures. This presents us with the question, for example, of whether they matter more than the woman (or man) whose gametes produced them. Fox thus suggests that this metaphor enables us to pose questions which lead us beyond current debates regarding the embryo's status. She notes that this not only confronts the dualism that dominates Western thinking but also compels us to rethink our notions of species.[89] She also notes that there are some who believe this metaphor might be a problematic for women, as it might write women out of the picture, 'given its conduciveness to

---

[83] Fox, 'Pre-persons, Commodities or Cyborgs', 171.
[84] Ibid.
[85] Ibid.
[86] Ibid., 182.
[87] S. Franklin, 'Making Representations: The Parliamentary Debate on the Human Fertilisation and Embryology Act' in J. Edwards and others (eds.), *Technologies of Procreation: Kinship in the Age of Assisted Conception*, 2nd ed. (Routledge, 1999) p. 131.
[88] Fox, 'Pre-persons, Commodities or Cyborgs', 182. Emphasis added.
[89] Ibid., 183.

technologism'.[90] However, Fox advances that the relational questions revealed by the cyborg metaphor will not leave the embryo 'free-floating', without the woman's body in the picture. This approach does not deny that the embryo's status is contestable, but nonetheless overcomes the current ethico-legal position of the embryo which Fox deemed unsatisfactory.

While the embryo is indeed a coupling between animal and machine to a certain extent (as humans are part of the animal species) – or, more accurately, a coupling between animal and technology – we can also pay attention to the environments in which this is happening. In particular, this coupling can be acknowledged to take place within a broader net-work of interaction between subjects and objects – that is, between gamete donors, the legal embryo that is created, between the researchers/technicians who create and use the legal embryos, as repro-ductive material or scientific objects for research (when this is the agreed intent), and the surrounding technologies that allow all of this to occur. Advancing relational questions regarding the embryo can thus not only resituate the legal embryo as a non-'free floating' being in the context of female reproduction but can also situate it within the complex of a network of actors in the lab (in a research context). A relational approach thus allows us to move beyond the notion of the embryo merely as a bounded subject-object within law (for it is not bounded in 'reality', either biologically or socially), towards a reflection of the complex scien-tific and social processes that the law itself regulates. Notably, a re-framing of embryos is also already taking place in some postmodern feminist scholarship.[91] For example, Valerie Hartouni argues that the embryo needs to be situated in a manner that makes its dependency upon the woman's body, or technology, more evident.[92]

The assemblage of technologies and biological matter used to create embryos *in vitro* blurs boundaries between the crude and broad categor-ies of 'technology' and 'person' – thus, in a way creating the 'cyborg' that Fox describes. The amalgamation of human and technology is becoming

---

[90] Ibid.
[91] Fox, 'Pre-persons, Commodities or Cyborgs', 181–182.
[92] V. Hartouni, *Cultural Conceptions: On Reproductive Technologies and the Remaking of Life* (University of Minnesota Press, 1997), p. 67. Also see S. B. Novaes and T. Salem, 'Embedding the Embryo' in J. Harris and S. Holm (eds.), *The Future of Human Reproduction* (Clarendon Press, 1998); and D. Haraway, 'Manifesto for Cyborgs: Science, Technology, and Socialist Feminism in the 1980s', reprinted in L. Nicolson (ed.), *Feminism/Postmodernism* (Routledge, 1985).

increasingly important and so, therefore, is the recognition of these new contexts – or regulatory spaces – within relevant regulatory frameworks. Discussing the 'everyday cyborg', Quigley and Ayihongbe comment that

> the subject-object boundary is taken to be an ontological one (i.e. an empirical reality). This is then imbued with a moral significance which we find reflected in law's structure and operative rules.[93]

Location of regulated entities (e.g. internal versus external to the body) is thus important for the law. While, as Quigley and Ayihongbe also point out, this division may seem pragmatic at first glance, it gives rise to some difficulties, as these authors detail in reference to the 'everyday cyborg'. For this analysis, the boundary between subject and object, for 'the embryo', is not fixed in legal reality, but it becomes inevitable through regulatory practice. While embryos have never been named under the category of 'property', 'object', or 'thing' either under statutory or common law, they at the very least become examples of the latter two by virtue of the research and *disposal* processes that the 1990 Act embodied. Thus, even if we baulk at attaching the legal label of 'object', the de facto reality of these legal provisions is that to all extents and purposes the legal embryo that is used for research ultimately is treated as 'thing'.

Law's 'boundary work'[94] concerning embryos is thus unclear. The embryo *in vitro* does not fall within any of the normative legal categories; it hovers on the bright line between what is subject and what is object. Advances in technologies may very well continue to provide challenges to the normative ontological divisions law has provided through, for example, the use of artificial wombs.[95] Embryos' transgressions of multiple normative biological and legal boundaries map onto other dichotomies, for example, that between the biological and the artificial.[96] Embryos created *in vitro* straddle the boundary between biology and artificiality. Yet, in the intellectual framework underpinning the 1990 Act (realised through the 'special status' that is bestowed on all embryos covered by this law), the Act does not place the embryo on the biology-artificial boundary, but instead fixes it firmly within the bounds of biology as a member of the human species. Following from this, further boundary work – where 'boundaries of science are episodically

---

[93] Quigley and Ayihongbe, 'Everyday Cyborgs', 303.
[94] See Taylor-Alexander and others, 'Beyond Regulatory Compression', 171.
[95] See Chapter 7 of this book.
[96] Discussed in the context of the blurred subject-object dichotomy, see Quigley and Ayihongbe, 'Everyday Cyborgs'.

established sustained, enlarged, policed, breached'[97] – has taken place by delineating embryos from other human cells (or tissue). Where this has taken place, what matters for law is whether something is pure matter:

> Thus, for the law it is clear that the types of materials at issue matter. But it is not just that 'matter matters'; that is, whether it is important that the materials themselves are biological or synthetic. The process of matter-ing – how material comes to matter – is significant.[98]

Nonetheless, when law was asked to capture 'the embryo' (and when Warnock was asked to advise on how this should happen), it was confronted with the problem that embryos are neither mere matter nor legal subject. Embryos did not fall into either of law's normative dichoto-mies, namely 'subject or object', and 'biological or synthetic'. Herein lies a contradiction, for the law also contains both processes of mattering and de-mattering embryos *in vitro* through use via reproduction or research. Processes of mattering,[99] or indeed de-mattering, are not captured by law, that is when a reproductive embryo is donated for research. Law has placed all *in vitro* embryos firmly in the same arena as it has already placed embryos *in vivo*: within the biological. The 'artificiality' of this placement was demonstrated clearly in *Quintavalle* and the 2008 Act, where admixed and cloned embryos were deemed as 'legal embryos', thereby not only continuing but *extending* the myth of the 'human' or 'biological' category to entities that are entirely artificial and that will never become human subjects.

As such, there is a two-fold 'problem' for law in regulating embryos: embryos neither have a fixed status, nor is it possible to 'fix' their status (practically speaking). Law, accordingly, struggles to capture and regulate what embryos *are* ontologically, as opposed to what the 'embryo' *is* descriptively. This may be, for example, because it does not reflect its biological processual complexities. Further conceptual steps are required if we want the law to better respond to the embryo's uncertain, *in-between* nature. Ultimately, by constructing embryos in law as 'the embryo' under one encompassing 'special status', law has fixed embryos *in vitro* in time and matter. Some might argue that this is untrue; the law's definition of 'embryo' within 1990 Act was amended in the 2008 Act to provide exception to the requirement that an embryo be 'human', to

---

[97] See T. Gieryn, *Cultural Boundaries of Science* (University of Chicago Press, 1999).

[98] Ibid; and J. Law, 'The Materials of STS' in D. Hicks and M. Beaudry (eds.) *The Oxford Handbook of Material Culture Studies* (Oxford University Press, 2010), p. 173.

[99] See Law, 'The Materials of STS'; Quigley and Ayihongbe, 'Everyday Cyborgs', 306.

include human admixed embryos (human–animal hybrids). Even if true, this does not invalidate the fixed, bounded, and all-encompassing category that 'the embryo' has become under the 1990 Act (as amended). Legally constructing embryos *in vitro* within the bounds of one 'special status' fixes multiple embryonic processes within one boundary. Thus, the problematic features of law associated with embryonic status (not all of which this analysis deals with) are also fixed.

3.4 Conclusions: From Process to Purgatory

Enduring uncertainty regarding embryos *in vitro* has led to legal stasis. Moreover, given the aforementioned issues faced by law in what, for this analysis, are symptoms of law's purgatorial response to uncertainty regarding the embryo, there are good reasons to consider that we need a new ethico-legal approach to thinking about the human embryo. This chapter has traced an emerging consensus amongst some academics that the time has come to revisit some of the core features of the 1990 Act framework, including, as Hennette-Vauchez puts it, the 'socio-legal (non)construction of the embryo'.[100] The legal boundaries discussed above highlight the challenges that embryos *in vitro* pose to prevailing legal ontologies, and 'perceived realities which get built into law's structure and operation'.[101]

The *in vitro* embryo itself, and increasing embryonic visibility (i.e. increased knowledge of its developmental processes), was brought about by research practices and thus sparked the inception of the 1990 Act. Understanding of these processes continues to this day and will unquestionably progress. Yet, as a response the 'fixed-ness' of law with respect to the legal status of the embryo is increasingly open to question, not least that we must assure ourselves of its ongoing fitness for purposes. More boldly, however, this 'special status' as a response to embryonic uncertainty is inadequate, and this has contributed legal ossification of the framework.

- This analysis posits, therefore, that between 1990 and today, the law has gone from process to purgatory, a state whereby it does not move beyond its original iteration. The embryo *in vitro* is a processual entity in legal stasis.

---

[100] Hennette-Vauchez, 'Words Count', p. 54.
[101] Quigley and Ayihongbe, 'Everyday Cyborgs', 303.

This has resulted in a legal gap between the intellectual set-up of the 1990 Act (as amended) and the realities of the multiplicity of processes it now allows for. To be clear, for the purposes of this research, reflecting process means neither (a) incorporating every new technology nor (b) that our social and biological understandings of the embryo have changed *extensively* since 1990. Rather, this book's approach about paying attention to the processes and transformations that occur in relation the regulated subject-object (the embryo) and those around it (donors, researchers, etc.). Further, a processual legal approach does not indicate that the law wholly reflects embryonic processes.

In other words, this 'legal gap' is typified by an intellectual mismatch whereby law treats embryos singularly as 'the embryo' by virtue of according one 'special status'. In reality, however, the 1990 Act (as amended) creates multiple categories of, and pathways for, embryos *in vitro* (with seemingly multiple statuses). Up until now, this work has referred to 'the embryo' as it is conceptualised as such in law. Hereinafter, however, this offering shall refer to 'embryos' – plural – to reflect and emphasise the multiplicity of embryonic entities that are created and led into various legal pathways. Considering the analyses of Chapters 1–3, there are two interrelated facets of this 'legal gap':

- Uncertainty surrounding embryos (*in vitro* and *in vivo*), for example with regard to how we feel about them and how we should treat them. This was reflected throughout history and in the deliberations within the Warnock Report; and
- The 'legal stasis' of the embryo *in vitro*, as regulated by the 1990 Act (as amended); in other words, the ossification of its legal development.

Further, it has been noted that there is not necessarily a disjunction between the 1990 Act (as amended) and the historical development of the early stages of human life. Conjoined, however, the analyses in Chapters 1–3 have shown that there is cause to better embody process and move beyond the 1990 Act's original iteration (per its intellectual basis), as law has done in the past. It seems that law almost blinded itself to process, including history of process, and scientific 'reality' of process post-Warnock.

The 'legal embryo' *in vitro* therefore needs to go through a legal and conceptual re-formation that captures the unfixed (processual, changing) nature of its own forms,[102] and the changing status of those who guide embryos through these varying legal contexts. Regulating for uncertainty

---

[102] E.g. whether as 'human', 'admixed', 'reproductive', or 'research'.

does not necessarily entail a commitment to eradicating uncertainty but rather to navigating it in a manner that addresses the multifaceted, as-yet-unspecified, and potentially ever-changing nature of these regulated entities: as we have seen, there is no such thing as the bounded and fixed 'embryo' in law. Moreover, once we acknowledge and embrace the fact that *in vitro* embryos are inherently uncertain, and difficult to conceptually 'freeze' by binding them in their regulatory space, law can be (re)formulated in a reflexive manner that also reflects the processes within its framework(s).

While appeals to 'redefine' the embryo in law, for example, provide justifiable starting points for any policy discussions, the 'legal gap' and relatedly legal stasis point to a need to redress the way in which law embraces and/or deals with the uncertain, changing nature of the embryo *in vitro* and our understandings of it. How might we navigate this? Is there a way in which law can better embrace the uncertain, processual nature of the embryo? There are further parallels between uncertainty, the stasis of law, and its anti-processual reflections of the embryo that are better understood by exploring the connection between the latter and 'liminality' itself. The 'problem' thus carved out by Part I of this book is: how we can understand process generally, legal process in particular, and legal regulation more deeply with respect to embryos, their protection, and their uses? The following chapters explore how law can better navigate and capture each element of this gap by way of a two-part analysis. The following chapter first discusses the utility of a framing associated with understanding those who are uncertain in nature, and our responses to them, namely that of the 'gothic'.

PART II

Through Liminality

Part I of this book has shown that while law has adapted to reflect changing biological and social boundaries, its creation of multiple embryos in modern law – while failing to account for the multiple processes at play – has created problems. These constitute or form a 'gap' between the intellectual foundation of the 1990 Act (as amended) and the reality of the processes it has helped to create. This gives rise to the question: how might the law fill this gap, both intellectually and practically? Part II of this book therefore considers how law might navigate this – as diagnosed by Part I – purgatorial state, by way of a twofold examination. It does so with the aim of providing a frame of analysis that can capture and explain the uncertain, processual nature of the embryo in ways that can inform legal and policy responses to their creation, use, and disposal in reproductive and research settings.

With a view to this, Chapter 4 looks at 'the gothic self' – an emergent concept that has evolved as a challenge to liberal idea(l)s of the 'self'. It draws parallels between this literature and embryos *in vitro* as a paradigmatic of 'gothic' and argues that there is benefit to legally realising them as such. As a framing, this enables us to explore the ways in which law deals with *uncertainty* regarding those who fall between boundaries of normative categorisation. This formalisation is a key step in filling the previously articulated legal 'gap', in that it enables an understanding of the nature of, and reasons for, it, yet it still leaves the question as to how we should legally treat the embryos that are categorised as such. This book therefore further argues that this residual question may be navigated by liminality – a concept concerned with processes and states of in-betweenness. Accordingly, Chapter 5 applies a liminal lens to the previous analysis regarding the static nature of the regulation of embryos *in vitro*. This chapter first introduces liminality as an anthropological concept, before going on to explain why the human embryo can be described as a liminal being. Liminality, which is inherently concerned with transformation, shall then be used as a means to

97

further analyse the law's navigation of processes and changes in this field. From this analysis, it will be argued that liminality's presence within embryo regulation is twofold: (1) within the nature of the regulated embryos and (2) within the nature of the law that governs them.

Overall, Part II of this book concludes that by viewing embryo regulation through a liminal lens, there are ways that law can better navigate and capture the contexts that it is leading the embryo *through*.

4

Navigating Legal Purgatory

The Otherness of Embryos

4.1 Introduction

As we saw in Chapter 2, a parallel public and moral discourse of what it means to be 'human' has shaped the construction of embryos under the 1990 Act (as amended). Within this, embryos *in vitro* are foregrounded as 'disputed territory and endangered bodies',[1] reflecting the irresolute discourse and 'rhetoric of fear'[2] in the buildup to the 1990 Act's inception. Amidst a 'rhetoric of hope'[3] for those who struggle to conceive 'naturally', rhetoric surrounding IVF and research included references to 'playing god',[4] 'Frankenstein',[5] and even Dr Mengele.[6] As we have seen, in reflection of the contentious and sensitive nature of this rhetoric, and the dispute over embryo research, embryos were given unique 'special' placement *between* normative legal categories under the 1990 Act.

This chapter draws parallels to the gothic trope that surrounded discussions on embryos *in vitro* in the 1980s as a frame of analysis that has grown in counter-response to law's tendency to place entities either within the category of a 'liberal, individual self' or outwith it (rarely *in between*). To explain, 'the gothic self is everything that [the] liberal self is not',[7] characterised by disorder, chaos, and dependency. It cannot be subsumed under the traditional 'self' that the law presupposes of its subjects. Further, within 'the gothic' lies the key concept of 'monstrosity',

---

[1] Fox, 'Pre-persons, Commodities or Cyborgs', 176.
[2] Mulkay, 'The Great Embryo Debate', 723.
[3] Ibid., 729.
[4] *Parliamentary Debates* (Hansard), Sixth Series, Commons Vol 171 (23 April 1990) (HMSO), para 9, cols 89–91.
[5] See Mulkay, 'Frankenstein and Embryo Research'.
[6] Mengele was a Schutzstaffel officer and doctor during World War II, infamous for his crimes against prisoners at Auschwitz. As Mulkay rightly states, in 'The Great Embryo Debate' these parallels were 'unjustifiable'.
[7] Ford, 'Nothing and Not-Nothing', 34.

at the margins of what we deem to be human: 'we stake out the boundaries of our humanity by delineating the boundaries of the monstrous'.[8] Overall, this is a useful frame of analysis for the purposes of this book because it provides a category for beings that are in a process of changing and those that do not fit into our normative forms of categorisation.[9] While the gothic trope does not explicitly centre around 'the in-between', it is argued that we should see gothic entities as such, because of their common placement – legally and sometimes socially – on the boundary between liberal, individualised human, and something akin to a science-fiction-esque 'monster'. The controversy that causes rhetorical parallels between new research and monstrous beings and mad scientists to be drawn is a major contributor to policymakers' reluctance to revisit the legal status of embryos *in vitro*.

This chapter situates embryos within emergent analytical responses to postmodern forms of categorisation, which often ignore those that fall in-between: the 'gothic self'.[10] In doing so, it provides an important step in navigating the contours of this book's previously articulated 'legal gap', which, as a reminder, are as follows:

- The intellectual basis of the law treats embryos singularly as 'the embryo', by virtue of according one 'special status'. In reality, the 1990 Act (as amended) creates multiple categories of embryos with seemingly multiple statuses.
- Similarly, the 1990 Act (as amended) accords embryos *in vitro* no 'rights', but also purports to protect their perceived 'interests'. I have argued that this is intellectually and legally incoherent.

The 'gothic self' is often described as an entity that occupies the boundary between that which we consider familiar and that which is unfamiliar. This quality, which can invite an uncomfortable mixture of 'distaste and sympathy'[11] from many persons, can easily be located in fictional gothic literature. Within this literature, 'monstrous' entities, characterised by their existence on the boundaries of humanity, may be found. The following section explores this in order to provide context for this analytical framing and offer relatable examples for those unfamiliar

---

[8] Z. Hanafi, *The Monster in the Machine: Magic, Medicine, and the Marvelous in the Time of the Scientific Revolution* (Duke University Press, 2000), xiii.

[9] See Ford, 'Nothing and Not-Nothing'.

[10] To be clear, while the gothic 'self' has been applied to persons in original discussions, the concept has since been extended to those that we might not count as 'selves' e.g. embryos.

[11] Ibid., 42.

with this theory. The rest of this chapter discusses scholarly adaptations of this concept, particularly as they apply to embryos *in vitro*, and an analysis will be offered of the regulatory lessons that we might learn from this concept.

4.2   An Account of Those *in Between*

4.2.1   The Literary Birth of the 'Gothic Self'

Classic gothic fiction often contains a mix of themes such as death, horror, humanity, and even romance. From classical literature to contemporary depictions of horror, writers create a sense of fear in the reader or onlooker through stories where the protagonist encounters creatures that occupy the boundaries between human and non-human.

Mary Shelley's 1818 novel *Frankenstein* is often described as the original 'gothic' novel, where scientist Victor Frankenstein sets about creating life from non-living matter. In doing so, he unintentionally creates an unsightly 'monster' that has all the features of a human being. Frankenstein is revolted by his creation, however:

> I had selected his features as beautiful. Beautiful! – Great God! His yellow skin scarcely covered the work of muscles and arteries beneath; his hair was of a lustrous black, and flowing; his teeth of pearly whiteness; but these luxuriances only formed a more horrid contrast to his watery eyes, that seemed almost of the same colour as the dun-white sockets in which they were set, his shrivelled complexion and straight black lips.[12]

It was the abnormality of the monster's apparently 'human' features that invited such a response from Frankenstein and, later in the book, from many others. Importantly, the monster was not necessarily a 'monster' within; it developed very human emotions and needs. Nonetheless, the monster's persistent rejection by society led to its demise at the end of the tale. Further examples of gothic literature include Robert Louis Stevenson's 1886 novel *Dr Jekyll and Mr Hyde*, which depicts a man troubled by an ever-changing, morphic split personality, and Bram Stoker's 1897 novel *Dracula*, which effectively invented the form of vampire that we so commonly see in horror fiction today.

There is also, of course, the classic children's fairy tale *Little Red Riding Hood*. While it is not generally typified as 'gothic' fiction, we can see elements of classic gothic themes in the story. The familiar tale, with

[12] M. Shelley, *Frankenstein* (Penguin Classics, 2003), p. 43.

which most people are familiar, tells of a little girl who encounters a talking wolf in a forest. The wolf has many human capabilities, like being able to speak and plan, but is very much a wolf in every other sense. This mixture of human and animal, and mal intent, is the root of the wolf's frightening quality. The story climaxes where the wolf kills and takes the place of the girl's grandmother. Even in modern entertainment some of the most acclaimed horror films (or testified as 'most scary') involve entities or creatures that are human-esque, such as ghosts or zombies. The source of our sense of horror regarding the depicted entities is not that these entities have no humanlike qualities, but 'rather, it is the fact that they seem to exist liminally, at the margins of the category of "human", and interstitially, across or between categories'.[13] Whilst traversing or existing between boundaries of categories of humanity, these beings also 'conform cleanly to none of them'.[14]

Although embryos and fetuses certainly do not invite such extreme responses of fear and adrenaline as the creatures of fictional horror, they certainly act as a very real example of the responses of abjection that the familiar-yet-unfamiliar can invite. Like Frankenstein's monster and Dracula, embryos exist not only at the boundaries of humanity but on the boundaries of what we know, experientially. Further, there is a strong link between the 1990 Act (as amended) and gothic tales more generally. As mentioned in Chapter 2, research by Michael Mulkay has, for example, found that in the public debate leading up to the legalisation of IVF in the United Kingdom, negative images from science fiction such as Frankenstein's monster were used heavily.[15] He suggests that in public appraisal of scientific advancements, such as IVF, the line between fact and fiction can become easily blurred; the imagery that goes along with this can play a powerful role in popular perceptions about the 'threat' of science and scientists.[16] Further, Andrew Tudor also argues that novels or films such as Frankenstein are expressions of society's long-standing 'cultural ambivalence' towards science, within which there is recognition of the power that science's sense of enquiry can have.[17] The link between fiction and reality is thus not tenuous; the line between science fiction and science fact is becoming increasingly blurred with the invention of new

---

[13] Ford, 'Nothing and Not-Nothing', 35.
[14] Hurley, *Gothic Body,* p. 24.
[15] Mulkay, 'Frankenstein'.
[16] Ibid., 158.
[17] A. Tudor, *Monsters and Mad Scientists: A Cultural History of the Horror Movie* (Wiley-Blackwell, 1991), discussed in Mulkay, 'Frankenstein', 157–158.

techniques such as implanted medical devices[18] and artificial wombs.[19] Further, new questions are arising regarding the blurring of traditional lines between other areas of health research (and medical law more generally). Examples include the blurring of the lines (or 'silos') between data and persons; genes and data; organs, persons, and property.[20] The blurring of ontological boundaries and legal categories through scientific advancement and social change presents a tremendous challenge for the law's framework. As the regulation of embryos *in vitro* exemplifies, this can lead to a conceptual and intellectual gap within the law. In order to explore this gap, the following analysis uses emerging academic responses to these blurred boundaries, particularly concerning those who exist/hover on the boundaries of normative legal subjecthood (as 'the embryo' *in vitro* certainly does).

4.2.2   Gothic Accounts of the Postmodern 'Other'

One's feelings towards the fictional beings mentioned earlier, whether in reading a novel or watching a horror film, can be explained by psychological theory of the 'uncanny'. Whilst this theory existed before Freud,[21] he developed it in a 1919 essay, *Das Unheimliche*, where he described the feeling of cognitive dissonance induced in a subject looking upon something that is uncanny:[22] to put it simply, an entity or object (or perhaps both) that one is simultaneously repulsed by and attracted to. The gothic fictional genre has used this unique combination to great success in the world of entertainment and publishing. Parallels to the interlinked concepts of 'the uncanny' and 'the gothic' have also generated much scholarly attention and have been used by academics in multiple disciplines.[23]

---

[18] See Quigley and Ayihongbe, 'Everyday Cyborgs'.
[19] H. Devlin, 'Artificial Womb for Premature Babies Successful in Animal Trials' (*The Guardian*, 25 April 2017), www.theguardian.com/science/2017/apr/25/artificial-womb-for-premature-babies-successful-in-animal-trials-biobag
[20] See Taylor-Alexander and others, 'Beyond Compression'; C. McMillan and others, 'Beyond Categorisation: Refining the Relationship Between Subjects and Objects in Health Research Regulation' 2021), *Law, Innovation and Technology*, 13(1) (forthcoming).
[21] These theories utilized a being that one sees a lot in modern horror films – lifelike dolls. See E. Jentcsh, 'On Psychology of the Uncanny' (1906), *Angelaki: Journal of the Theoretical Humanities*, 2(1), 7–16.
[22] S. Freud, *The Uncanny* (Penguin, 2003).
[23] For example: in music, see E. Hinds, 'The Devil Sings the Blues: Heavy Metal, Gothic Fiction and "Postmodern" Discourse' (1992), *The Journal of Popular Culture*, 26(3), 151–164. In literature, see Botting, *Gothic*, and R. Helyer, 'Parodied to Death: The

As a genre, and as a mode of analysis for those who have been 'Othered',[24] it offers narrative to those who fall between the cracks or outside of modern (or indeed postmodern) norms.[25]

The gothic trope, in its scholarly form, arose in order to debunk conventional narratives around certain norms, including females[26] and those with a disability.[27] As Allan Lloyd Smith points out in his introduction to *Modern Gothic*, there are 'striking parallels between the features identified in discourses concerning postmodernism and those which are focused in on the gothic tradition'.[28] Yet 'the gothic' does not only apply to those permanently between the cracks of norms; Botting posits that gothic novels warn others of 'social and moral transgression by presenting them in their darkest and most threatening form ... when the rules of social behaviour are neglected'.[29] Heyler – who argues that these gothic narratives rely on an emotional response rather than an intellectual one – explores this in her analysis of the postmodern gothic of the characters in the novel *American Psycho*.[30]

Explorations of the 'gothic self' and 'monster' have emerged in the legal field as a scholarly counterpoint to legal liberalism (the idea that law presupposes individuals to be competent and self-sufficient). As Ford points out, these concepts are both 'literary precursors to, as well as contemporary examples of, the postmodern Other'[31] (the former having been exemplified in the literature discussed above). Otherness, in and of itself, is often a transgressive way of being (transgression, according to Ford, means a state of 'non-compliance' with existing norms).[32] 'Others', particularly new forms of Otherness that have formed in the past half-

---

Postmodern Gothic of American Psycho' (2000), *Modern Fiction Studies*, 46(3), 725–746. In law, see D. Punter, *Gothic Pathologies: The Text, the Body and the Law* (Springer, 1998).

[24] Simply explained, based on the notion of duality, that definition of self is embedded in having an opposite. The notion of 'Othering' has been used (and indeed rejected) in a number of theoretical discourses, including feminist theory.

[25] Notably some feminist theorist have rejected postmodernist critiques entirely, see J. Parpart, 'Who is the "Other"?: A Postmodern Feminist Critique of Women and Development Theory and Practice' (1993), *Development and Change*, 24(3), 439–464.

[26] For example: M. Shildrick, *Leaky Bodies and Boundaries: Feminism, Postmodernism and (Bio)ethics* (Routledge, 2015); B. Creed, *The Monstrous-Feminine: Film, Feminism, Psychoanalysis* (Psychology Press, 1993).

[27] For example J. L. Scully, *Disability Bioethics: Moral Bodies, Moral Difference* (Rowman & Littlefield, 2008).

[28] Sage and Smith, *Modern Gothic*, 6.

[29] Botting, *Gothic*, 7.

[30] Helyer, 'Parodied to Death'.

[31] Ford, 'Nothing and Not-Nothing', 33.

[32] Ibid.

century (e.g. the 'everyday cyborg') on the boundaries of the norm, are often overlooked in law.[33] As a result, law remains ill-equipped to deal with those that fall in between the cracks of its normative realms of categorisation. Within the concept of the gothic, the notion of monstrosity plays a vital role. It is closely linked with the notion of the 'abhuman': 'the abhuman subject is a not-quite human subject, characterised by its morphic variability, continually in danger of becoming not-itself, *becoming* other'.[34]

This quality of being 'almost, but not quite' is close to Freud's aforementioned concept of 'the uncanny'. It is this sense of social and moral 'transgression' that can be located in regulatory discussions surrounding embryos *in vitro*, both in the 1980s and today. This peculiar type of familiarity invites negative responses: 'abjection (distancing, casting-out), disgust, shame and revulsion'.[35] Ford adds that this language can be easily located in law, particularly in areas of case law such as end of life or disability. If 'gothic' beings are in opposition to the liberal, they are also in opposition to the legal, for the law embodies liberal norms.[36] The gothic is not only free from the law but also 'extra-legal'.[37] According to Punter, the gothic body is 'perpetually unamenable to the rule of law'.[38] The 'monster', that which is not one normative category, nor another, does not fall under any of the law's categories either and thus poses a challenge to regulation; it is therefore something that is difficult to capture effectively in legal frameworks.

The 'liberal self' and the 'gothic body' are thus contrasting models of selfhood. One is individuated and self-contained, while the other 'disordered, leaky and lacking in self-sovereignty'.[39] Leakiness, discussed in Margret Shildrick's *Leaky Bodies and Boundaries: Feminism, Postmodernism and (Bio)ethics*,[40] is used to refer to the literal physical 'leakiness' of women's bodies, and also the leaks and flows between bodies of knowledge and matter once traditional boundaries (such as the gender binary) are deconstructed. She points out that the normative categories that organise us are discursively unstable, and balance is

---

[33] In the sense that robust frameworks are not, or sometimes cannot be, in place to deal with them.

[34] Hurley, *Gothic Body*, pp. 3–4.

[35] Ford, 'Nothing and Not-Nothing', 35. Also see Karpin, 'Uncanny Embryos'.

[36] Ibid., 34.

[37] Punter, *Gothic Pathologies*, 218.

[38] Ibid.

[39] Ford, 'Nothing and Not-Nothing', 34.

[40] Shildrick, *Leaky Bodies and Boundaries*.

usually obtained by reiterating them repeatedly over time. Take, for example, the constant societal reiteration of women's 'body standards'; sometimes changing with trends, but ever iterated all the same. Shildrick argues that we should embrace embodiment as a process and that we should resist formalisation: 'an acceptance of the leakiness of bodies and boundaries speaks to the necessity of an open response'.[41] While 'the embryo' may not be described as a typical liberal 'self', neither can the 'selves' expounded in works such as Shildrick's. Both are fluid, occupying unstable categories. These 'gothic' associations are born from embryos' placement in women's bodies, and the challenge that they pose to traditional social and legal norms of subject- and object-hood.[42] Therefore, despite clear differences in levels selfhood/personhood, there is much to be drawn from 'leaky' and other 'gothic bodies'. In particular, liminality, as a lens, helps us to account for the fluid yet bonded nature between people and 'things'. This point is built upon later in this book (Chapters 6 and 7) to explore the importance of relationality for embryonic pathways through the law.

4.3   The Otherness of Embryos: A 'Gothic' Framing

Drawing parallels between regulated embryos *in vitro* and the 'gothic' trope helps to articulate the complexities that law encounters when faced by embryos' processual, uncertain, 'transformative and transgressive'[43] nature. This 'gothic' framing is important for the purposes of this book because it helps to navigate the contours of the 'legal gap' carved out in Part I. This subsection thus invokes two key pieces of legal scholarly work on embryos as 'uncanny' and 'gothic' (on which relatively little work has been done so far) before going on to build upon these works in order to draw lessons from them.

In her chapter 'Nothing and Not-Nothing: Law's Ambivalent Response to Transformation and Transgression at the Beginning of Life', Ford draws upon literature on the 'gothic', characterised by 'ambivalence and uncertainty',[44] which, as described above, is in contrast to legal liberalism. In doing so, she adds to the 'gothic' discourse, as the gothic character of the embryo/fetus is largely absent from postmodernist critiques of the liberal self, and recognises that this has not occurred with

---

[41] Ibid., 217.
[42] See C. McMillan and others, 'Beyond Categorisation'.
[43] Ford, 'Nothing and Not-Nothing'.
[44] Botting, *Gothic*, 3.

a view to challenging assumptions underpinning this portrayal.[45] This 'powerful critique' has rarely been extended to embryos/fetuses, even though they are some of the most paradigmatic cases of transformation and transgression (key elements of being 'gothic') that one can find in a human context.[46] In 'Uncanny embryos: Legal limits to the human and reproduction without women', Karpin invokes the idea of 'the embryo' as *unheimlich*, or uncanny, in reference to the technologically produced embryo that exists outside the body of the woman. Karpin posits that the 'technologically produced embryo is constructed as a phantasmal pre-monition of the child to be'.[47]

The rest of this section builds upon the aforementioned literature and posits that embryos *in vitro* have 'gothic' qualities, not only because of what they *are* – as something that is not quite 'nothing' yet not 'person' – but also because of three other factors: (1) origins, that is as Ford argues, where embryos originate from and what we associate them with (women); (2) contexts, that is where they are, amongst technology; and (3) ends, that is the premonitional considerations we make of embryos *in vitro*. Each allows us to understand, more deeply, the legal uncertainties surrounding embryos *in vitro*.

4.3.1 Origins: The Female Body

While the 1990 Act (as amended) provides for implantation of embryos *in vitro*, and their use for reproduction and the creation of life, it also provides for their scientific use and disposal. Do these practices in some way dissociate embryos from women? If so, does this make embryos potentially even more monstrous or gothic? Arguably it does; not only do the associations of being born from women remain, but embryos' physical placement in technology, sometimes being part 'human', part animal (for example),[48] furthers their 'abhuman' nature. Yet even where research embryos *in vitro* are not human–animal hybrids, or even if they could be dissociated from their feminine origins and associations, 'the embryo' would nonetheless remain intrinsically gothic: 'its very body, and existence, refute and transgress liberal norms of subjecthood'.[49] For this

---

[45] Ford, 'Nothing and Not-Nothing', 42.
[46] Ibid., 37.
[47] Karpin, 'Uncanny Embryos', 599.
[48] Permitted under s4A of the 1990 Act (as amended).
[49] Ford, 'Nothing and Not-Nothing', 40.

book, there are important parallels between the gothic trope and embryos *in vitro*, not only because of their technological origins, but for a certain subgroup of them, their technological futures (i.e. as research embryos). Yet, no matter whether any particular embryo or category of embryos is destined for technological futures or not, their origins dualistically lie in technology and women/sex. It is only relatively recently that the possibility of creating embryos without the use of male and female gametes has been introduced through, for example, *in vitro* gametogenesis (discussed in Chapter 7).

Ford argues that all embryos may be described as 'uncanny', and in contrast to Karpin, she holds that this is particularly so if they are located *inside* the body. She also argues that embryos' (all embryos, but especially embryos *in vivo*) 'gothicness' comes, in part, from their origins. They are created through processes that inspire fear and awe: sex and science.[50] Both are powerful yet exposing and threatening in their own ways.[51] Embryos and fetuses originate in either one or the other, or sometimes both, of these 'profoundly exciting but profoundly troubling institutions, so they are, from their very inception, ambivalent and challenging beings'.[52]

Not only are women 'leaky', but a brief survey of past legal judgments, for example refusal of treatment cases, shows a depiction of the woman as unreasonable when 'in the throes of labour'[53] (though women's autonomy has been more recognised in this area in recent times).[54] These depictions stand in contrast to another typical caricature of the woman and her body, namely, as a powerful and threatening being, 'one capable of containing the male both in intercourse and in pregnancy, and performing hidden and profound transformations'.[55] Embryos and fetuses are, of course, tied up in this narrative, as it is contained within – or destined for – the woman's womb. Ford claims that 'the embryo' 'absorbs' the negative associations associated with contemporary (mis) understandings of female corporeality.[56] Ford points out that her latter argument might be open to critique from the standpoint that 'the

---

[50] Ibid., 38.
[51] Ibid.
[52] Ibid.
[53] For example: *Rochdale Healthcare (NHS) Trust* v. *C* [1997] 1 FCR 274.
[54] See *St George's Healthcare NHS Trust* v. *S; R* v. *Collins and others, ex parte S* [1998] 3 All ER 673.
[55] Ford, 'Nothing and Not-Nothing', 39.
[56] Ibid.

embryo'/fetus is often imagined as 'free floating',[57] that is, isolated from the woman in public discourse. However, she writes, these two arguments are not mutually exclusive. While, with the increased visibility of the early stages of life, the entire process of pregnancy has become more of a 'public event', it is exactly because pregnancy has become so prevalent in the public imagination that the association between pregnancy and 'the embryo'/fetus has been severed.

Even where an embryo is technologically predestined, its associations with the female body contribute to embryos' gothic parallels, which itself can be inherently negative given feminist critical literature on 'the monstrous feminine'.[58] For Karpin, this embryonic existence

> evokes sympathy and horror in the same moment. Unhinged from the all-encompassing female body and equipped with its own genetic identity it attains an individuality that pre-figures its birth. In this way even in the absence of the mother, the embryo is assigned a holding place in the (human) family. But the hybrid/manipulated embryo amplifies its uncanniness evoking the horror of an alien presence, apparently the same but yet not so.[59]

It is no news to those familiar with feminist literature that women have often been caricatured in everyday social and legal discourse as weak (emotionally and physically), vulnerable, dependent, and unstable.[60] Feminist discourses have challenged the dominance of liberal notions of the self in the case of narratives surrounding those who might be seen in a process of transformation, or as transgressing modernist norms, including female, 'vulnerable', disabled, and transgender persons.[61] Embodying or occupying transformational dimensions causes their marginalisation and thus invites responses of abjection.[62] Michael Thompson, for example, has argued that within the 1990 Act, the association of the feminine with monstrosity has been exacerbated by the Act's regulation of reproductive technologies; it combines the 'monstrous feminine' with concerns regarding new technologies to produce an image of the female as 'an object of horror and fascination'.[63] The dual

---

[57] See Karpin, 'Uncanny Embryos', 604.
[58] Creed, *The Monstrous Feminine*.
[59] Karpin, 'Uncanny Embryos', 599.
[60] Ford, 'Nothing and Not-Nothing', 39.
[61] Ibid., 36–37.
[62] Ibid, 37.
[63] M. Thompson, 'Legislating for the Monstrous: Access to Reproductive Services and the Monstrous Feminine', (1997) *Socio Legal Studies* 6(3), 401–424.

origins of women and technology intensify the gothic nature of embryos *in vitro*. Not only are they born from technology, but in some cases (i.e. freezing, research), they remain amongst technology.

4.3.2   Contexts: Placement Amongst Technology

All embryos *in vitro*, whether created for reproduction or research, are created, used, and stored amongst technology. Moreover, embryos are additionally transformative *in vitro*. They are taken through processes of freezing and unfreezing, and moreover 'spare' embryos created for reproduction are often donated to research. For some gothic writers, technology is gothic in and of itself:[64]

> Technology ... becomes threatening when it emerges as a dangerous supplement that supplants and exceeds its control. Like the vampire ... technology monstrously undoes the system which designed it.[65]

As we saw in Chapter 2, some original gothic novellas, each with their own gothic–technological associations[66] (briefly discussed at the beginning of this chapter), were regularly cited in media debates leading up to the original 1990 Act.

For some, 'Frankenstein's dream of systematic, science-based control over the creation of human beings can be seen as having become a reality in the modern fertility clinic'.[67] Mulkay cites Christopher Toumey, who posits that many mad scientist stories (like Frankenstein) are presented to us not as enjoyable fiction but as a warning about scientists and science.[68] These warnings have been easily transferred to media coverage of reproductive scientific advancements, especially IVF.[69] In the lead up the 1990 Act, both sides of the debate supported their arguments using this imagery.[70] While direct reference to science fiction was not always present in parliamentary debate or the media, the negative construction of scientists' motives and the temporal extension of the scientific

---

[64] F. Botting, *Limits of Horror: Technology, Bodies, Gothic* (Oxford University Press, 2010).
[65] Ibid., pp. 43–44.
[66] F. A. Kittler, *Literature, Media, Information Systems* (Routledge, 2013).
[67] Mulkay, 'Frankenstein', 157.
[68] C. Toumey, 'The Moral Character of Mad Scientists: A Cultural Critique of Science' (1992), *Science, Technology and Human Values*, 17(4), 411–437, 434, quoted in Mulkay, 'Frankenstein', 159.
[69] See Mulkay, 'Frankenstein'.
[70] Ibid.

narrative beyond the matter at hand ('slippery slope' arguments, for example) mirrored some of the more direct Frankenstein-esque rhetoric used in the news media when the issue first aired. The notion of the mad, malicious scientist continued to work behind the scenes. The connotations of embryos within technology, as reproductive or research subject-objects, thus undoubtedly has gothic associations.

4.3.3 Ends: Physical Placement within a Woman

In discussions surrounding the advancement of science, reproductive technologies, and changes to the law, the embryo is always foregrounded. These discussions produce connotations of a 'free-floating', phantasmal embryo, associated with the 'leakiness female' of embodiment but at the same time the uncanny because of its suspension in the lab/in law without the end/context that we normally associate embryos to be placed in: the womb.

Karpin suggests that instead of focusing on the embryo as a phantasmal premonition, we should instead focus on another: the '*not yet pregnant woman*'.[71] In this way, Karpin infers that where there are embryos, there are also women who will be become pregnant with them. Therefore, they are 'premonitionally pregnant'; the effect of this is to highlight provisionality of embryos *in vitro*.[72] Indeed, *in vitro* embryos, whatever path they are on, can only ever achieve personhood through gestation within a woman.[73] Therefore, such embryos remain entirely subject to the decisions that any woman makes regarding her pregnancy or non-pregnancy. To add to Karpin's analysis, this is a more 'processual' way of framing *in vitro* embryos, especially those created for reproductive purposes (this is the case for most *in vitro* embryos) because it recognises processes have to take place for (a) women to become pregnant and then (b) birth to take place.[74] A policy focus on the phantasmal child, rather than the premonitionally pregnant woman, is uncanny because it misses out *process*, something that we have seen in Chapter 1 is important for the interrelation of society, medicine, and the law. Process, here gestation, is a piece of the embryo *in vitro*'s social, scientific, and legal story that is missing. The effect of this is that embryos are suspended in an almost unearthly, alien-like manner in

---

[71] Karpin, 'Uncanny Embryos', 599.

[72] Ibid.

[73] At the moment, unless/until artificial wombs (ectogenesis) are available.

[74] Notwithstanding prior processes such as harvesting the eggs, collecting sperm, and fertilisation.

policy debates, devoid of the broader context in which they grow and exist. Herein lies the uncanny thread running through the lead-up to the 1990 Act and recurring discussions surrounding how we regulate embryos today.

With new technologies, new contexts arise. With the possibility of the creation, use, and storage of embryos *in vitro*, another 'end' – in addition to the womb – became possible. As we have seen, with the 'end' of the womb/the mother, the phantasmal embryo's potential 'ends' (and the processes it takes to get there) are given little attention in social and legal discourse. This too applies to the new end for embryos *in vitro*, introduced by the new process of research: disposal. Would paying attention to 'ends' make a difference to how we discuss policy, and how we regulate? As Karpin argues in the context of reproduction: yes, as it puts the woman back in the picture, centrally. In fact, it puts the whole process back in the picture, legally and publicly, and moreover, it enables us to be more alive to the biological and (now) scientific processes that need to take place for these ends to be reached. Conceptualising 'embryos' as they are, 'phantasmal' and 'free-floating' in law or in rhetoric surrounding law, has meant that a key/central part of the picture has been omitted. While 'ends' for research are conceptualised in this book as 'disposal' for embryos, as this is what happens in a physical, literal sense, it is also important to recognise that there are ends to the embryo beyond reproduction or disposal. For the research, the information gained might be social ends such as public interest, public benefit, advancements in fertility treatment, and so on. For reproduction, it might be ends such as making, or adding to, one's family. Karpin and Ford, who have framed embryos as uncanny/gothic (a framing hitherto rather uncommon), have advocated for law to recognise the uncanny and gothic nature of embryos. Literature has yet to answer how the law might take its next steps towards encompassing such a framing. The next section uses academic literature to pinpoint key lessons for the law moving forward, by way of drawing from Part I's analysis and the analyses summarised earlier.

4.4   Lessons from a Gothic Analysis

This section builds on the previous analysis to pose two important facets of the law's framework for embryos *in vitro* that require deeper understanding: (1) the nature of embryos *in vitro*, and more importantly for this book, (2) the nature of the law that regulates them. However, these lessons leave some vital questions which cannot be answered by any of the analyses made so far. We thus need an additional framing in order to move forward – one concerned with navigating processes and states of in-betweenness: liminality.

4.4.1 Embryonic Ontologies are a Challenge to Conventional Subjecthood

As discussed above, a gothic analysis provides a way to conceptualise and articulate those on the bounds of legal subjecthood. The first lesson, therefore, is that if we conceptualise embryos as such, then we can bring them out of the outskirts of legal awareness.[75] As we have seen, conceptions of the gothic self are a useful tool for challenging commonly conceived, liberal notions of legal subjecthood. Legal subjecthood, amongst other classifications, denotes a certain 'category', distinguishing subjects from other (non-liberal) persons or things. The law struggles with the 'self' who is not a liberal subject (e.g. those who defy bodily norms, such as the conjoined twins in Re A,[76] or the 'everyday cyborg');[77] selfhood commonly signifies independence and full personhood. Law struggles even more so with those who do not qualify as persons (a 'self'), but also do not fall within the ambit of property. The gothic body is one that stands in 'stark contrast' to the liberal self;[78] it is everything that the liberal self is not: 'Whereas the liberal self is autonomous, the gothic self is dependent.'[79]

'Selfhood' is a problematic term to use when discussing embryos. This, however, does not discount embryos from 'gothic' analysis, even in reference to arguments about legal subjecthood. As we have seen, there are still many parallels between the gothic trope and embryos. While embryos cannot be said to have selfhood, their legal and social oscillation between the latter and 'property' still places them in stark, somewhat uncomfortable contrast to the aforementioned 'liberal subject'. In other words, the law does not (at present) class embryos as property (whether or not it *should* is outwith the ambit of this work) nor as person; by failing to do either, the law leaves embryos to sit in awkward relation to both

---

[75] Discussed in Chapter 4 of this book.

[76] See A (children) (conjoined twins: surgical separation) [2001] Fam 147.

[77] See Quigley and Ayihongbe, 'Everyday Cyborgs'.

[78] P. Atkinson, 'Book Review: Gothic Imaginations' (2005), *Social Studies of Science*, 35(4), 653–664, 660.

[79] Ford, 'Nothing and Not-Nothing', 34.

legal categories. As such, the familiar humanlike qualities of the embryo (amongst other things such as its 'potential'), along with its dependence upon others (namely the woman), render 'the embryo' a problematic (non)category of entity for the law. The law places it in a 'category of its own':[80] not quite human, not quite inhuman, but 'abhuman'.[81]

Thus, as a challenge to conventional subjecthood, embryos' lack of fit within law's normative bounded categories of person or property has provided an ontological challenge for the law. This challenge has resulted in what this research has diagnosed as the 1990 Act's 'legal gap'.

4.4.2   A Deeper Understanding of the 1990 Act's 'Legal Gap'

A gothic framing of embryos *in vitro* also aptly highlights some of the contours of what this book has previously articulated as the 'legal gap' between the 1990 Act's conceptualisation and its practical effect(s). This gap has been ossified in the 1990 Act's realisation of the Warnock Report's 'special status'. This status treats embryos with both favour and disregard in that it not only gives them 'special protection' but also does not disallow research on them and disposal of them.

It is worth noting a potential criticism of a gothic framing of embryos *in vitro*: if the liberal law's response to the 'gothicness' of 'the embryo' has been to 'cast it out', why does the law appear to show 'the embryo' or fetus a degree of favour?[82] For example, the law accords the embryo *some* goodwill by according it a 'special status'. Ford's answer to this is that seemingly positive statements do not necessarily negate the abjection response.[83] Abjection is ambivalent and not necessarily without a sense of approval. It combines fear and revulsion with a sense of identification and sympathy.[84] Nonetheless, there is more to this. It does not automatically follow that because embryos *in vitro* have a 'special status', the law shows embryos *complete* favour. Yes, it favours all embryos, including research embryos, by giving them a special status in one sense and has thus given them nominal and somewhat symbolic protection via the fourteen-day rule. However, in another sense, this special status does not show 'complete' favour because it still allows for these embryos to be

---

[80] *Attorney-General's Reference (No 3 of 1994)* [1998] AC 245, [255] (Mustill LJ).
[81] A separation from human existence, with different moral rules but not insofar that it is an 'object'.
[82] Ford, 'Nothing and Not-Nothing', 43.
[83] Ibid.
[84] Ibid.

researched upon and destroyed. The difference between special status and law's practical effects is thus a prime example of how responses to something 'gothic' can play out, an apparent (and confusing) mixture of favour and disregard.

Further, gothic parallels help us to understand more granularly the difference between reproductive embryos and research embryos, based on the contexts from which they were born and are associated with. We need to account (more), for example, for the importance of the woman and the processes in her womb for embryonic/fetal evolution, a link that has become disconnected through legal stasis. But how can we understand these processes more deeply? There is a gap in the literature here. The following section considers this gap, before going on to propose the answer in more depth in Chapter 6.

4.5 Conclusions: From Conceptualisation to Realisation, What Is Missing?

This book posits that our understandings of the importance of process are deepened by a gothic analysis. If one accepts the above parallels between embryos *in vitro* and the gothic category, then this enables us to understand more deeply why there has been a 'legal stasis'. A gothic framing of embryos *in vitro* highlights that there are logical reasons for this stasis, as embryos in and of themselves as liminal entities invoke an uncanny response. Embryos are well situated within the gothic category and as a constituent of this category invite abject responses (from people *and* law). As such, as Beebee points out, 'to counsel against such responses is tantamount to claiming that the embryo/foetus does not really belong in that category at all'.[85] This, however, is not what this book intends to do. Rather, it seeks to use the gothic as a frame of analysis in order to better capture postmodern responses to embryos. We must accept embryos' gothic character. We need to do so in order to better understand (a) our own responses to them and, more importantly for this book (b) the law's responses to them (which has been the allocation of a 'special status' under the 1990 Act). There is also a gap in gothic/uncanny discussions of embryos, in that process seems to be part of being gothic. Further, while this framing is undoubtedly revealing, it does not tell us, legally (or morally), how embryos should be treated.[86]

---

[85] Beebee, 'Introduction to Part 1', 14.
[86] Ibid., 17.

This book also argues that we need to go beyond explaining the controversy; we need to understand uncertainty surrounding the 'special' status of embryos in a deeper sense. Thus, while a gothic conceptualisation is undoubtedly useful for capturing *those in between*, it leaves the key question of how the law might navigate that liminality. In other words, what are the (a) contours and (b) consequences of doing so? Although 'gothic' work is not framed in terms of liminality, there is insight to be gained by adding the concept of liminality to the analysis. Liminality draws our attention to the importance of a threshold, that is, having the quality of being 'betwixt and between' states.[87] The next chapter situates 'the gothic' within liminal literature. Combined, these concepts (the gothic and liminality) provide a powerful explanation and articulation of why we (as persons) and the law (as an institution) treat embryos as we do. Chapter 5 of this work therefore explores liminality as an essential component of realising 'gothic' natures of embryo in law, as something that we should indeed embrace if we are to understand normative legal and social responses to embryos, before finally discussing what it might mean for the regulation of embryos *in vitro*.

---

[87] V. Turner, *The Ritual Process: Structure and Anti-Structure* (Aldine Transaction, 1969), p. 95.

5

A Liminal Lens

5.1 Introduction

So far, we have seen that embryos *in vitro* sit firmly on the boundaries of normative legal categories and, moreover, that they represent an essence of process and transformation that law is seemingly unable to capture. What further complicates the matter for the law, as this chapter shall explore, is the variable *physical* research and reproductive contexts which embryos *in vitro* are moved *into*, *through*, and *out* of, namely:

- Research within the lab
- Subsequent, and inevitable, disposal post-research
- A woman's womb.[1]

Yet, how can the law better capture this, and thus close the intellectual and practical gap between conceptualisation of 'the embryo' in law and the *multiple* physical contexts they are moved through? This book argues that to answer this, we need a concept that deals with the navigation between boundaries, uncertainty, and processes; for this work, that concept is liminality.

This chapter introduces liminality, an anthropological concept, before going on to explain why human embryos may be described as liminal beings. As an entity in a state of constant and rapid change, embryos sit 'betwixt and between' the various realms of legal categorisation. As such, the core problem for law is twofold: 'the embryo' has neither a fixed status nor is it possible to 'fix' its status. Law, accordingly, struggles to capture and regulate what embryos *are* ontologically (as opposed to what the 'embryo' *is* descriptively).[2] The challenge in capturing these ontologies is perhaps part of the problem – if, indeed, this is what law has sought to do. This chapter argues that an embrace of liminality – both as a state

[1] And out of the uterus, either by birth, or by 'natural' or medical termination.
[2] See Chapter 3 of this book.

embryos are led into and as a lens for analysing that state – fully reveals the multiplicity of contexts in which embryos are used and created. This chapter posits the 'special' legal status of embryos *in vitro* is outdated, if not problematic, and if we want legal frameworks to take *process* seriously – as a key component of regulating something that is rapidly changing – then it is time for the law to recognise explicitly the separate contexts and processes through which it is leading embryos. This chapter shows that a liminal perspective demonstrates that there are vital aspects of embryos – some of which the law itself creates – that the law might better recognise, namely its contextually variable and relational qualities. To some extent, focus has already been thrown on these matters by Chapter 4's analysis of the gothic, Frankenstein-esque trope that often surrounds new scientific developments, but, that analysis alone has not gone far enough to close the 'legal gap' outlined in Chapter 3.

Liminality is important to this work because its application as a lens helps us to understand processes in a scholarly sense. Further, it can also inform practical solutions and approaches concerning how we legally treat embryos. Yet if a key facet of liminal process is being led out of liminality, one must ask where exactly are embryos being led? The next section of this chapter argues that we must consider whether embryos have a 'telos.' The term is used here in an elementary sense[3] in order to cast light on the purpose, or perhaps more accurately, the *end-stage* of embryonic processes within law. This analysis is important for Part III of this book, which draws on lessons from this chapter in order to look more closely at the ways in which embryos are led through and out of processes *in vitro*. The final section of this chapter assesses the common (and indeed uncommon) threads that may be drawn between lessons from liminality and the previously discussed lessons from a deeper understanding of the 'gothic' features of embryos *in vitro*. It builds on Chapter 4's 'lessons' in order to carve out a further contour of this book' contribution: the explicit and important link between the *uncertainty* surrounding embryos in law and a liminal lens .

5.2   Rites of Passage

The realm of the liminal is entered when we participate in cultural rituals that transcend everyday life.[4] The term is derived from the Latin term

---

[3] As opposed to its philosophical or theological use, which is far more complicated.
[4] Squier, *Liminal Lives*, 3.

'limen' (a *threshold*), which simply denotes a situation where ritual and temporal limits are removed 'in order to facilitate a "passing through"'.[5] The concept, coined by anthropologist Arnold van Gennep in his 1909 book *The Rites of Passage*, emerged from an ethnographic study of ritual practices.[6] These 'rites of passage', often highly staged ceremonies, were commonly found in tribal communities.[7] These were used to stage, often in a ceremonial or formal manner, 'a sensitive point in transition between states or statuses in a person's life or in the life of a collective'.[8] In some communities, for example, children might undertake an initiation rite to mark their transition to adulthood when they come of age. Van Gennep described these transitions, where one crosses a *threshold*, leaving their old state and entering the new in the following terms:

> Life itself means to separate and be reunited, to change form and condition, to die and to be reborn. It is to act and to cease, to wait and to rest, and then to begin acting again, but in a different way. And there are always new thresholds to cross: the thresholds of summer and winter, of a season or a year, of a month or a night; the thresholds of birth, adolescence, maturity, and old age; the threshold of death and that of the afterlife – for those who believe in it.[9]

These rites of passage, for example birthdays, weddings, christenings, and funerals, bring us from one state of being to another: a transitional phase.

Arnold van Gennep sought to understand social transformations and identified 'liminal rites' as a ' key component of the reproduction of social order'.[10] Within these rites of passage, suspension of social order is nonetheless spatially and temporally limited, and therefore 'rites of passage' allow a social transformation to occur without disturbing broader organisational structures.[11] He posited that these transitional moments have three stages:

> [1] the rites of separation from a previous world, *preliminal* rites, those executed during [2] the transitional stage *liminal* (or *threshold*) rites, and

[5] Á. Szakolczai, 'Liminality and Experience: Structuring Transitory Situations and Transformative Events' (2009), *International Political Anthropology*, 2(1), 141–172, 155.
[6] van Gennep, *The Rites of Passage*.
[7] P. Stenner, 'Liminality: Un-Wohl-Gefühle und der affective turn' (2016), *Transcript Verlag* 45–68, 46.
[8] Ibid.
[9] van Gennep, *Rites of Passage,* 189–90.
[10] Taylor-Alexander, 'Beyond Regulatory Compression', 155.
[11] Ibid.

[3] the ceremonies of incorporation into the new world *post-liminal rites.*[12]

Put simply, these stages are 'a separation from everyday life, a move into the margin or limen ... and finally a return to everyday life, though at a higher level of status, consciousness or social position'.[13] 'Liminality' refers to the middle phase in transition, where the aforementioned suspension of structural order occurs. This suspension marks the sense of *becoming* that happens, where someone enters a threshold as one type of entity and leaves it as another. This sense of becoming is paradigmatic of the liminal phase.[14] A young man may thus enter a rite of passage as a child and leave it as an 'adult' or 'man'.

Anthropologist Victor Turner later built upon Arnold van Gennep's interpretation. His work studied the role of liminality in ritual performances, such as initiation rites, and described the way in which liminal experiences may be both transformative and a powerful lens that reveals the underlying values and structure of society. He posited: 'Liminal entities are neither here nor there; they are betwixt and between the positions assigned and arrayed in law, custom, convention, and ceremony.'[15] Turner also noted that liminality is an 'inter-structural situation' that involves a concurrence of opposite symbols; thus, in the second (liminal) stage, opposite processes and notions coincide in a single representative. This representative is characterised by the unitary quality of the liminal: 'that which is neither this nor that, and yet is both'.[16] We may apply this analysis to a multiplicity of transitions, where, for any period of time, persons are neither their old selves nor yet their new selves, for example during a marriage ceremony or where someone changes their nationality.

Since van Gennep and Turner, liminality has been extended further in modern theory. Building upon the work of Árpád Szakolczai,[17] anthropologist Bjørn Thomassen suggests that there are further concepts that help to reveal both the dangers and the 'analytical potential of liminality'.[18] These are mimesis, trickster, and schismogenesis,[19] each

---

[12] Emphasis in original. van Gennep, *Rites of Passage*, 21.

[13] Squier, *Liminal lives*, 4.

[14] Taylor-Alexander and others, 'Beyond Compression,' 157.

[15] Turner, *The Ritual Process*, 95.

[16] Ibid., 7.

[17] See A. Szakolczai, 'Permanent (Trickster) Liminality: The Reasons of the Heart and of the Mind' (2017), *Theory and Psychology*, 27(2), 231.

[18] See B. Thomassen, *Liminality and the Modern: Living through the In-between* (Ashgate, 2014).

[19] G. Laurie 'Liminality and the Limits of Law' (2017), *Medical Law Review*, 25(1), 58.

with their consequences for those 'in between'. These three concepts reveal the danger of *remaining* liminal, otherwise known as 'permanent liminality'. Here lies an anti-structural, constant state of chaos where the entity does not or cannot emerge out of its liminal state to the other side. Thus, reincorporation into society is, in some cases, simply not possible.[20]

Mimesis may be described as a mode of unreflexive imitation through imitative behaviour or patterns in the absence of a clear path out of liminality.[21] As Szakolczai puts it, 'a real-life situation of transition – unless meticulously regulated in law, as in political elections – starts by a weakening and eventual suspension of the ordinary, taken-for-granted structures of life. The search for a solution usually involves an escalating process of imitation.'[22]

Yet, where imitative situations arise, *who* convinces people to follow this model? The next concept reveals the risk that a 'trickster' emerges where, again, there is an absence of a clear path out of liminality. This 'trickster', or 'shaman of the liminal', may claim to lead the way out of this situation but instead exploits it for nefarious ends.[23] Tricksters are outsiders, figures who cannot be trusted, often associated with jokes and storytelling. They exist on the margins of society until a situation arises where the attention of the community is diminishing, and they can place themselves as a central figure; this is where they become dangerous. As Szakolczai explains: 'The condition of possibility for such trickster takeovers is a liminal situation where certainties are lost, imitative behavior escalates, and tricksters can be mistaken for charismatic leaders.'[24] This figure can be easily located in pre-liminal literature, myths, and folktales – for example, Hermes and Prometheus in Greek mythology, Loki in Scandinavia, or the North American Coyote.[25] To add to this, more modern familiar examples might include Rumpelstiltskin, Jareth (from Jim Henson's *Labyrinth*), and (perhaps controversially) The Doctor (from *Doctor Who*). Tricksters thus emerge to present a seemingly 'rational' strategy that can hook others into following them, and where this occurs, liminality can be endlessly perpetuated rather than following through to the abovementioned third

---

[20] Szakolczai, 'Permanent (Trickster) Liminality', 231.
[21] Laurie, 'Liminality and the Limits of Law', 58.
[22] Szakolczai, 'Liminality and Experience', 156.
[23] Laurie, 'Liminality and the Limits of Law', 58.
[24] Szakolczai, 'Liminality and Experience', 155.
[25] Ibid., 154; For an interesting exploration of these types of figures with liminal analysis, see G. Hansen, *The Trickster and the Paranormal* (Xlibris, 2001).

stage (a return to normality),[26] otherwise known as Schismogenesis.[27] Schismogenesis may be described as a

> risk that the transformative process will not be completed because of the (negative) cumulative interaction between parties. This can result in either a state of permanent liminality where a state of crisis is perpetuated, or the incorporation of a 'schism' into society itself at the re-integration phase and a 'splitting off' of groups.[28]

In other words, where society is continually stuck in a state where unity has been broken, yet those who have been split are forced to stay together – facilitated by a trickster – it can produce an unpleasant state for all and may, for example, induce violence.[29]

It should be noted that Thomassen[30] also argues that liminality should be used to examine, rather than explain, social phenomena.[31] As a mode for examination, he argues, it 'opens the door to a world of contingency where events and meanings – indeed "reality" itself – can be moulded and carried in different directions'.[32] However, this research argues that it can, and perhaps should, be used both as an exploratory and an explanatory power in the context of embryos. This is because liminality reveals the array of subjects, objects, actors, and non-actors involved in the day-to-day life of those regulated under and affected by the 1990 Act. It is a lens that enables us to explore possibilities, but it also explains, in tangent with Ford and Karpin's work on the gothic/uncanny embryo (discussed in Chapter 4), the predominant regulatory attitude towards the status of embryos. In other words, it is important to note that for this work the analytical power of liminality comes from the ways in which the lens can reveal, more deeply, the dynamics of process. For scholars like Thomassen, liminality is not normative but just 'is'.[33] This work concedes this, but for the purposes of this book, liminality helps us to understand more than how things are; this work focuses on transformational process rather than on (subjective) experience. I argue that it helps to reveal an understanding of how liminality goes beyond the gothic because it

---

[26] Szakolczai, 'Liminality and Experience', 155.

[27] Coined in G. Bateson, *Naven* (Stanford University Press, 1958).

[28] Laurie, 'Liminality and the Limits of Law', 58.

[29] Szakolczai, 'Liminality and Experience', 155; also see Bateson, *Naven*.

[30] Thomassen, *Liminality and the Modern*.

[31] Taylor-Alexander and others, 'Beyond Compression' 155.

[32] Thomassen, *Liminality and the Modern*, 7.

[33] Laurie, 'Liminality and the Limits of Law'; Taylor-Alexander and others, 'Beyond Compression', 155.

informs normative responses, but importantly it is not signalling any particular normative outcome as such (see Chapter 7 of this book).

5.3 Widening the Lens

This section widens the liminal lens beyond rites of passage and explores the liminality of embryos *in vitro*. It argues that they are liminal in two key ways. First, and perhaps the most obvious, embryos are biologically and physically liminal – rapidly changing, from one state to another, from a ball of cells to (potentially) a baby. Within that, in certain situations embryos are also physically frozen, with a somewhat unknown future. It is an ongoing process of becoming (what it is becoming will be addressed shortly). Secondly, it is legally liminal, neither person nor property:[34] it hovers between these two legal categories, suitable for almost everything else we regulate. In many ways, it is thus defined by being 'not yet something else', legally, biologically, socially, and so on.

5.3.1 The Liminality of Embryos

Human embryos may be described as liminal entities, aside from the liminal states that the law has created for them, by delineating categories of being, for they are in an ongoing process of 'becoming'. Embryos, as 'liminal lives', occupy the second stage, the marginal, or 'in-between' zone. As Squier states, 'these liminal lives test the boundaries of our vital taxonomies, whether social, ethical, biological or economic'.[35] Building upon this, Taylor-Alexander and others stress the need to move away from the tendency present in some of the liminality literature to use the word as a synonym for a person who occupies merely 'marginal' space.[36] In the context of health research, as well as others, liminality is central to subjects and objects of regulation, and the spaces that they go through certainly do not occupy the periphery of everyday life.[37] As an entity regulated by the 1990 Act (as amended), embryos occupy a realm of 'pure possibility';[38] there are multiple 'ends' to its liminality: research (eventually disposal), reproduction, and 'freezing'. For example, 'the embryo' as

---

[34] See Chapter 3, Section 3.3 of this book.
[35] Squier, *Liminal Lives*, 4.
[36] Taylor-Alexander and others, 'Beyond Compression', 154.
[37] Ibid.
[38] To echo Turner, *The Ritual Process*; Taylor-Alexander and others, 'Beyond Compression', 166.

a resource for SCR 'is defined by its being "not yet" something else, that is a stem cell is defined more in terms of a biological possibility – its pluripotency – than a well-defined actuality'.[39] It is arguable that there is room for law to recognise this 'pure possibility' more. After all, as we have seen there are many possibilities for embryos under the framework. Possibility is a key facet of the processes it regulates, for example, exact futures are unknown when an embryo is created (unless it is created to be researched on). All there is here is one possibility, especially at the stages where embryos are frozen or tested via PGD (where possibilities are truly unknown at those stages.) The transitory state of embryos has been recognised in other cultures, for example in *mizuko kuyo*, a Japanese tradition for grieving miscarriages that recognises liminality in embryonic life *in utero*.[40]

To return to the above point about liminality's normative quality for this work, Squier, writing on excess embryos, argues that 'contemporary medicine necessitates a significant revision of Turner's book, one that acknowledges the shifting, interconnected, and emergent quality of human life'.[41] Her work explores how science fiction has paved the way for changes in biotechnological science and uses liminality to explore how science and fiction have altered the contours (ontologies) of human life through several contemporary examples, such as hybrid embryos. She draws upon Paul Rabinow's work to bridge writings on liminality with his concept of 'purgatory'. According to Rabinow, with biological and social ambiguity comes 'purgatorial anxiety'.[42] In combining the sense of responsibility associated with the latter, and the sense of possibility associated with liminality, Squier uses both as a reminder for the long-term implications of biotechnological interventions alongside the inventive capacity of human beings to change or redirect the trajectories of our development.[43] Quoting Victor Turner, she adopts the following meaning of liminality:

> Liminality, literally 'being on a threshold' – is Turner's term for an in-between state, 'betwixt-and-between the normal, day to day cultural and

[39] L. Eriksson and A. Webster, 'Governance-by-Standards in the Field of Stem Cells: Managing Uncertainty in the World of "Basic Innovation"' (2008), *Science and Culture*, 27(2), 99–111, 105.

[40] E. Harrison and I. Midori, 'Women's Responses to Child Loss in Japan: The Case of "Mizuko Kuyō"[with Response]' (1995), *Journal of Feminist Studies in Religion*, 11(2), 67–100.

[41] Squier, *Liminal Lives*, 6.

[42] P. Rabinow, *French DNA: Trouble in Purgatory* (University of Chicago Press, 1999).

[43] Squier, *Liminal Lives*, 8.

social states and processes of getting and spending, preserving law and order, and registering social status'.[44]

Liminality is thus a conceptual lens that challenges us to engage with, and perhaps even embrace, the processual nature of regulated (and unregulated) subjects and objects, and their interactions. Through this lens, we can 'see and experience the most basic elements of common humanity'[45] and thus 'engaging with process and change helps reveal existing social structures and ordering practices'.[46] As Squier points out, liminal lives function relationally.[47] In some ways, embryos may function 'less as *nouns* – whether subjects of experience or objects of other's actions – than they do as *verbs*, enacting a reciprocal exchange between science and culture'.[48] Embryos are thus a prime example of an entity caught between humanity's sense of 'tremendous possibility of the new biomedicine, and our purgatorial anxiety to account responsibility for its implications'.[49] The rest of this book draws regularly from the above, yet Squier's work, unlike this, has no legal focus. Further, this work adds Chapter 4's gothic 'framing' to the liminality of embryos *in vitro*.

To recap, as we have seen in Part I, there are multiple processes and ends to embryos *in vitro* under law. These may be identified as:

1. Where embryos are to be used for reproductive purposes
2. Where they are to be used in research
3. Where they have an uncertain future, that is if used for PGD, their future could be either state 1 or 2 (above).[50]

If an essential component to being liminal in nature is being led *out* of this state, then one must ask: if the law is to embrace the liminal, processual nature of human embryos, then where is it leading embryos *to*? This might be cast as a form of the question: what is/are the telos/teloi[51] of human embryos? The short answer, discussed in the next section, is that it has no single telos but multiple ones, which have been facilitated further by new reproductive and research technologies.

---

[44] Ibid., 3; V. Turner, 'Frame, Flow and Reflection: Ritual and Drama as Public Liminality', in M. Benamou and C. Caramello (eds.), *Performance in Postmodern Culture* (Coda Press, 1977).
[45] Taylor-Alexander and others, 'Beyond Compression', 155.
[46] Ibid.
[47] Squier, *Liminal Lives*, 9.
[48] Ibid., 10.
[49] Ibid.
[50] As above-mentioned, this reflects Turner's description of a state of 'pure possibility'.
[51] 'Teleology' is intended in the Aristotelian sense e.g. purpose, final end, or end goal.

5.3.2   Do Embryos Have a 'Telos'?

The teloi available to embryos (in a legal sense) in turn impact on the ontology of the regulated embryo(s). Here, telos is used to describe a destined end-point. For example, if a particular embryo or group of embryos is put on a research path, because we can apply new technologies to them, they then become research artefacts. To be clear, the 'teleology of embryos' could be interpreted to support a variety of arguments. For one, it is often employed based on the idea that biological entities have an inherent teleology: 'A teleological definition would view the developmental pathway typically followed by an embryo to be what nature "intends" or as what it is the gene code's pre-designed "purpose" to achieve.'[52] The brief analysis in this subsection focuses on teleology of embryos *in vitro*, which has arguably been disrupted by *technology*. This technological disruption of teleology has, of course, been facilitated by law – in the United Kingdom, the 1990 Act.

What is the telos of *in vitro* human embryos? The short answer, discussed further later, is that many embryos created *in vitro* have no single telos but multiple ones, as facilitated further by the regulation of new technologies. Indeed, the 'natural' telos of embryos has never been singular. Once conceived, embryos may be lost naturally from a couple of days in age, right through to the later, foetal stage. Alternatively, they may of course undergo successful gestation within the mother's womb and be born into the world. The development of modern medicine has brought about more than two telos for human embryos. While, as aforementioned, there has never been a guaranteed continuity to embryonic life, modern technology has brought about a more explicit disruption to the latter than ever. As Waldby and Squier state:

> Stem cell technologies introduce a decisive disruption into any imagined continuity between embryonic life and infantile or adult life. Any biotechnology that changes the temporal trajectory of human life has implications for ways of being human.[53]

New research and reproductive technologies demonstrate that embryos are not 'proto-human',[54] meaning that we cannot simply read the biography of human life, and biology, back to our moment of origin. The

---

[52] D. Gamble, 'Potentialism and the Value of an Embryo', *Public Affairs Quarterly*, 19(4) (2005), 271.

[53] C. Waldby and S. M. Squier, 'Ontogeny, Ontology, and Phylogeny: Embryonic Life and Stem Cell Technologies' (2003), *Configurations*, 11(1), 27–46, 32.

[54] Ibid., 33.

temporal implications of stem cell technologies, for example, 'demon-strate the *perfect contingency* of any relationship between embryo and person, the non-teleological nature of the embryo's developmental pathways'.[55] The boundaries of human existence are therefore increas-ingly unstable – 'imprecise at best, contested at worst'.[56] As research and conception practices are evolving and changing, so does the narrative(s) of embryonic life:

> [A]ssisted conception practices had already unsettled the teleological end point of embryos that places it within a sequential, linear narrative of 'life': gametes-embryo-foetus-child. . . . For instance, the teleological sequence of embryos may include one or more of the following: be frozen and stored, allowed to perish, implanted into the 'mother' who then miscar-ries, used for implantation into a woman other than the source of the oocyte (egg), or used by clinicians to practice assisted conception tech-niques and further understanding of human reproduction.[57]

Certain embryos thus lack a 'human' teleological trajectory, for example admixed embryos. Some argue even further that if they lack that trajec-tory, perhaps it is a misuse of language to even call them 'embryos' at all: 'An embryo reflects an evolutionary history and a developmental future. If cloned human blastocysts lack this teleological trajectory, it would be a misuse of language to continue to call them "embryos".'[58] Whilst this book does not claim that the term 'embryo' should be retired from use in certain cases, it is nonetheless worth noting the modern redundancy of the connotations, and teleological implications, of using the term 'embryo' in all contexts.

It seems, then, that modern science, facilitated in law, affects the teleologies of embryos in at least three ways:

1. It interrupts
2. It pauses
3. It creates teleologies for embryos.

It is *interrupting*, in that it can change the liminal 'path' that embryos are on. They can go from PGD to implantation, or to research. They can go

[55] Ibid.
[56] Squier, *Liminal Lives*, 7.
[57] S. Parry, '(Re)constructing Embryos in Stem Cell Research: Exploring the Meaning of Embryos for People Involved in Fertility Treatments' (2006), *Social Science and Medicine*, 62(10), 2358.
[58] I. Hyun and K. W. Jung, 'Human Research Cloning, Embryos and Embryo-like Artefacts'(2006), *Hastings Centre Reports*, 36(5), 34–41, 39.

from the developmental process to being terminated where a woman wishes it. It *pauses* it, in that it allows embryos to be literally frozen in time, in a state of 'permanent liminality', unmoving along any trajectory at all. The law also *creates* teleologies for embryos, in that it creates new situations, possibilities, and paths in which they can exist (liminally), and from which they can be led out (teleologically) that did not exist before. For example, embryos can now be used as a supply of stem cells, the telos of which is to be disposed of or turned into something new, such as an advanced therapy for the treatment of others or a research tool.

One might argue that the use of teleology in this context is misplaced. If, as according to Aristotle, the ultimate telos of all humans is 'flourishing' and living a virtuous life (etcetera),[59] then it would seem nonsensical to use it to support practices which result in embryo disposal. Yet this is not necessarily implicated by use of the word 'telos'. Here it is used to emphasise the third, hitherto unarticulated stage(s) of embryonic legal processes. As Karpowicz and others argue, teleological arguments do not preclude or necessarily support, for example, the creation of chimeras.[60] Whether merging human and non-human tissues, or altering the 'path' on which an embryo might sit, the nature of teleological guidance leaves room for endless speculation on the 'natural' purposes of any living thing without providing guidance on what is 'right':

> [I]t is not clear whether a teleological view would consider heart transplants or *in vitro* fertilization natural or unnatural. By their very artificiality, these would seem to violate the natural ends of the human components involved and of those who possess them, rather than restoring them to their teleological functions. Yet the same interventions would help humans achieve their natural ends, respectively, of being alive and reproducing.[61]

Scientific intervention has clearly defined, and redefined, the possible telos of human embryos. Yet what role should the law play here? The answer to this is of course subjective, but there are considerations it might better embrace if it wishes to take a sincere stance on the

---

[59] Or happiness, or pleasure, any teleological theories could apply here.

[60] P. Karpowicz, C. B. Cohen, and D. Van der Kooy, 'Developing Human-nonhuman Chimeras in Human Stem Cell Research: Ethical issues and Boundaries' (2005), *Kennedy Institute of Ethics Journal*, 15(2), 114; for an alternative analysis see C. Palacios-González, 'Human Dignity and the Creation of Human-nonhuman Chimeras' (2015), *Medicine, Health Care, and Philosophy*, 18(4), 487.

[61] See Karpowicz, Cohen, and Van der Kooy, 'Developing Human-nonhuman Chimeras in Human Stem Cell Research', 107–134.

processual nature of embryos. Physical reintegration into the community, as per Turner,[62] is neither possible nor desirable for all embryos *in vitro*.[63] Reintegration may occur in other ways; however, for example, research carried out on *in vitro* embryos contributes to public goods, for example improving fertility treatment. Perhaps, then, the answer to this is not that the law should necessarily lead them somewhere, but to recognise that by virtue of being entities 'betwixt and between', they are already being led out of liminality by technology and society, facilitated in law. Yet, as the following shows, this is not always possible.

5.3.3 Permanently Liminal?

As argued in the introduction to this chapter, liminality literature can add to Mulkay, Ford, Kaprin, and others' gothic analysis of embryos *in vitro* in order to help us understand our (non) engagement with the 'abhuman'. Recall that according to liminal literature, the ultimate *telos,* or end-point of liminal beings, is to be led out of liminality. Some, however, may experience 'permanent liminality': a constant state of chaos where the entity does not or cannot emerge out of their liminal state to the other side; reincorporation into society is, in some cases, simply not possible. Thus, some entities can remain (permanently) 'in between'.

Like all that is gothic, and all that is liminal, embryos are 'always on the point of dissolving into something else'.[64] It is unstable, tenuous, and incomplete. According to liminal literature, the permanently liminal becomes a perpetual 'outsider'. While this has a marked overlap with aforementioned theories of the 'gothic self', nonetheless, as aforesaid, this does not necessarily *always* place them at the margins of moral and social life. Permanent liminality has been used in disability literature to discuss and challenge the experiences of *some* disabled persons in society. Willet and Deegan confront our 'hypermodern society', which 'creates permanent liminality for most people with disabilities' and is full of barriers for the latter such as 'forbidden spaces' (e.g. those without wheelchair accessibility).[65] Persons with disabilities have also been described as

---

[62] Turner, *The Ritual Process;* also see Thomassen, *Liminality and the Modern*, 92.
[63] Some might say that it would be immoral to make 'birth' possible by implanting a 'research' embryo (including a cloned embryo, or an admixed embryo) into a woman (or even an artificial womb).
[64] Punter, *Gothic Pathologies,* 200.
[65] J. Willett and M. Deegan, 'Liminality and Disability: Rites of Passage and Community in Hypermodern Society' (2001), *Disability Studies Quarterly,* 21(3), 137–152.

experiencing responses of legal abjection.[66] As an 'inchoate',[67] partially formed being, embryos are a model of the various hallmarks of the gothic and liminal (yet not necessarily marginal).[68] Some embryos' liminality is perpetuated in law, their in-between state ossified either physically (by being frozen) or symbolically by what may be interpreted as failing to provide an effective 'out' or 'third stage of the liminal process. Teleologically speaking, law arguably treats research embryos as 'artefacts',[69] yet their *telos* (as an artefact) has arguably been limited by the fourteen-day rule.

Perhaps the most obvious form of permanent liminality for embryos, then, is their physical freezing within a lab context. 'Good quality'[70] embryos may be frozen for use in future treatment or research. The 'quality' of embryos is unaffected by the amount of time they are frozen. According to the HFEA website:

> The embryos will be put in a special substance, which replaces water in their cells. This will protect the embryos from damage caused by ice crystals forming. They'll then be frozen, either by cooling them slowly or fast freezing (vitrification) and stored in tanks of liquid nitrogen until you're ready to use them.[71]

At the end of the standard storage period (ten years, but in some special cases this can be extended to fifty-five years),[72] where one's embryos have not been used for treatment, there are a number of options: donate them to someone in need; donate them to research; donate them to training; or discard them (the most commonly selected option).[73] Where embryos are used for training, research, or are discarded, their final (legally governed) process is their disposal, where according to the HFEA, they are 'simply removed from the freezer and allowed to perish naturally in warmer temperatures or water'.[74] These embryos thus never really 'emerge' out of liminality to a new 'flourished' state. Further, one could

---

[66] Ford, 'Nothing and Not Nothing'.

[67] J. Seymour, *Childbirth and the Law* (Oxford University Press, 2000), 135.

[68] Ford, 'Nothing and Not-Nothing', 40.

[69] Mason, *Human Life*, 94.

[70] Human Fertilisation and Embryology Authority ('HFEA'), 'Embryo Freezing', available at www.hfea.gov.uk/treatments/fertility-preservation/embryo-freezing/ accessed 29 January 2020.

[71] Ibid.

[72] Human Fertilisation and Embryology Authority, 'Code of Practice' (9th ed., 2019, first published 2009) 17.13.

[73] HFEA, 'Embryo Freezing'.

[74] Ibid.

also argue that permanent liminality also applies to embryos used for research in particular; never going beyond the fourteen-day stage and thus all they ever have been (since conception), or will be, is 'in between'. It is therefore arguable that embryos, as 'research artefacts',[75] are prevented from becoming the best possible artefact they can be (teleologically, in terms of an object of scientific value), as opposed to the common norm where their use is limited, despite their inevitable disposal.

Accordingly, there is little in the way of substantive 'feedback loops'.[76] To explain, feedback loops are outputs of a regulatory system routed back as inputs to the various actors implicated in an enterprise. Taylor-Alexander and others argue:

> Using the frame of command-and-control regulation as a particularly acute instance of regulation given effect through law, we posit that such responses often compress and dislocate the 'feedback loops' needed for robust and dynamic steering of behaviour, thus stunting the development of flexible regulatory tools that can better address health research .... To consider command-and-control in particular, such an approach is characterised by what we call regulatory compression. While feedback loops – outputs of a regulatory system routed back as inputs to the various actors implicated in the enterprise – exist between research and regulatory spaces, they are bound by the organisational structures in which they arise. The temporal dimensions of health research regulation play a central role in mediating the resolution of ontological issues (of what something 'is' that is to be regulated) and of democracy (how can we decide appropriate and socially acceptable ways of regulating). When the regulatory space is viewed this way, we can see the effects of respective regulatory approaches in health research practices.[77]

We discuss them in the context of health research regulation more generally, but embryos are rather representative of this point in context:

> Embryo regulation is a form of static, hard law, and the question of the status of the embryo – as laid down by Warnock – has not been revisited since the creation of the original HFE Act in 1990. Even the debacle over cloned embryos was effectively shut down by the House of Lords in 2005 in Quintavalle. This is arguably an example where potential for new, more public input into the regulation of embryos has been blocked, thus maintaining the rigidity and inflexibility of one of the core focuses of the HFE Act, viz., the status of the embryo. Accordingly, there is little in

---

[75] Mason, *Human Life*.
[76] Taylor-Alexander and others, 'Beyond Compression', 164.
[77] Ibid., 151.

the way of substantive feedback loops, and the statute itself is quite inflexible in this regard.[78]

Embryos may also be framed as liminal in law. This state is, thus far, unchanging. Notably this is not necessarily a 'bad' thing, nor is permanent liminality more generally. It is important, nonetheless, that this state is realised so we might move beyond and *out* of it (discussed further in the next subsection). Therefore, two of the three liminal states summarised earlier may be identified as not only 'liminal' but also 'permanently liminal' (1 and 3). Nonetheless, as discussed further in the next section, not only are embryos *in vitro* liminal entities or indeed permanently liminal within the framework that governs them (as argued above), but so too is the *law* that governs them. Overall, this section has drawn out one of the key facets of this book's original contribution: the positive potential of permanent liminality. Next, I argue that considering it in this manner allows us to move beyond what we have (if we so desire, although whether or not we desire it is beyond the scope of this book), or rather, it provides a framework for discussion when considering moving beyond what we have (and which we have had for almost thirty years, at the time of writing).

5.3.4   Liminal Law?

This section argues that liminality may not only be identified as a feature of embryos themselves but also of the law that governs them. Here it is argued that the static, unchanging regulation of embryos *in vitro* identified in Chapters 3–4 is a form of permanent liminality, building upon academic calls for 'frozen' medico-legal concepts to 'unfreeze'.[79]

From what we have seen thus far, a diagnosis of permanent liminality seemingly paints a bleak picture. Szakolczai has termed the aforementioned permanent states of crisis as 'permanent liminality', a never-ending chaotic state.[80] While he describes this state as negative, as with mimesis, schismogenesis, and trickster, it is arguable that 'permanent liminality' has positive potential, at least as an analytical lens. In revealing the permanence of an inherently processual legal and physical condition, this analytical process leaves scope for this purgatory's disruption. Indeed, calls have already been made by some to 'ditch durability' as

---

[78]   Ibid., 164.
[79]   See. Jacob and Prainsack, 'Embryonic Hopes', 514.
[80]   Szakolczai, 'Permanent (Trickster) Liminality'.

a hope for law in this ever-changing field.[81] This book argues that permanent liminality can create a new 'condition of possibility' when this state of stasis becomes apparent, a condition for change.

One aspect of these concepts particularly speaks to the United Kingdom's regulation of embryos *in vitro*. Mimesis, the blind following of certain practices without reflection, might arguably be located in the 1990 Act's iteration and apparent reiteration of embryos' 'special status'. Recall that the question of the status of 'the embryo', as laid down by the Warnock Report, has not been revisited since the creation of the original 1990 Act. It is arguable that Parliament has been unreflexively iterating embryos' 'special status' since the 1980s, without revisitation or reflection. It has not been questioned in Parliament since its inception and in fact has been specifically noted as *not* up for discussion in deliberations leading up to the 2008 amendments to the Act.[82] This correlates with the previous discussion of 'feedback loops'.

While this may seem bleak, it is nonetheless worth noting what this book calls the 'positive analytical potential' of liminality. Szakolczai has termed the aforementioned permanent states of crisis as 'permanent liminality', a never-ending chaotic state. While he describes this state as a negative, as with mimesis, schismogenesis, and trickster, it is arguable that 'permanent liminality' has positive potential, as an analytical lens. In revealing the permanence of a particular situation, whether it be the regulation of embryos or others, the analytical process leaves scope for the disruption of this permanence. Indeed, calls have already been made by some to 'ditch durability' as a hope for law in this ever-changing field.[83]

In a collection of papers entitled 'Embryonic Hopes', Fox and Murphy posit that contemporary law-making on embryos cannot and should not be durable: 'We think that durability has to go: it can no longer be our hope for the law in this area.'[84] In expecting law to fail, and for failure to be made 'ordinary', their hope is that law will become more workable, as change is a necessary feature in regulating this field. They advance that if we articulate our hopes (as reference points for scenarios and decision-making) for law, and settle conflicts regarding meanings and boundaries (whether potential or actual) in a pragmatic way, then these expressions

---

[81] Fox and Murphy, 'Response to Sarah Franklin', 510.
[82] House of Commons Science and Technology Committee, 'Human Reproductive Technologies and the Law: Report of the Fifth Session 2004–5' (2005), 51.
[83] See Fox and Murphy, 'Response to Sarah Franklin', 510.
[84] Ibid.

of emotion can yield to reasonable legal solutions,[85] such as amendments that have a positive impact on family structures.[86] For the authors of this collection, hope and failure seem to go hand in hand in law, each the flipside of the other. Failure 'breaks open a consensus agreement once it is no longer capable of responding to real-world problems in a satisfactory manner'.[87] It thus enables us, and particularly stakeholders in policy such as those affected by infertility, to revisit and re-actualise hopes (in terms of what we might want for law) in reaction to this.

Legal constructions of embryos thus have considerable power to make and break research and family-making practices. I argue, therefore, that we must be receptive to change in its normative characterisations and not allow them to stagnate as social and scientific understandings change. 'Durability', then, where science and society are changing relatively rapidly in the field the 1990 Act regulates, may be framed as a form of permanent liminality. If we do not hope or intend for permanence of law, however, we need to be cognisant of embryos' regulatory purgatory. To explain my argument further, and a return to Squier's work and her connection between Turner's 'liminality' and Rabinow's 'purgatorial anxiety', allows parallels to be drawn between Rabinow's diagnosis and the unrevised legal status of embryos today. Rabinow describes this experience of social and biological ambiguity as

> a chronic sense that the future is at stake; a leitmotif among scientists, intellectuals, and sectors of the public turning on redeeming past moral errors and avoiding future ones; an awareness of an urgent need to focus on a vast zone of ambiguity and shading in judging actions and actors conduct; a heightened sense of tension between this-worldly activities and (somehow) transcendent states and values; and a pressing need to define a mode of relationship to these issues.[88]

In Squier's elicitation of the intrinsic relationship between possibility and responsibility in contemporary health research,[89] a core feature of embryo regulation is unveiled. To extend this analysis, we have seen this tension in recent debates surrounding embryos on the extension of the fourteen-day rule, surrounded by the very tensions described earlier by Rabinow. Yet I argue that as we have seen, law's characterisation of

---

[85] Ibid., 514.
[86] E.g. the removal of the 'need for a father' from the 'welfare of the child' provision in the original 1990 Act.
[87] Fox and Murphy, 'Response to Sarah Franklin', 515.
[88] Rabinow, *French DNA*, 17–18.
[89] Taylor-Alexander and others, 'Beyond Compression', 156.

this tension often occurs in the fixation of boundaries in order to balance the weights of possibility and responsibility in rapidly advancing fields of technology. I thus suggest that this fixedness, when unvisited, becomes purgatorial.

Although there are, quite commendably, regular consultations on certain proposed incremental amendments to the 1990 Act,[90] notwithstanding the small extent to which this is done in consultations, there have been few supplementary opportunities for this fundamental issue to be addressed. Recall that the key issue at hand for this research is that the 'special status' of embryos, a core facet of the Act that regulates the use of embryos in the United Kingdom in multiple contexts,[91] has been made entirely inflexible by the law. In the years since the law has seen examples such as *Quintavalle*,[92] where potential for new and more *public* input into the regulation of embryos has been blocked. This serves to maintain the rigidity and inflexibility of one of the core focuses of the 1990 Act (as amended), the 'special status' of embryos *in vitro*. Yet can we move beyond this, out of liminality, by applying the positive potential of permanent liminality offered here? This book explores the answer to this in Part III.

Jacob and Prainsack end their collection by asking: 'If the law's facing of its own failure (and resilience) is more inspiring than disconcerting, could this be because embryos have had an effect on the law as well as being produced by the law?'[93] 'The embryo' in law is just one of many representations of embryos. Indeed, Jacob and Prainsack 'challenge law as an instrument of order and its reliance on the distinction between persons and things'.[94] The 'liminality of things' helps to reveal the fluid and bonded relationship between health research subjects and objects,[95] for example tissue and its donor. It also helps to reveal the nature of entities that might be classed as 'subject-objects' (here, neither subject nor object, yet both) where their states in respect of the latter are fluid and subject to change. While law in this area has continued to be reactionary

---

[90] For example on mitochondrial replacement therapy in 2014, which resulted in the Human Fertilisation and Embryology (Mitochondrial Donation) Regulations 2015.

[91] Broadly, research and reproduction.

[92] This case raised the question of whether embryos created by cloning fell under the 1990 Act. It was held on appeal to the House of Lords that they did, and the Act was subsequently amended to reflect this. See *Quintavalle* [2003].

[93] M.A. Jacob and B. Prainsack, 'Unfreezing Embryos?' (2010), *Social and Legal Studies*, 19 (4), 515–516.

[94] Ibid.

[95] Taylor-Alexander and others, 'Beyond Compression', 162.

and piecemeal,[96] it has not necessarily dictated embryos' liminal nature, for liminality is 'not easily amenable to direct influence or control'.[97] It has, however, facilitated new forms of liminality, each with their own end. If the production, use, and disposal of embryos *in vitro* for reproduction and research are to continue in light of the advancement of scientific techniques in this field, a nuanced legal approach is required in order to take embryos out of regulatory purgatory. This approach, which draws from the analysis made in this part, shall be explored in Part III.

5.4   Lessons from a Liminal Lens

So far, the key lessons from a liminal lens (for this book) are as follows:

- The positive potential of 'permanent liminality' with regard to the regulation of emerging technologies and scientific processes
- The centrality of relationality and experiences of the regulated embryo[98] as subject-object, and embryonic processes as it travels through legally and scientifically produced 'pathways'
- The liminality of law itself, permanently in a state where it does not renew, or emerge *out* of this state to a new one.

There are several key parallels to be drawn between liminal literature and hallmarks of the gothic trope that often surround public discussion of *in vitro* embryos. Both can draw lessons from the other, and the following aims to synthesise these lessons in the context of the regulated embryos *in vitro*. It does so with a view to debunking current legal norms surrounding the singular 'special status' of 'the embryo'.

As we have seen, scholars such as Squier have already cast embryos as liminal beings, and this book does not purport to make a new claim re embryos as liminal. What this book does do, however, is make a key and arguably much-needed link between embryos as 'gothic' and embryos as 'liminal'. As discussed in Chapter 4, a gothic framing of embryos *in vitro* enables us to appreciate the way we treat embryos and the reasons for that, but this perspective still leaves the key question of how it may be

---

[96] See R. Storrow, 'Quests for Conception: Fertility Tourists, Globalization and Feminist Legal Theory' (2005), *Hastings Law Journal*, 57(2), 295–330; K. Webster, 'Whose Embryo is it Anyway? A Critique of *Evans v Amicus Healthcare* [2003] EWHC 2161 (Fam)' (2013), *Journal of International Women's Studies*, 7(3), 71–86.

[97] See Laurie, 'Liminality and the Limits of Law', 61.

[98] By persons e.g. researchers.

encompassed in law. Analysing law through a liminal lens may answer this. Yet, why, one might ask, is a gothic framing required at all? I argue that it is important because it reveals essential facets of the law that would be absent from the employment of a liminal lens alone: it reveals both the *nature of* and *why* there is a 'legal gap', as identified in Part I. It thus provides an essential intellectual step between the gap in the law as *is* and the intellectual closure of this gap, from conceptualisation to realisation.

Both 'gothic' qualities and the liminal condition commonly include those who are in a state of fluidity and flux; they conform to neither one category nor any other. Further, there are multiple categories or ways of 'being' for embryos (this is in part facilitated in law); this is discussed further in Part III. This section therefore draws together some of the distinct yet currently underexplored links between 'gothic' and liminality literature. Thus far, it identifies three main qualities as sites of interconnection between the two concepts, all concerned with those who fall between normative boundaries: 'in-between', 'becoming', and 'relationality'. There is, however, one glaring disparity between 'gothic', its related literatures, and the liminal literature: marginality.

5.4.1 'Marginal'?

A key feature of the gothic trope is to challenge the marginalisation of, and debunking of conventional narratives surrounding, those who stand in contrast to liberal norms and thus may be perceived as sitting on the outskirts of 'normal' society. For some, their personal/physical opposition to liberal (legal) norms causes these groups' marginalisation in society.[99]

Marginality, however, is a key divergence between liminality and the gothic trope that should be addressed here. It is important to challenge the common conception that 'liminal' can be used as shorthand for 'marginal'. Rather, in the context of health research regulation liminal spaces are central to every day practice:

> [W]e stress the need to move away from a tendency of some of the liminality literature to employ the word as a synonym for something or someone that occupies a 'marginal' space. When viewed in the context of health research regulation, these liminal spaces do not occupy the periphery. On the contrary, our analysis shows that liminality is central to the everyday research practices and the regulatory mechanisms that surround them.[100]

---

[99] Ford, 'Nothing and Not-Nothing', 37.
[100] Taylor-Alexander and others, 'Beyond Compression', 154.

While other 'gothic' entities may rightly be described as 'marginal', this book argues that embryos may not. Literature on the gothic trope does not say that embryos are marginal per se, but it does point out that there are parallels between them and 'monstrous bodies', who are often classified as marginal persons. And indeed Ford has argued that we ought to be willing to acknowledge that 'the embryo' can invite abjection responses from the law and others.[101] Nonetheless, liminality shows us that it is important not to frame embryos as something that is liminal *because* it is marginal. It is important to articulate that while gothic entities are indeed 'extra-legal', 'unamenable to the rule of law',[102] and they may sometimes be liminal, one does not necessarily give rise to the other. Liminality is central to the physical transformation of embryos because these entities are subject to perpetual change towards well-defined (legal) ends, and thus this realisation has significant implications for the way in which the law regulates them. To be clear, this book draws an important distinction between being placed on the margins (whether in law or society) and *being* marginal (intrinsically). The key point, here, is *not* that embryos are not marginal in any sense, but that liminality cannot be used as a shorthand for marginality, which it seems that 'gothic' sometimes can be. Moreover, a label of 'gothic' is a mere descriptor: it tells us nothing about law as regulation, nor indeed about law as process. If regulatory objectives are to be met, including those with regard to embryos which will necessarily change status in the pursuit of those objectives, then we require better ways than we have at present of understanding the processes in play.

Liminality, whether experienced by subjects, or experienced by onlookers in relation to subject-object, or indeed (not) experienced by objects, is central to every day social and political life. The law may indeed 'cast out' non-liberal individuals, and as we have seen in Chapter 4, whether by default or by design, embryos *in vitro* have been slowly disappearing from the legal landscape, but this does not imply that they are marginal (either as research objects, or reproductive subjects-to-be). In other words, while the law may have 'cast out' certain individuals or entities, they remain central to scientific, societal, and political life. Herein lies one of the key problems for this book: the law has placed embryos on the margins, whereas in reality, embryos are liminal, *not* marginal. This is because embryos are central to research and

---

[101] Ford, 'Nothing and Not-Nothing'.
[102] Punter, *Gothic Pathologies*.

reproductive practices. Yet, what might we do about this? In answer to the legal 'casting out' of embryos, Ford suggests:

> For a start, instead of *embedding* the notion of the foetus as 'monstrous' or as 'outcast' . . . or excluding discussion of the embryo/foetus altogether as most postmodernist discourses on corporeality and subjecthood do, we ought to be alive to the parallels between the body of the embryo/foetus and other 'monstrous' bodies. We ought to be willing to acknowledge the possibility that the embryo/ foetus invites responses of abjection – from academic commentators and judges, as well as from ordinary members of the moral community. It would be strange if the embryo/foetus were able to *avoid* such responses, given how readily it maps onto concepts of the monstrous and the abhuman. As such, any notion that the incomplete, unstable body of the embryo/foetus can be excluded from serious attempts to critique liberal subjecthood, particularly in the bioethical context, must be regarded as problematic.[103]

A liminal lens does not necessarily stand in contrast to this recommendation, but to add to this, this book recommends that while we should be alive to the parallels between embryos and 'monstrousness' or 'Otherness', their liminal qualities have placed it centrally within the moral community, albeit with mixed responses. This does not negate that the law has had an 'abject' response to 'the embryo', quite the opposite; these abovementioned parallels place 'the embryo' in a particularly unique place in law, where it is there left relatively untouched yet remains central to moral and scientific knowledge exchanges. Instead of naming this legal response to 'the embryo' as a 'casting out', it might be better to call it a 'regulatory purgatory'. And if this is accepted, then this brings another reason to consider the issue through a liminal lens: liminality, as stated previously, is about leading through and out of a state of stasis. It requires us to ask: what lies beyond legal stasis?

5.4.2   Between Boundaries: 'A Confusion of All the Customary Categories'

Building upon Freud's above-mentioned theory of *das unheimliche*, psychologists have since referred to the 'anxiety' that can be facilitated by the uncanny.[104] This may be linked to Susan Squier's adoption of

---

[103] Ford, 'Nothing and Not-Nothing', 44.
[104] See G. Diatkine, 'Le Séminaire, X: L'angoisse de Jacques Lacan' (2005), *Revue française de psychanalyse*, 69(3), 917–931.

Rabinow's 'purgatorial anxiety', and liminality. When we come across the liminal, this sensation is created not only in concern over what we should or should not do, for example with regard to biotechnologies, but interestingly adds that 'in the ambivalence and ambiguity of our responses to them, we also confront our own in-between state'.[105] From what we have seen of accounts of the 'gothic self', one could say that 'gothic' persons, or onlookers upon 'gothic entities', can experience the same kind of anxiety. When encountering the gothic, the sense of familiar–unfamiliarity arguably leaves the onlooker in his or her own emotional purgatory. This book argues that the 'gothic' thus invites people to experience their own 'in-between state'. Purgatory, even if it concerns another, is a fearful state of being for many, which has been reflected in classic gothic literatures such as Dante's *Divine Comedy* ('limbo' or 'purgatory' being the first circle of hell).[106] Embryos' own purgatorial state has put the law, an onlooker, in its own moral, social, and regulatory purgatory. This is an effective explanatory power behind the law's ever more apparent 'step back' from the human embryo over the past twenty-seven years.

Recall that Turner describes liminal beings as 'neither here nor there; they are betwixt and between the positions assigned and arrayed in law, custom, convention, and ceremony'.[107] There are striking similarities between this, and 'gothic selves' described by literature, who often do not quite belong to one societal group, or another, or fall under a particular category of person that the law prescribes (e.g. gender). Being in an 'inter-structural situation' involving a concurrence of opposite symbols,[108] a quality of liminality, is equally as important a hallmark for those who are thought to be 'gothic'. Occupants of the liminal, and the gothic, both sit betwixt and between, being neither one nor other, occupying a liminal space between societal taxonomies 'whether social, ethical, biological or economic'.[109] Yet those who have been delineated as gothic in nature, in many cases, cannot reach the 'third stage' of liminality, emerging out of the other side and returning to everyday life. These people or entities may therefore be described as 'permanently liminal'.

Human embryos are the epitome of Turner's description of the liminal social condition: 'a confusion of all the customary categories'.[110] While

---

[105] Squier, *Liminal Lives,* 9.
[106] D. Alighieri, *The Divine Comedy* (Vintage Books, 2013).
[107] Turner, *Forest of Symbols* 95.
[108] Ibid.
[109] Squier, *Liminal Lives* 4.
[110] Turner, *The Forest of Symbols,* 97.

embryos are not in a 'social' condition per se (for that might require personhood), the latter analysis can still apply. It is physically and structurally absent from society; it is in many ways invisible. According to Turner, liminality is often accompanied by seclusion of those in transition, 'since it is a paradox, a scandal, to see what ought not to be there'.[111]

One can see how this effect of liminality applies to those who have also been centred in gothic literature, which argues that we should not necessarily see this quality as something that is negative; it is an 'inescapable feature of humanity'.[112] Those who feel that they do not fall within the normative gender binaries, for example, have certainly experienced (and indeed suffered) responses of abjection, yet some may also be described as liminal ('between genders'). There is an androgynous quality to embryos, as are many of those who are in a liminal state.[113] Their sex organs, whether male or female, are not visible via ultrasound until the nine-week stage, and in fact do not even develop before the sixth week. This adds to the paradoxical, ambiguous quality of embryos, qualities that also characterise liminal beings.[114] Dually, gothic and liminal literature helps to frame and reveal these qualities, ever underlying discourse, but never articulated.

Moreover, recall Chapter 4's consideration of embryos *in vitro* as 'boundary objects', of which there is a degree of 'interpretive flexibility'. This point was made to demonstrate that embryos are on the thresholds of various boundaries that we recognise; for example, they are simultaneously 'nothing and not-nothing'.[115] This analysis, conjoined with the previous, is helpful to a point for this work. A further step is required here, however, because embryos are not only *between* boundaries, but also *becoming*.

5.4.3 Becoming

Embryos are very much in a state of constant change, ever *becoming* (unless frozen). It should be noted that the notion of *becoming* is much centred within the liminal literature, rather than the gothic literature. While we can see echoes of this notion within some applications of 'the gothic', there is still a significant divergence between the two concepts on this front. Kelly

---

[111] Ibid., 98.
[112] Ford, 'Nothing and Not-Nothing', 34.
[113] Turner, *The Forest of Symbols*, 98.
[114] Ibid., 97.
[115] See Ford, 'Nothing and Not-Nothing'.

Hurley describes an abhuman subject: 'a not-quite human subject, characterised by its morphic variability, continually in danger of becoming not-itself, *becoming* other'.[116] The latter part of this description very much echoes the liminality literature. Nonetheless, a divergence should be noted, in that becoming 'not itself, becoming other' is a 'danger' here, rather than a rite of passage with the positive connotations of reintegration into society. The 'danger' (if any) in liminality is not sourced from an entity's *becoming* but that it might stop *becoming* – the possibility that that state might become 'permanent', or subject to mimesis, a trickster, or schismogenesis. To apply this to embryo regulation, as argued earlier, one could say that the fourteen-day rule prevents embryos from *becoming*: here, they are stuck in a limbo from which there is no emergence.

Thus, one parallel may be drawn here, however, in that if a liminal being is in 'danger' of these three concepts, it is in danger of becoming 'Other' by virtue of not being able to emerge from liminality. For the purposes of this research, a distinction of Hurley's analysis of the abhuman may thus be made between something's morphic variability and sense of becoming, and its danger of becoming 'Other'. Embryos may thus still be situated as 'abhuman' as per the parallels it has with 'gothic selves', yet it is important that we differentiate between *becoming* as part of liminality, and becoming 'Other' as part of permanent liminality.

It is also worth noting that for those to which 'gothic' literature typically lends its analysis their 'Otherness' is often not a development but something they have been born with (albeit not always, disability can of course be acquired) and thus often cannot (and do not necessarily want to) 'emerge' out of as per liminal literature. Thus, for those who are 'gothic', there is much more of a sense of negotiating their 'being' as opposed to negotiating 'becoming'.

In the two permanent liminalities described above the law is thus preventing embryos from *becoming*. I posit that permanent liminality, like a gothic framing, can enable us to begin positive shifts in liberal law's bounded frameworks.

5.4.4   *Relationality*

Some liminality literature applies the concept to experiential contexts; thus, a subject is often described as *experiencing* liminality.[117] Why, then,

---

[116] Hurley, *Gothic Body*, pp. 3–4.
[117] Thomassen, *Liminality and the Modern*, 99.

might we still apply liminality to embryos? To explain (at least in part), by connotations of 'experience' itself, it is clear that embryos do not yet have the conscience to 'experience' in the normal sense. Notwithstanding, this is not problematic for the use of this lens in an embryonic context for this book. Thomassen highlights in his work the multitudes of applications that liminality may have, from moments, to places, to objects.[118] However, he also remarks that experiences of liminality can relate to three types of 'subjecthood' (individuals, social groups, and whole societies).[119] While this might have opened up the possibility of liminality to some extent, as a lens, in some ways it is also rather restrictive. As we note in 'Beyond Regulatory Compression': 'this typology is rather limiting, especially when we observe how much of health research regulation focuses on objects – tissue, data, embryos, genes and so on – rather than on the person to whom these objects relate'.[120]

We argue that Thomassen's typology arguably does not take account of the network of participants (subject or object) who can be involved in a liminal process or setting. Subjects and objects in these settings can be moulded and defined by their interaction – in other words, their experiences of each other. To provide a basic example, when parents christen a baby, he/she is not aware of what is going on or why; the process, in many ways, is for the parents. Liminality thus helps to account for the changing relations between people, things, and the world around them. It is not only people who can go through processes, 'things' are also capable of transitioning in a manner which leads to new, or renewed, understandings of the thing itself, and their connections to people.[121] As demonstrated by the previous discussion, it is important to recognise the 'fluid but bonded nature of the connection between subject and object'.[122] Thus, in order to use liminality's full analytical potential, we cannot only talk about the liminality of things (objects) but of those who experience objects' (or indeed subject-objects') liminality. Policy and its construction affect the way that people experience the thing being regulated; it is entirely relational. Human embryos are arguably paradigmatic of that, in that their subjectivity and objectivity are fluid depending upon the regulatory path they are put on (e.g. research or reproduction). These pathways shall be discussed in more detail in Part III. As mentioned

[118] Ibid.
[119] Ibid., 89.
[120] Taylor-Alexander and others, 'Beyond Compression', 158.
[121] Ibid.
[122] Ibid., 162.

above, after all, the 1990 Act does not actually regulate embryos, but persons' actions/inactions regarding embryos.

To tie this analysis into liminality's normative potential, it is arguable that we could continue to talk about liminality of things as a standalone category, or, we could argue that the thing itself is going through experience, but this is being experienced by the actors who are implicated in the transformations being done to the thing in question. A multiplicity of actors can affect embryos *in vitro*, from the decisions of their progenitors, intended parents, or the scientists who research upon and dispose of them. These relations can all have different meanings, in different contexts; for example the relation between an embryo and its donor is rather different depending upon whether it is decidedly a 'research' or 'reproductive' embryo.

Herein lies the relational lesson from liminality. Overall, it is arguable that the 1990 Act (as amended) overlooks experience as a transformative part of the liminal process, although embryos do not 'experience'. In other words, if experience is one revealing component (in that it can inform normative discussions) of the liminal lens (with regard to our regulatory structure), another is the dynamics of process. Yet, if the process is incomplete, and embryos do not reach their telos, then we are at risk of 'permanent liminality'.

Further, application of this *relational* framing to a legal context helps forge connections between the law, regulatory subject-objects (embryos are often treated as both simultaneously in law, for example when frozen), and the human subjects from which they were derived.[123] In these situations, law facilitates the modification of the subject-objects' states of affairs, for example 'consent' acts as a mechanism for 'unused' reproductive embryos to be used for research purposes.

5.5 Conclusion: Navigating *through* Liminality

While law in this area has continued to be reactionary and piecemeal,[124] it has not necessarily dictated embryos' liminal nature, for liminality is not easily amenable to direct influence or control.[125] It has, however, facilitated new forms of limen, each with their own end.

---

[123] For example, Isabel Karpin argues law bypasses the 'constitutive role of women's embodiment' in I. Karpin, 'The Legal and Relational Identity of the "Not-Yet" Generation' (2012), *Law, Innovation and Technology*, 4(2), 122–143, 123.

[124] See Storrow, 'Quests for Conception'; Webster, 'Whose Embryo is it Anyway?'.

[125] See Laurie, 'Liminality and the Limits of Law', 60.

Both 'gothic' qualities and the liminal condition commonly include those who are in a state of fluidity and flux; they neither conform to one category nor the other. Further, there are multiple categories or ways of 'being' for embryos (as, in part, facilitated in law), which is discussed further in the Part III. A gothic analysis emphasises embryos' (liminal) placement between 'person' and 'non-person', and provides convincing explanation as to the 'step back' the law has taken from them in the past thirty years. As an aside, this is not to say that the reason for this is not also grounded in policy. Baroness Warnock, for example, recently advocated that we should not alter the fourteen-day rule, so that embryo research is not opened up for discussion again:

> We should note that every time the law about embryo research has been changed or amended the opposition has rallied its forces, and I think it would do so again if we try to get the 14-day rule extended . . . The risk is that all the progress we have made since 1990 would be lost. I think we should stick to the 14-day limit.[126]

Whether or not one agrees with this, it is nonetheless grounded in legal (and social) ambivalence towards embryos. This ambivalence would not be there (at least in part) if it were not for the parallels that human embryos have with the 'gothic self'. Yet, how can the law cope with this ambivalence? The Warnock Committee's original answer was, as aforementioned, according 'the embryo' a 'special status' and thus attaching limits to its use in research context. Nonetheless, as very recent debate over research time limits has shown,[127] the advance of science has proven problematic for this static form of regulation, placing embryos and law in regulatory purgatory. This is where liminality becomes relevant. Liminality helps to reveal how law might better engage with the liminal, processual treatment of embryos. It emphasises that our regulation of embryos is already somewhat context-based, in that it treats reproductive and research embryos very differently. Moreover, if we want law to embrace that further, there are certain distinctions it can make between certain 'types' of embryos, based on recognising the different processual pathways on which we – and the law – place different categories of embryo.

---

[126] Baroness Warnock speaking to the *Observer*, quoted in, R. McKie, 'Row over allowing research on 28-day embryos,' (Guardian Online, 4 December 2016) available at: www .theguardian.com/society/2016/dec/04/row-over-allowing-research-on-28-day-embryos accessed 29 January 2020.
[127] Ibid.

Yet what has liminality revealed about these pathways? Recall that the 'liminality of things' helps to reveal the fluid and bonded relationship between health research subjects and objects, for example tissue and its donor. It also helps to reveal the nature of entities that might be classed as 'subject-objects', where their states in respect of the latter are fluid and subject to change. 'The paradox is that while liminality has failed hitherto to account for things, regulation all too often fails to account for experiences of subject in relation to things.'[128] Thus, for example, we can see this argument reflected in feminist literatures (e.g. critiquing the law as having failed to articulate the vital relation between embryo and woman). Further, while embryos do not, of course, subjectively experience liminality (as far as we know), science and the law turn them into liminal entities in the sense that they are in transition (or stasis) towards diverse ends. These factors necessarily impact on their legal and moral status in different ways, but the law at present does not recognise this, let alone accommodate it.

It might be the case that law will always be liminal, and this is something we should embrace. Recognising its liminality means we can revisit, and grow, almost in a Hegelian sense. This analytical frame thus suggests that there is a way for law to better capture and navigate process, and enable moving out of law's 'permanent liminality' (previously identified as 'legal stasis') at some point. If we move away from permanent liminality, perhaps the associated negativities of this state can be lost as that state is lost (namely, the lack of a coherent framework). This is not to say that permanent liminality is always a 'bad' thing: on the contrary, here its realisation enables us to move beyond stasis.

To recap, the key lessons from Part II of this book are as follows:

- A gothic framing articulates research embryos' permanent liminality within law
- Utilisation of a liminal lens has diagnosed law, too, as permanently liminal. This framing has positive potential, which can enable law to emerge out of its stasis
- A liminal lens has brought a new facet to a gothic framing of embryos: that being on, or between, boundaries do not and should not denote marginality. Those in between, per this research's analysis of embryos, are central to everyday lives of donors, potential parents, and research

---

[128] Taylor-Alexander and others, 'Beyond Regulatory Compression', 159.

practices. However, as Part I has shown, there is a disparity between the reality of these everyday lives and practices, and the law's framing of them

- Law treats embryos *in vitro* as marginal, because of their gothic nature, yet as a liminal analysis has shown, this is not the reality in practice. This articulates more deeply a key facet of Part I's 'legal gap'
- Relationality and experiences by persons who produce or use regulated embryos are central to their use, as subject-object that travels through legally and scientifically produced pathways, one of the key original contributions of this book (to liminality literature)
- Overall, this conjoined analysis acts to articulate, and navigate, the contours of this gap, where law has seemingly struggled to capture the uncertain, processual nature of embryos *in vitro*.

The next step for this book, then, is to identify how Part II's articulation and navigation might take place in order to lead embryos out of liminality. This work's final question is thus: how can law better reflect the uncertain nature of embryonic processes, and the technologies that create them?

PART III

Out of Liminality

The lessons from Part II, as applied here, make evident that there are more ways to define embryos than by biology; everything that happens to them is because of actors along the way. Moreover, these actors relationally define their embryos through their experience of them. Thus, future parents and their IVF clinicians experience embryos differently than the donor couple and the researchers who conduct research on embryos qua research artefacts. A context-based approach, for this book, provides a more intellectually robust basis for regulating embryos *in vitro*, especially in light of the ever-changing nature of science, technology, and society.

With a view to addressing the lessons from Part II, Chapter 6 explores how an embrace of liminality (as a lens that also allows us to see this as a quality of embryos) reveals the multiplicity of contexts in which embryos are used and created. I argue that if we wish for law to continue to take process seriously (as it has done in the past), and that if liminality teaches us about the permanent liminality of law in this area, then it is this book's 'context-based' approach that provides a framework to consider the separate contexts that law is leading embryos into, through, and *out* of. Importantly, this book does not claim that doing so would change what we have in terms of the prevailing legal and regulatory framework in any seismic way, but rather in a nuanced way that allows us to ask questions about how we want to treat embryos, legally.

Building on Chapter 6, Chapter 7 then considers the ways in which this lens might help the law to consider contemporary debates on embryos *in vitro* as well the broader implications that those debates may have. Importantly, it does not assess what we should do, but the ways in which the lens of liminality helps us to think about what we could do. It emphasises that liminality and 'the gothic' can add to legal, ethical, and social discussions on embryos *in vitro*.

6

A Context-Based Approach

6.1 Introduction

Part II of this book, by way of a twofold analysis, highlighted the legally liminal nature of embryos *in vitro*, particularly when it comes to embryos that are to be used for research purposes, and/or disposed of. Yet recall, from Chapter 5, that the liminal process has three stages: 'a separation from everyday life, a move into the margin or limen ... and finally a return to everyday life, though at a higher level of status, consciousness or social position'.[1] The first and second stages of embryos' legal liminality have been examined by Parts I and II of this book, but what of the third stage? If an essential component to being liminal in nature is 'being led out the other side', then one necessary question that a liminal analysis has made evident is: if the law is to embrace the liminal, processual nature of human embryos, then where is it leading embryos *to*?

With a view to answering this question and building on Part II's analyses of the gothic rhetoric surrounding embryos and the liminality of embryos and Part I's diagnosis of the 1990 Act's 'legal gap', this chapter explores and articulates embryos' 'pathways' through the law. The analysis in this chapter emphasises that there can only ever be two places that law, in its present state,[2] can lead embryos: to a woman's womb, or its own destruction and disposal. Ultimately, this chapter has been developed with a view to answering a question left by Part II's analysis: how might we use a liminal lens to bring lessons from 'the gothic', from conceptualisation to realisation? This chapter does so in four sections:

- First, it briefly takes stock of the analysis and 'lessons' highlighted by the book so far, before going on to synthesise this analysis, and in doing

[1] Turner, 'Frame, Flow and Reflection', 34.
[2] Although, as Chapter 7 discusses, other physical contexts (i.e. artificial wombs) are now a reality.

so, considering the ways in which law can lead embryos out of liminality.

- Second, it focuses on the roles of persons in embryonic processes *in vitro*.
- Third, it draws out the contours of a context-based approach, including what the approach *is not*.
- Finally, it, discusses the potential effects of a context-based approach for the issues (i.e. the contours of the 'legal gap') discussed in Part I of this book (listed in Section 6.5). It suggests that a context-based approach has the potential to justify affording embryos *in vitro* different 'statuses' depending on the relationally guided and defined pathway on which it is, or onto which it is put.

It is important to note that by advocating a context-based approach, this work does not intend to imply that different contexts in which embryos can be used are entirely ignored by the law. As discussed in Part I, the 1990 Act (as amended) has recognised these contexts (and thus embryos' processual nature) to some extent with, for example, its separation of 'human' embryos and hybrid embryos.

6.2   Synthesis: Leading Embryos *into* and *through* Liminality

As we have seen from Part I, well before the development of modern science, law dipped in and out of the special relationship between mother and embryo/fetus. The legal regulation of embryos *in vivo* has been variable but heavily influenced by common understandings of embryonic process at any given point in time. It is important to reiterate that there is, of course, no such thing as 'the embryo' under law. However, recall that in the United Kingdom, all embryos *in vitro* do fall under one 'special status'. We thus have a multiplicity of embryos implicitly delineated in law, and these vary depending upon the context in which they appear. The following briefly summarises these legal contexts and the extent of the law's involvement in embryonic/fetal processes in each.

To start at the beginning, as it were, the first context in which embryos appear may be described as (once a woman is pregnant) through 'natural' reproduction.[3] Where the mother intends to take an embryo to full term, the

---

[3] Although women can also self-inseminate via 'DIY assisted conception'. See E. Jackson, 'The Law and DIY Assisted Conception' in K. Horsey (ed.), *Revisiting the Regulation of Human Fertilisation and Embryology* (Routledge, 2015).

law in the United Kingdom does not interfere. It does get directly involved,[4] however:

1. Where a woman wishes to terminate her pregnancy. This is governed by the Abortion Act 1967.
2. Where a woman wants to refuse medical treatment that would prevent termination.[5]
3. Where the woman and partner are in conflict over an unborn embryo/fetus, the law has traditionally been very involved. Today, however, the law has (at least relatively speaking) taken a step back. In many cases the interests of the woman trump those of the unborn embryo/fetus[6] or those of any other parties involved, including the father. There are some exceptions such as the *Evans* case,[7] where it was ruled that frozen embryos could not be implanted without both parties' permission.
4. Where the woman wishes to take an unborn embryo/fetus to full term but it is not medically possible: medical futility.[8] This of course existed before the development of modern medicine, but has become more articulated as science, and the ability to intervene in pregnancies, has advanced.

With the growth of modern (technological) science, however, embryos can exist in more contexts. All the aforementioned may be classed as 'reproductive' embryos; however, the teleologically based categorisation of embryos becomes slightly more complicated *in vitro*. The creation and biological processes of embryos/fetuses *in vivo* are only touched upon by the law in limited situations, and even then, in those situations, law can only be called upon after the fact.[9] In this way, the law relating to reproduction *in vivo* is very much outcome-oriented. Unlike the *in vivo* gestation, law is greatly involved in every stage of embryonic processes *in vitro*.[10] It goes

---

[4] Although there is a lot of discussion surrounding 'nudging' pregnant women. See for example: M. Hilhorst and others, 'Nudge Me, Help My Baby: On Other-Regarding Nudges' (2007), *Journal of Medical Ethics*, 43(10), 702–706.

[5] For cases on this, see for example: *Paton v. British Pregnancy Advisory Service* [1978] 2 All ER 987, [1979] QBD 276; *Re T (Adult: Refusal of Medical Treatment)* [1992] 411 ER 649; *Re S (Adult: Refusal of Treatment)* [1992] 4 All ER 671; *Burton v. Islington Health Authority and De Martell v. Merton and Sutton Health Authority* [1992] 3 All ER 833; *MB (an Adult: Medical Treatment), Re* [1997] 38 BMLR 175 CA, [1997] 8 Med LR 217; *St George's* (n54).

[6] *Kelly v. Kelly* [1997] SC 285; also see S. McLean, 'The Moral and Legal Boundaries of Fetal Intervention: Whose Right/Whose Duty' (1998), *Seminars in Neonatology*, 3(4), 249–254.

[7] *Evans* [2008].

[8] See Laurie and others, 'Medical Law and Ethics', pp. 516–542.

[9] E.g. 'wrongful life' and 'wrongful injury' actions.

[10] Although public health policy is heavily involved in *in vivo* gestation, for example through adverts discouraging smoking and drinking during pregnancy.

beyond merely 'getting involved' in variable situations and outcomes for the embryos created outside of the body to actually *governing* all stages of the process. Yet, as this book has argued, while the 1990 Act (as amended) governs all these stages, it does not encompass them as well as it should.

Traditionally, medical law has been heavily involved in the first three contexts listed earlier. As a result, in the present day, the interests of the *pregnant* woman often trump those of the unborn embryo/fetus or the biological father (importantly though, not always).[11] The fourth context of medical futility remains a far more complicated area. For the purposes of this research, however, we turn to a fifth context:

5. The fifth context and the one central to this book – creation *in vitro* – has multiple sub-contexts that an embryo may go through. These are listed in further detail later. These contexts, as aforementioned, may be broadly categorised as either 'reproductive' or 'research' embryos.

An all-encompassing statutory framework governs the *in vitro* context: the 1990 Act (as amended). As summarised in Chapter 2, legal provisions for embryos *in vitro* fall under the Warnock Report's 'special status' in one way or another (the extent and nature of this special status being, in and of itself, vague). Yet, in juxtaposition to this *singular* status, within the Act's framework for 'context 5' there exist several legal 'pathways':

(a) Creation of a 'human' embryo *in vitro*, and subsequent implantation into a woman's womb, intended for reproduction.
(b) Creation of a 'human' embryo *in vitro* with a view to implantation in a woman's womb, which is subsequently, but prior to implantation, deemed as surplus or tested upon for genetic disorders (resulting in positive or negative selection). Here the intended use of an embryo is 'reproductive' at the time of testing, but may change to 'research' subject with the permission of its 'parent(s)'.
(c) Creation of a 'human' embryo *in vitro* for the purposes of research only, researched upon for up to fourteen days, then disposed of.
(d) Creation of a hybrid (legally 'non-human') embryo *in vitro*,[12] researched upon for up to fourteen days, then disposed of.

It should be made clear that not all these legal pathways are available – or indeed applicable – to every embryo *in vitro*. Some embryos are created in a manner that means they can never legally be used for reproductive

---

[11] Particularly when the embryo is not *in utero*, see *Evans* [2008].
[12] 1990 Act (as amended) s4A.

purposes, either (a) as a hybrid embryo, (b) as a cloned embryo, or (c) because they were created especially for research purposes with donor gametes. This work is particularly interested in the regulation of 'human' embryos *in vitro*, for they (unlike admixed embryos, at least at the moment) have multiple possible *teleologies* under the 1990 Act (as amended).

By according a 'special status' that applies to all embryos *in vitro*, the fourteen-day rule places 'research embryos' in permanent liminality, per Chapter 5's analysis. Part of this book's contribution to the literature is its argument that permanent liminality, as it applies to embryos, is not always a negative experience and, in fact, can give rise to positive change if realised. This reflects the consequences of schismogenesis, per Chapter 5's liminal analysis, that eventually results in permanent liminality. For embryos *in vitro*, per pathways (b) and (c) here, there are several stages within these legal pathways where they sit at a crossroads between potentially becoming a 'being' or becoming 'artefact'. This reflects the 'splitting off' of groups at the re-integration phase of the liminal process.[13] Those which are led down the research route (undoubtedly by relational means), as we know, may no longer be implanted into a woman's womb. An embryo on this route or 'pathway' may therefore only ever be treated as research 'artefact'[14] under the 1990 Act's framework. If an embryo is on this route of 'no return' as an 'artefact' or (essentially) a legal 'object', then there are reasons (legally speaking) to treat these embryos as the 'best' object they can be, per a liminal analysis. To use the teleological analysis from Chapter 5, in asking where law leads embryos to, it becomes evident that at some point, some embryos are split off from others and essentially become treated as 'objects' under law.[15] 'Reproductive' embryos, on the other hand, remain legally liminal (as subject-objects) until they (hopefully) emerge out of legal liminality by being born. Further, there are multiple liminal processes beyond the 'reproductive' embryo *in vitro*'s 'end stage' of implantation in the uterus (i.e. once it is *in vivo*). Two possibilities spring to mind: the first being the implantation process and the second the process of birth. However, as this book has shown through its processual analysis, this end stage for embryos *in vitro* is by no means the only stage of importance for law.

---

[13] Laurie, 'Liminality and the Limits of Law', 58.

[14] Mason, 'Human Life', 94.

[15] Although certainly not explicitly. In fact, maintaining a 'special status' implies quite the opposite.

The overlap of embryonic categories and their presence betwixt and between thresholds of categories define embryos. The fluid corporeality of embryos has, in a way, typified the law's response to them. However, we have a version of law that only partially recognises embryos' inherent instability – an instability that the law itself has facilitated:

> By virtue of this process of becoming, it makes little sense to categorize [the embryo] as a singular entity. Moreover, not only does the ontology of the embryo change as it moves into different time-spaces, the ability to engage with the therapeutic possibilities of the embryo for research is co-produced at the intersection of regulation, biology, and laboratory approaches technologies.[16]

Where embryos are given a 'reproductive path', their treatment as a subject, rather than as an object, is intensified. To be clear, they are not treated as subjects (with personhood) in law but more as a *subjects-to-be*. For example, the Abortion Act 1967 makes it increasingly difficult for the fetus to be terminated as it develops. Liminality, as a lens, makes evident not only the law's treatment of embryos as subjects-to-be or objects but also the importance of relationality; connections with subjects that already enjoy full personhood, namely the biological (or non-biological) creators of the embryo, 'ought not to be too easily or quickly severed'.[17] This raises the question: if a particular embryo is a research object, should it be led to be the 'best object it can be', that is, the 'best possible' research object? The answer and corresponding implications of this shall be discussed in Chapter 7.

Combining the analyses of Chapters 3–5 of this book allows us to consider embryos' pathways into, through, and *out* of the law. For ease of reference, this can be depicted in the manner shown in Figure 6.1.

From this we can see the thresholds in place for embryos *in vitro*, beyond which they sometimes cannot return (e.g. after being created 'for research' or after being implanted). The flowchart shows the overlap of the embryonic categories and their ontologically based teleologies that occur under the 1990 Act. For example, there is an overlap between the 'not-selected' or 'spare' embryo created for reproduction and embryos created for research. This is not to say that they *always* overlap, but at key (liminal) moments in legal processes, they certainly do. Yet how, practically speaking, are these changes in 'path' made? They are only partially determined in law. If, as Part II has shown us, relationality is a key aspect

---

[16] Taylor-Alexander and others, 'Beyond Compression', 166.
[17] Ibid.

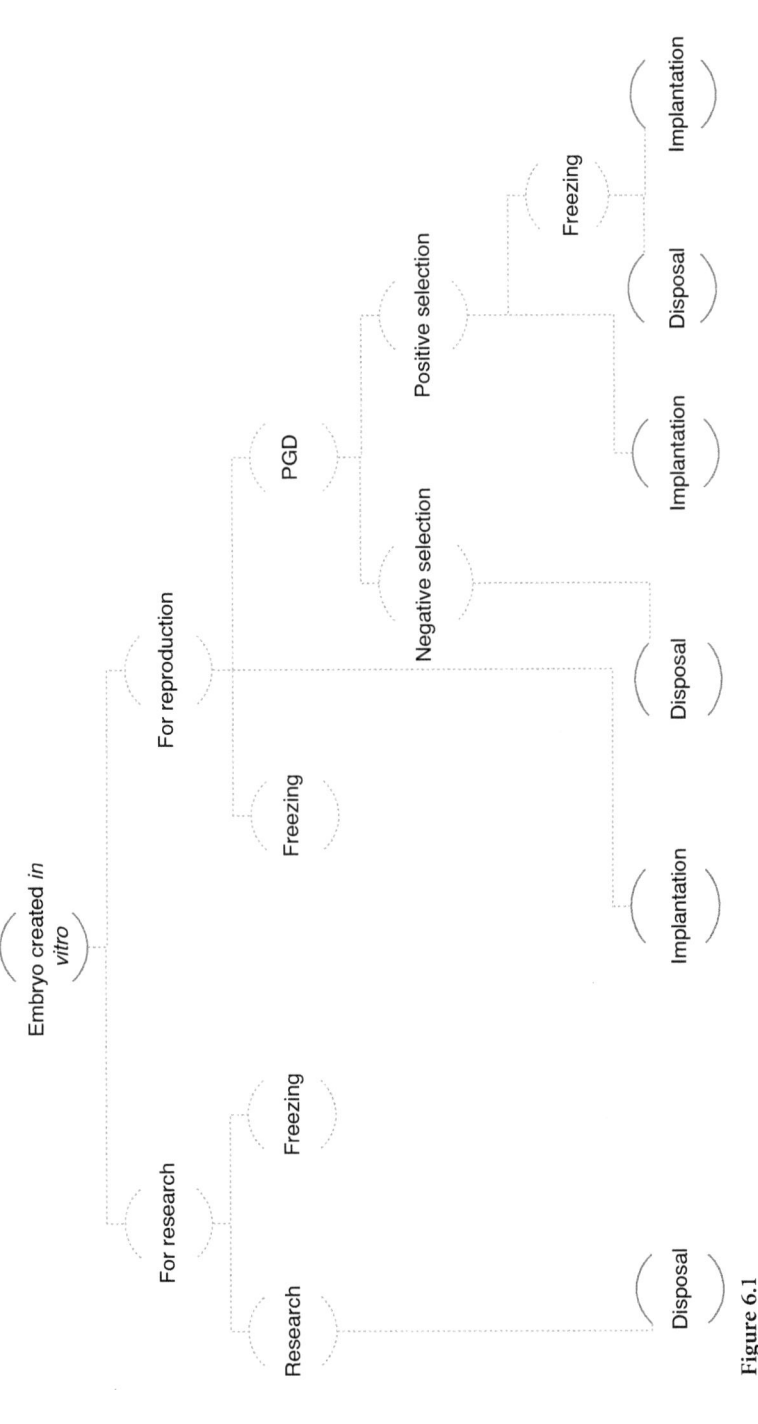

Figure 6.1

of liminal embryonic processes, then it is pertinent to ask: who creates these changes in embryonic onto-teleological pathways? The exploration of the dynamics of these processes, aside from a focus on process itself, also reveals the importance of persons and relations for these processes. After all, it is *people* who place embryos in the womb, gestate, research upon, or dispose of them. This is the subject of the next section.

6.3   *Who* Leads Embryos *into, through,* and *out* of Liminality?

If what embryos might *become* is variable, the outcome is largely at the behest of external actors (at least in the context of the 1990 Act).[18] Given that the 1990 Act (as amended) does not regulate embryos or objects but the people who produce, use, and come into contact with them, the embryo's various contexts are realised through persons. This subsection focuses on the relational aspect of embryonic pathways. It does so because Part II has shown us that a focus on embryos *in vitro* alone, as part of a broader network of actors, would be limiting.

Figure 6.1 helps to make this broader network evident for embryos and accounts for the changing relations between 'persons', 'things', and 'non-things' in the variable pathways that an embryo can take. Depending upon the pathway an embryo is placed on, a different actor might lead it through this pathway, in its liminal embryonic state. A woman, for example, leads it through gestation, while a researcher takes it through the research process. Both are essential to the respective processes; without these actors, the processes could not take place. Relatedly, at the point in time where the progenitors of an embryo make their decision with regard to donation, freezing, destruction, or implantation, their intention begins to shape the legal status of the embryo, thus indicating the context within which its value (whether reproductive, therapeutic, or other) will be determined. These actors are the vehicles that lead embryos through liminality. They are thus key players in the technologically produced biological processes embryos are put through. Moreover, as Squier has pointed out, liminal lives function relationally.[19] In some ways, embryos may function 'less as *nouns* – whether subjects of experience or objects of other's actions – than they do as *verbs*, enacting a reciprocal exchange between science and culture'.[20] Embryos are

---

[18] It is notable that in 'natural reproduction', the embryo's different outcomes may also be affected by biological factors not in the control of the mother or others.

[19] Squier, 'Liminal Lives', p. 9.

[20] Ibid., p. 10.

a prime example of an entity caught between humanity's sense of 'tremendous possibility of the new biomedicine, and our purgatorial anxiety to account responsibility for its implications'.[21]

The fluid quality of embryos and those that lead them *into, through,* and *out* of liminality highlights this area of law as transgressing thresholds, boundaries, and time; the 1990 Act (as amended) regulates a space of uncertainty. In other words, there are things that have been (and continue to be) revealed by the lens of liminality that the law has yet to embrace fully. Yet why should the law do so? Ingram Waters points out that evolving scientific knowledge has come paired with an increased scientific awareness of the multiple 'uses' that embryos now have:

> Human embryos are no longer defined only as those things that become human; now, human embryos have the potential to become other things, such as research subjects, stem cell repositories, and facilitators of therapeutic cloning research. Their value is increased by their enhanced utility. For Squier, biotechnical innovations and their accompanying discursive constructions alter the liminal space in which science and human bodies interact. The liminal space can be seen as a field of knowledge production where the contestation of claims happens in numerous ways.[22]

Embryos are paradigmatic of the scrutiny that the ontological status of novel entities undergo, in which 'the near future and recent past'[23] is a central feature.[24] There is an inherent relation here between our knowledge of embryos, their process of *becoming*, and the rules that society and the law apply to them. Liminality thus helps reveal the network of actors at play in the regulation of embryos, both in health research and in artificial reproduction. Embryos are a site of crossover between epistemology[25] and ontology[26] (*episteme* and *ontos*),[27] where knowledge and existence intertwine. A context-based framing further highlights that the outcome of the actions of these actors, which are facilitated by law, is that embryos *in vitro* now have the potential to be led through a number of paths. On most paths, an embryo will reach some sort of end or *telos*, but they may also be frozen for periods. There is

---

[21] Ibid.

[22] M. Ingram-Waters, *Unnatural Babies: Cultural Conceptions of Deviant Procreations* (ProQuest, 2008), p. 75.

[23] P. Rabinow, *Anthropos Today: Reflections on Modern Equipment* (Princeton University Press, 2003), 55.

[24] Ibid.; Taylor-Alexander and others, 'Beyond Regulatory Compression', 156.

[25] Simply put, theories of knowledge.

[26] Simply put, theories of the nature of being.

[27] Taylor-Alexander and others, 'Beyond Regulatory Compression', 156.

thus a distinction between: (a) an embryo that is likely to emerge out of liminality and (b) an embryo that is 'permanently liminal'. While ultimately embryos may only ever be used for reproductive purposes or researched upon (and then disposed of), the liminal lens highlights a key aspect of embryonic ontology that the law does not articulate: their relationality.

There are strong links between Quigley and Ayihongbe's analysis of law and the 'everyday cyborg', and law and embryos *in vitro*. As they point out, for some – though not all[28] – STS scholars, materiality is 'relational, about the interrelationship between the material and the social'.[29] Using this understanding of materiality, Quigley and Ayihongbe draw attention to relationality and process in their analysis of the interaction between 'everyday cyborgs' and law.[30] They go on to comment:

> [W]hen we say that challenges arise because of the linking of the biological with synthetic materialities, we do so to highlight not only that materials (i.e. biological or synthetic) matter for law and law's approach, but this mattering occurs as part of particular contexts, processes, and relations. For everyday cyborg technologies, and indeed everyday cyborgs themselves, the interrelationship is not only between the materials and the social, but also the legal, the conceptual, and the normative.[31]

As previously discussed, the law's boundary work is clear when it comes to most of the entities it regulates. Yet when it regulates embryos *in vitro*, not only are these boundaries unclear, but they come under immense pressure. This is because of embryos' changing materiality as they travel through legal processes. These processes are all made (and broken) by their relations to persons, just as it is with implanted devices, per the analysis quoted previously. Moreover, these boundaries are further pressured by the way in which science (a processual field) changes the materiality of embryos (see Chapter 7, Section 7.3).

Embryos also pose further questions for law: not only whether or not they are 'matter', but also, to use the word in another sense, *how much* they matter, and to whom. This, as discussed in Chapter 2, was answered

---

[28] For discussion on this see Quigley and Ayohingbe, 'Everyday Cyborgs'. Also see E. Sørensen, 'The Time of Materiality' (2007), *Qualitative Social Research*, 8(1); Latour, *We Have Never Been Modern*.

[29] See Quigley and Ayohingbe, 'Everyday Cyborgs', 306; Sørensen, 'The Time of Materiality', 3.

[30] Ibid.

[31] See Quigley and Ayohingbe, 'Everyday Cyborgs', 306–307.

through the 1990 Act's (as amended) instantiation of a 'special status' for embryos. It seems that for law, how much something matters has everything to do with the type of matter it is:

> For the law, the question of what matters and how when it comes to technologies is one which traditionally delineates persons from things along multiple dimensions (subject-object, internal-external, biological-synthetic).[32]

To explore this further, one can see which of each of these binaries has been deemed to matter more to the law. For example, harsh sanctions have been imposed against bodily harm (all subject, internal, biological), yet less (generally speaking) for damage to personal property (object, and often synthetic and external).

Yet what of embryos *in vitro?* It obviously does not fit clearly into any of the three binaries Quigley and Ayihongbe mention in the aforementioned quote. This material binary, as this book has argued, is not problematic in and of itself,[33] but is nonetheless a key component of the intellectual gap between the intellectual set up and the 'real effect' of the 1990 Act (as amended). Further, as discussed in Chapters 3 and 4, embryos' legal straddling of the subject-object binary (and indeed other legal binaries) may be explained through their rapidly changing, processual nature and their gothic associations therein. Embryos' gothic, uncanny nature has challenged law's normative boundary works and has placed them (as a liminal entity) in a legally liminal space. Thus, to add to Quigley and Ayohingbe's analysis, the law's non-articulation of the multiple processes is unsatisfactory: it ignores either subject- or object-focused concerns,[34] depending on the legal pathway an embryo is on. This is not to say that embryos should be viewed as one or the other within this binary. Quite the opposite. A context-based approach may be a way of navigating embryos' in-between quality, by recognising the processual as a key element of embryonic and legal processes here. Therefore, viewing embryos relationally helps reveal the way these pathways evolve and take place; law does not actually regulate embryos but the people who produce and come into contact with them. These actors are thus, in some sense, the ones who lead embryos through liminality. Nonetheless, they do not get to completely determine what happens to

---

[32] Ibid., 307; Also see Sørensen, 'The Time of Materiality', 3.
[33] Again, the question of how we should treat embryos morally is not within this book's ambit.
[34] McMillan and others, 'Beyond Categorisation'.

embryos, as the state has an overarching protective role through the 1990 Act (as amended).

6.4   A Context-Based Approach

The previous analysis and diagram give rise to at least two questions: (1) If these contexts are already available under the current framework, how does drawing them out add to contemporary literature and debate? (2) What would the contours of a context-based approach be? Parts I and II of this book have already answered the first as follows:

- the intellectual basis of our framework is not robust as there is a 'gap' between the intellectual set-up of the 1990 Act (as amended), under a singular 'special status', and the realities of the pathways embryos are led through under this framework;
- this gap can be understood more deeply by better understanding the processes that are regulated, the dynamics of which (explored by 'gothic'/liminal analysis) are not adequately recognised in law; therefore
- an approach based on the findings of Chapters 1–5 could inform regulatory reform in a manner that reflects the above.

The explorations in this section are made with a view to answering the above-mentioned second question.

A context-based approach to regulation is required in order to move the lessons from Part II from concept to 'reality'[35] and to better fill the legal gap identified in Part I. This approach thus draws on the lessons from this work so far. While this approach does not claim to answer all perceived flaws with the 1990 Act's (as amended) regulation of embryos *in vitro*, it is more appropriate[36] than the basis for our current framework as it addresses the above-identified 'legal gap' and embraces processuality therein.

In order to mark out the dimensions of this context-based approach, this section first provides some background and brief reiteration of support for this framework. The next subsection then draws out the exact contours of a context-based approach, which emphasises embryonic processes through 'pathways' (5(a)–(d), and in Figure 6.1, both

---

[35] By 'reality' I do not mean to comment on what this might look like in statute. Rather, I provide a framework for moving these concepts closer to being useable in contemporary legal discussions.

[36] As above, 'appropriate' meaning apt for the embryonic pathways.

above). Finally, two possible criticisms of this approach are responded to: that it is an approach based on intent and that redefining 'the embryo' would serve the same purpose – notably, that this analysis does not go as far as to map out the practical application of this approach within statute (or guidelines). The contention for this analysis, however, is that this is not necessary for the purposes of the current exercise and that an important lesson has been exposed regarding the limits of law and thinking to date.

6.4.1 Background

The legal boundedness of 'the embryo' is contestable. It is important at this stage to recall that there has already been a call to analyse embryos on a contextual basis. Yet also recall that these analyses are missing grounding beyond the conceptual. For example, Jacob and Prainsack describe the outcomes of the workshop entitled 'Embryonic Hopes' (discussed in Chapter 3):

> In the interactions at our workshop . . . we found an unanticipated level of agreement across disciplines on the unbounded character of the concept of the embryo, on the need to analyse embryos in the context of networks of social and biological relations that they are embedded in, and even on which methods yielded the most meaningful insights into understanding the ways that embryos are enacted in social realities. At the same time, and despite this explicit reference to embryos-in-practice (to paraphrase Timmermans and Berg's (2003) concept of technology-in-practice), the agreement remained at a conceptual level . . . In other words, when discussing definitions, definability, and even the possibility of the undefinability of concepts such as the embryo, agreement was easily achieved across disciplines. However, as soon as the discussions moved to how concepts could be mobilized towards something else – action, further analysis, etc. – mutual understanding proved more challenging.[37]

This book does not – and *cannot* – provide a framework on which there might be mutual consensus. Instead, the aim is to provide a framework for discussion, underpinned by a robust intellectual framework that could mobilise previous calls for a more context-based approach.[38]

As we saw in Chapter 3 and built upon further in Chapter 4, embryos *in vitro* may be subject to two outcomes only: reproduction and research.

---

[37] Jacob and Prainsack, 'Embryonic Hopes', 497–498.
[38] A common thread between which being law's inability, as it stands, to fully cope with embryonic uncertainty, discussed in Chapter 2.

Indeed, Sarah Devaney refers to the 'dual reproductive identity' of 'the embryo':

> Thus, at the point embryo progenitors make their decision; their intention helps to shape the embryo's legal status, indicating the context within which its value (whether reproductive, therapeutic or other) should be determined. This has been termed the 'dual reproductive identity' of embryos consisting of past attempts to conceive a child and the future capacity of science to transform the vital power of individual cells into colonies of regenerative cells.[39]

There are thus currently two broad onto-teleological[40] options for an embryo: will it become a 'research artefact',[41] or a (potential) 'person'? Emphasising this question and its answer(s) undoubtedly acts to further situate embryos within the technological, relational aspect of their existence.

To explain further, the 'reintegration' – or third stage of liminality – that we want (or at least expect, as the outcome we intend does not always come into fruition) for embryos impacts upon the ways in which we consider/use and/or store them at present. Each possible pathway is led by people, and to some extent, their intent towards a pre-defined end point.[42] These intentions can of course change – for example, if an embryo is rejected for implantation but relevant consent has been acquired for research use – but then, so does our present treatment of them in accordance with the new target that we have for its future use. The key point, however, is that while it is indeed important to situate embryos *in vitro* as technologically and relationally produced beings, we must move beyond thinking about them in terms of how they are *produced* or what they *are* as separate considerations. Instead, the intellectual set up of the 1990 Act (as amended) must be brought beyond the ambit of production, through to how embryos are used and what the legal results of that use will be. In this way, embryos' technological and relational qualities would be more fully encompassed by any governing legal framework. In doing so, it does not take away from the original objective of attributing some sort of 'respect' for 'the embryo' as per the Warnock Report. Instead, and in accordance with a later comment by

---

[39] Devaney, *Stem Cell Research*, 15–16.

[40] I use this term to emphasise that our categorisation of this entity is very much dependent on our intentions for its future (of course, not *always*, natural termination can occur at any stage).

[41] Mason, *Human Life*, 94.

[42] This is of course limited by several factors, including other persons and law.

Warnock herself (that you cannot 'respect' something that you end up throwing away), it better reflects and articulates not only current understandings of biological processes but the ways in which the law has engaged and can continue to engage with them. I thus advocate a 'context-based approach' to human embryos *in vitro*.

6.4.2   The Dimensions of a Context-Based Approach

Based on lessons from this chapter and Part II of this book, this subsection draws out the exact contours of a context-based approach. This is done in order to show that the law *can* navigate embryonic processes in a way that closes the gap between the intellectual set-up of the Act and the 'reality' of the 1990 Act (as amended). Taking the analysis offered in this book into account, the dimensions of this context-based approach may be summarised as recognising the following:

> Our response to embryos *in vitro* has thus far been one of uncertainty, and not wrongly so. This uncertainty can be explained by the gothic origins, associations, and technological placement of embryos *in vitro*. With this in mind, it is thus important to recognise the context from which embryos *in vitro* come into being and the effects that they have on how we treat them, namely:
>
> - the multiplicity of pathways law leads embryos through (see Figure 6.1);
> - at the end of these paths, there are only two possibilities: birth or destruction;
> - importantly, there are several thresholds that embryos can cross in order to reach those pathways; therefore
> - if deemed a research 'artefact', there is only one telos: destruction; and
> - if on a 'reproductive' pathway, much has to happen for the original telos of that pathway (birth) to occur; and finally
> - these pathways are greatly affected by actors/persons and are thus relational.

Notably, this approach entails that we do not give embryos a single status in law; indeed, depending on their path, their telos is going to be different, morally, socially, and legally. In turn, the actors influencing embryos' progress towards their telos will also change. One might ask, then, if the contexts are there within law, why draw them out in this fashion? But the point being made is not to make the telos (more) explicit, per se, but rather to provide a way of thinking about embryos *in vitro* that focuses on process.[43]

Overall, this is proposed because analysis from Parts I and II has shown that it is important to regulate embryos *in vitro* in a way that recognises their processes of becoming (as opposed to regulating them based on what they could be).[44] In this way, a regulatory framework could be constructed in a manner that recognises embryos' relational properties, a key facet of making the 'becoming' happen. One might conflate this approach to one which hinges on the intentions of the creator or user of the embryo. This is not the case. While intent is an important part of this approach because actors' intent affects the telos of embryos and the processes they are put through, it is not the *only* part. The intent of people, whoever they are, who put embryos on various pathways, shapes the latter's travels from the first stage of liminality to the last. This approach allows us to account for the flexibility and change-ability of intent regarding embryos. Intention alone is not sufficient as an intellectual basis for regulating embryos. This is the subject of the next subsection.

6.4.3   More Than Intent

It is important to clarify that the proposed approach, in its utilisation of telos, aims to better capture the entirety of embryonic processes, rather than focus on the proposed end point, which would be purely based on intent. As explained in Chapter 5, telos, for the purposes of this book, means 'destined future end', an end which is defined for the purposes of the 1990 Act, that is IVF or research.

Context here does not necessarily mean the given (static) state that an embryo is 'in' (i.e. 'what it is' and/or 'where it is'), but rather a combination of these and intention:

> [E]mbryos are not fixed, universal biological entities but are defined by, and acted teupon in relation to, their social context, that is, by their location in time and space.[45]

---

[43] See the Introduction of this book for discussion of the normative element(s) of process for the purposes of this argument.

[44] I.e. potentiality.

[45] E. Haimes and others, '"So, What Is an Embryo?" A Comparative Study of the Views of Those Asked to Donate Embryos for hESC Research in the UK and Switzerland' (2008), *New Genetics and Society*, 27(2), 113–126, 124.

Embryos' intended destiny alone is insufficient to demarcate the status of embryos under law. This, again, is why context – within which intention may be included as a consideration – is so important. This type of reasoning accepts that a process is yet to happen; whereas looking at intention alone almost skips the importance of biological process (and the mother) entirely and looks at the 'end goal' (a baby), this new/my proposed type of reasoning accepts that a process is yet to happen.[46] An implanted embryo could thus be said to be different from a non-implanted embryo (although not necessarily in terms of legal definition, see below).

Aside from the extent to which intent is problematic as a basis for treating something a certain way, legally speaking, it is important to clarify why intent is not practical. This, in turn, means that intent is not the only consideration in this context-based approach:

(a) intent does not account for the entirety of embryonic processes biologically and legally available (as revealed by a liminal analysis); this is because:
(b) it does not account for factors that influence reaching that intent; further,
(c) basing an approach on intent raises the question of 'whose intent?'; and
(d) depending on the answer to (c), intent may also change throughout the process.

Intent alone is thus not a viable starting point for this analysis, because it is mutable.

Overall, this highlights that intent alone does not provide a robust basis for a framework. For example, one can intend for an embryo (or group of embryos) to be successfully researched upon and yield useful results, but there are multiple events that have to take place between the creation of that embryo and it becoming a useful, successful 'research artefact', including (to name a few) people, time, the correct scientific conditions, and an element of luck. Ultimately, intention alone ignores the various processes that need to take place to actualise this intention.

A context-based approach incorporates intent by accounting for embryonic processes (of which intent nonetheless is a vital part) and the role of actors in directing them but also looks more holistically at the legal pathways available under the 1990 Act (as amended).

---

[46] In a similar way to potentiality, although these two concepts are still different.

6.4.4   More Than Definition

One could argue that simply by redefining embryos we might solve the problem at the heart of this book. This has been partially disproved in Chapter 4 but deserves further consideration here. While embryos in the United Kingdom are generally defined by what they are,[47] this only affects potential embryonic processes in part – being 'human', 'alive', and 'not admixed' is a necessary ontological threshold for the law that embryos must pass in order to go through certain processes (e.g. implantation). In other words, in any particular situation, what an embryo is, if it is human, does not tell us much more than whether or not it can legally be placed inside a woman's womb. If an embryo is not purely 'human', then, of course, there is only one legislative option for it: research and/or disposal.

An analysis of law based on embryonic definition leaves elements of embryonic biological-legal processes unarticulated. The central concern of this book is not with defining or redefining embryos under the 1990 Act (as amended). Defining embryos, or categorising them, does not account for the multiplicity of biological possibilities and pathways that are available under the 1990 Act (as amended). Definition is an important threshold for certain pathways (as the flowchart above demonstrates), but once that threshold is met, much more (in terms of actors, scientific processes, biological processes, etc.) has to occur in order for the full process to occur. While one could change embryonic definitions under the 1990 Act (as amended) to account for the purpose for which embryos are created, this would neglect the utility of 'spare' embryos that were originally created for fertility treatment services – the most common source of 'research' embryos. Though the latter could possibly be accommodated by a new doctrine, a robust analytical framework must be behind any such definition. Definition and 'legal status' (admittedly both very loaded terms) are of course different. Regarding the latter, the predominant legislative attitude towards embryos in the United Kingdom can be described as recognising 'the embryo's' potential but not treating that potential as sufficient to merit legal protection from research and disposal (at least before the primitive streak). Further, definitions afforded under the 1990 Act (as amended) do not affect the 'special status' of regulated embryos. Limits that famously reflect this 'status' – for example the fourteen-day rule – are the same for all 'kinds' of

---

[47] See F. Baylis and T. Krahn, 'The Trouble With Embryos' (2009), *Science and Technology Studies*, 22(2), 31–54.

embryos. Legally defining, or redefining, embryos is thus not this book's aim.

6.5   Does It Close the Gap?

So, does a context-based approach address the 'intellectual gap' articulated in Part I? This section argues that this context-based approach may be used to close the 'legal gap' between the intellectual basis of the 1990 Act (as amended) and the realities of the pathways it has facilitated. As a reminder, the key facets of the 'gap' within the 1990 Act (as amended), as initially identified by Part I and the nature of which is explored more deeply in Part II, are as follows:

- Uncertainty surrounding embryos (*in vitro* and *in vivo*), for example with regard to (a) how we feel about them and (b) how we should treat them;
- The 1990 Act's 'legal stasis'. In other words, the ossification of its legal development.

A gothic framing and liminal analysis in Part II revealed the nature of this gap even further:

- these uncertainties derive from the contexts from which embryos are born, are associated, and exist in (technology);
- the relational nature of embryos affect (a) the way in which we view them, and (b) the pathways they are led along through law;
- the above uncertainty, that is the gothic nature of embryos *in vitro*, has contributed to the 'legal stasis' and has discouraged revisitation.

Building on the lessons from Part II (see Section 4.5 of this book), this chapter has advocated a context-based approach, which recognises that

- There are a multiplicity of pathways law leads embryos along (see flowchart in 6.1 above).
- At the end of these paths, there are only two possibilities: birth or disposal. Importantly, there are lots of ways that embryos can reach those possibilities.
- *If* deemed a research 'artefact', there is only one *telos*: disposal.
- *If* on a 'reproductive' pathway, much has to happen for the original telos of that pathway (birth) to occur.
- These pathways are affected by actors and are thus relational.

In these ways, these sections and chapters have each respectively answered the four questions set in the Introduction of this work, namely:

1. Part I: in what ways does UK law engage with embryonic processes, if at all?
2. Part II: how can we understand legal process and legal regulation more deeply?
3. Part III: how can law better reflect the uncertain nature of embryonic processes and the technologies that create them?
4. Overall, does law reflect and embody processual regulation, and if so, what does this look like? And if not, what form could it take if reform were thought to be desirable?

Yet in answering these questions, this work has left us with one final question: does all of this 'bridge the gap' between the intellectual basis of the law, and the realities of the processes it regulates? A context-based approach raises questions regarding the extent to which it accounts for facets of this 'legal gap' iterated previously. These are addressed in what follows.

1. Does the approach of this book create more legal and/or moral certainty? If not, how does it embrace uncertainty?

As a reminder, 'uncertainty' for this book refers to two things: (1) moral ambiguity and plurality towards embryos, and (2) relatedly, how to treat them (in law).

Importantly, a context-based approach does not purport to dissolve uncertainty, nor provide certainty. As we have seen in this book's discussions, especially in Chapter 5, we will always have a degree of ambivalence when regarding embryos in a morally pluralistic society. Relatedly, certainty does not 'fit' well with this book's argument that we should be alive to the permanent liminality of law in this field. If we accept that as a society we will always feel some degree of uncertainty regarding how we feel about embryos or how we should treat them,[48] what we need is a transparent, coherent, and robust framework that is open to revision and which, to a large extent, embraces this ambiguity. In other words, the aim of Chapter 5's approach was to provide a framework for *navigating* (not dissolving) that uncertainty which, as Chapter 3 has argued, we should accept if we want to provide a sound intellectual basis for our legal framework.

---

[48] Also see Ford, 'Nothing and Not-Nothing'.

But, relatedly, what does it mean to embrace uncertainty? Without repeating the above, this approach accounts for parallels revealed through gothic framing, lessons which show an innate sense of transformation and becoming.[49] Further, it highlights the relational aspects of embryonic development – a key aspect of navigating these uncertainties. This has been shown, for example, in the debates surrounding abortion, where embryonic/fetal existence is entirely relational to the gestational mother.

Overall, this approach recognises that there is uncertainty here and accepts that embryo regulation has an inherent, prevalent element of uncertainty. This work thus enquired how we might navigate this uncertainty. Moreover, it has considered what it means to take a processual approach to regulation, therewith revealing the importance of changing contexts over time (e.g. from being created as a 'reproductive' embryo, but moved onto a research 'path'). That analysis requires us to ask: (1) which processes and telos(es) are at play in these contexts, and relatedly (2) how are these affected by what embryos are *becoming*?

Accordingly, this work then considered the mismatch between the language of the singular, all-encompassing 'special status' of 'the embryo' (which in some sense suggests something fixed and immutable), which sits in opposition to the sense of becoming and processes within the inexplicit pathways the 1990 Act (as amended) regulates. Moreover, as this work has made clear, it is not that our values are necessarily any different but that our frame of reference has changed. If we accept the latter, then this work's analysis inherently disrupts the 'special status' of 'the embryo'.

2. Would this approach affect the singularity of the 'special status' underlying our current framework?

This approach has the potential to disrupt the singular 'special status' of 'the embryo' in favour of an approach that more accurately reflects the multiplicity of processes (and thus inexplicit 'statuses') embryos are led *into, through*, and *out of.* This work does not purport to envision every possibility but to give some examples. If we accept that it dissolves the singularity of embryonic 'specialness' under law, then a context-based approach has the *potential* to capture the following:

- a recognition of the multiplicity and overlap of embryonic pathways through law;

---

[49] van Gennep, 'Rites of Passage'.

- this can justify affording embryos *in vitro* more than one 'status' depending on the pathway(s) they are on, rather than the singular, all-encompassing 'special status' that (as we have seen) has come under much critique;[50]
- 'reproductive embryos', once implanted, may only ever be used for reproductive purposes (and this would hold true whether or not gestation was or was not ultimately successful); and
- embryos that have no distinct pathway as of yet (i.e. they are frozen or undergoing the process of PGD) are neither, but may be treated as reproductive embryos (if that is the goal of their creation) until that path is evidently not an option anymore; and further that
- 'research embryos' may be either created specifically for research or become so through becoming 'spare' when the reproductive pathway is no longer an option (and per appropriate parental consent).

Equally, it does not follow that 'research embryos' are no longer subject to our moral value framework nor that regulatory *carte blanche* would apply to them. There remain very good reasons for considering what is at stake and permissible with research on the 'research embryo'. This context-based approach, however, more overtly brings into discussions surrounding embryo regulation the end points that are envisioned, as well as the fact of 'use' of the entity in question towards those ends. These value preferences become a separate consideration and are highlighted in the answer to the next question.

3. If a 'special status' has meant that embryos do not fit into law's normative subject-object, person-property binaries, etcetera, does this book's approach affect these binaries?

A context-based approach does not dissolve this binary and this book is not arguing for or against such dissolution. Nonetheless, this work does have the potential to disrupt a binary approach. For example, it may be decided that research embryos – as 'artefacts' – become clear objects, even though they are 'not nothing'[51] in moral and legal terms. Indeed, many legal objects and 'artefacts' have engendered considerable amounts of legal protection that reflects the ways in which we 'value' them, such as celebrated works of art. This is not to compare embryos to an object in the traditional sense of the word (as a mere thing, *res* or indeed property); rather, it is to

---

[50] See Chapter 5.
[51] See *St George's*.

suggest that recognition of object-hood does not render embryo as 'nothing', especially if it is deemed inappropriate to do so.[52]

Alternatively, this work's analysis might prompt discussions around the status of reproductive embryos as subject-objects. This has the potential to provide a framework to embrace the relationality of embryos *in vitro*, per their telos of being placed *in vitro*. In other words, this book's framework can help us to move away from the (much critiqued) notion of the 'free-floating embryo' in law towards embryos being reliant upon, and having an innately special and interconnected relationship with, their intended and/or gestational mother(s).

Yet, for this book, the importance of this framework does not lie in attempting to reach any of these ends per se, but in informing our decisions about them in a manner that is coherent and transparent. Indeed, a relational focus is also key for research embryos. For example, donor couples might have more of a say in what kinds of research is done with their embryos and/or might have a stronger claim to know about the social value or other benefits that came of donating their embryos for research. This is a possible consequence of a frame of analysis that focuses on the value of the telos and the interests that parties have in the achievement of that telos. We return to the feature of this point next.

Whether we want to continue our current legal framework, or change it, can be informed by this approach, but the approach herein does not give any normative answers in that respect. To reiterate, the normative part of this book is that spaces in-between, and processes therein, need to be navigated by robust, coherent, defensible, and justifiable law.

4. Would accounting for relationality actually have any practical effects on assisted reproduction and research, in practice?

A context-based approach can have implications for actors on multiple levels, including donors, embryos, and parents. For example, the liminal quality of embryos has the potential to greatly influence scientific researchers. A study by Svendsen and Koch challenges the idea that 'spare' embryos are a biological fact. They suggest instead that embryos are constituted by the decision-making of researchers; this 'ongoing fact-making' reveals a network of relationships and conflicts in which researchers are involved.[53] Further, while this is not a book rooted in feminist theory in the strict sense, a context-based approach supports the

---

[52] See McMillan and others, 'Beyond Categorisation'.

[53] M. Svendsen and L. Koch, 'Unpacking the "Spare Embryo": Facilitating Stem Cell Research in a Moral Landscape' (2008), *Social Studies of Science*, 38(1), 93–110.

growing argument in feminist literature that women are marginalised within our present legal frameworks. This approach helps us emphasise that actors, however involved in embryonic processes, have *different* relations with embryos. It might enable us to support the above-mentioned proposition, for example, that the prospective mother (and father) should have a much greater say in what happens than if an embryo was to be used for research purposes.

Further, this approach also has implications in information disclosure practices regarding the (consented) use of 'spare' embryos for research. As Jonlin comments, there are some donors who

> firmly reject the option of donating their excess embryos to other infertile couples because they do not want 'someone else raising our child' and do not want their current children to have one or more siblings 'out there'. Therefore, destruction is the only remaining option, and destroying them for research purposes is preferable to throwing them away.[54]

Therefore, she adds, many of those who decide to donate

> hope that their embryos will do some good, and are relieved and even thankful there is a use for them. Some donors feel it is incumbent upon them to give back to research because research enabled them to have a family. Many donors ask scientific questions about stem cell research, including how tissues are made from pluripotent stem cells. Some want to know about the political climate for funding stem cell research. Occasionally, donors need assurance that their identities will not be made public. Although some donors seem to convey a sense of resignation, and comment on the finality of the decision to donate, others express their enthusiastic support for stem cell research and for science in general.[55]

Given that this approach encourages transparency and coherency, including regard for relationality and feedback loops,[56] it gives reason to provide a framework that allows us to tell donors more accurately and clearly what will happen to their donated embryos. Some have described the voices of donors as having been 'marginalised' in the research process.[57] Indeed, donors themselves could be described as experiencing their own liminality. Yet, as above-mentioned, liminality

---

[54] E. Jonlin, 'The Voices of the Embryo Donors' (2015), *Trends in Molecular Medicine*, 21 (2), 55–58, 56.

[55] Ibid.

[56] Outputs of a regulatory system routed back as inputs to the various actors implicated in an enterprise; see Taylor-Alexander and others, 'Beyond Regulatory Compression', 164.

[57] Parry, '(Re) Constructing Embryos in Stem Cell Research'.

is not, and should not be, used as a shorthand for marginality in the context of health research regulation. Here, the actions and decisions of donors are central to research practices, given that their donated embryos are the primary source of 'research' embryos in the United Kingdom. With a liminal framing in mind, a context-based approach could thus give donors more options for additional engagement in the research process, if they so wished, and might entitle them to find out more about the benefits and/or results from research carried out on their 'spare' embryos.

Ultimately, this allows us to consider more deeply who has a say in various embryonic processes. Indeed, if an option for further donor involvement in research were deemed desirable, the framework might enable us to more fully address the critique that donors can feel disengaged in the research process.[58] In other words, perhaps the framework might enable some donors to 'emerge' out of their own experience of permanent liminality, with regard to their donated embryos.

5. Does this context-based approach address the permanent liminality of law, identified in Chapter 5?

As discussed in the conclusion to Chapter 5 (Section 5.5), this analysis enables us to think about how we can move past our present legal framework, if we decide that revisitation and/or renewal is something we want to do. It therefore enables us to move out of our unreflexive iteration of a singular 'special' (yet practically not special) status. Further, an acknowledgement of the permanent liminality of law, and indeed of some embryos in law, allows us to ask questions surrounding where they are/could be led after emerging out of that liminality: what is/are the telos(es) of embryos *in vitro*?

6. What is the effect of the teleological aspect of the context-based approach?

From this, three interrelated sub-questions arise:

(a) When taking a teleological approach, is there a normative imperative to achieve the 'best' outcome possible?

This question is for others to decide. If, however, the answer is yes, we might then have a reason to revisit the fourteen-day rule. The questions arising from this particular example are discussed in the next section. A teleological approach, seen through a liminal lens, encourages consideration of the *full* process. It helps us consider not only that embryos *are*

---

[58] Ibid.

becoming but *what* they are becoming, and asks us to contemplate whether we want to attach importance to that and acknowledge who is implicated in these diverse processes.

(b) If we decide that a particular embryo is bound for a reproductive pathway, what does that mean per its teleology?

One might take a teleological approach to mean that I am arguing that we must follow that teleology's imperative to the letter, that is that all 'reproductive' embryos should be implanted in a woman. This is not the case. As the flowchart in this chapter has shown, an important part of a context-based approach is recognising that these pathways are not straightforward and can overlap. To focus on ends alone would ignore the importance of process, which is the central focus (and normative claim) of this work; a focus on ends alone masks how we get there. Again, the utility of a liminal lens is that it does not only give us any particular normative imperative but also allows us to consider, more deeply, the dynamics of the variant transformations that embryos can go through.

The above questions also give rise to another, similar question: If 'research' embryos are subject to an argument that they should be the 'best' research embryos they can be, does this suggest that a 28-, 60-, or even 180-day rule could be defended? Not necessarily. The reasons for this answer are discussed in more detail in Section 7.3.

Overall, a context-based approach, as described earlier, encourages thinking about the processual nature of embryonic development but still allows us to 'value'[59] embryos in a way that recognises the multiplicity of factors necessary for that process to take place (e.g. the mother, time, biology) for embryos to eventually become persons, or not. This is not the only potential outcome of a context-based approach, but it is one that addresses Part I's 'legal gap', as it considers embryos *in vitro* more processually and moves us beyond the incoherent framework we have at the moment.

6.6   Conclusions

It is possible that in failing to place liminality and uncertainty at the centre of the legal framework behind research and reproductive practice, the law is perpetuating a myth of the single 'status' of the human embryo *in vitro*. Thus, the variable, relational liminal states of embryos are important for the future of artificial reproduction and embryo research.

---

[59]   If we deem it appropriate to do so, in the name of moral pluralism.

Overall, this chapter's analysis and approach is problematic for *the* status of 'the embryo' under UK law. It is flawed to conceive of 'the embryo' as a unitary entity. The disruptive potential of liminality has helped highlight the static scientific and ethical assumptions that the law has crystallised within the 1990 Act (as amended):

> Liminality forces us to recognize the differences in status that the embryo may experience depending on the paths upon which it is put. With changeable contexts come fluid boundaries. In particular, liminal boundaries are fluid because contexts can change.[60]

We have seen, for example, that an embryo used in pre-implantation genetic diagnosis may end up following one of several paths ending in reproduction or research and/or termination. The variable contexts that we apply to stages of embryonic process, whether in the lab or in the womb, are thus open to change. The term 'embryo' itself is a temporally based definition;[61] it denotes a particular demarcated point in early human development.

How, you might wonder, can this book's analysis inform contemporary discussions surrounding the regulation of the creation, use, and storage of embryos *in vitro*? The final chapter of this book applies the above context-based approach, based on a liminal analysis, to three contemporary (and controversial) developments in reproductive science.

---

[60] Taylor-Alexander and others, 'Beyond Regulatory Compression', 168.
[61] Ibid.

7

Looking Forward

The Fourteen-Day Rule, *In Vitro* Gametogenesis, and Ectogenesis

7.1 Introduction

In previous chapters it was argued that there are better ways for the law to regulate for uncertainty in the context of embryos *in vitro*. At this point, it seems pertinent to return to one of the first points made in this book. In the Introduction, it was stated that the regulation of embryos *in vitro* affects at least three strands:

1. Embryos *in vitro*
2. Science (persons and practices, e.g. research practices and researchers)
3. The family (in the broadest sense, e.g. donors, potential parents, hypothetical mothers, and hypothetical children).

This book has focused primarily on the first, but thus far, we have seen that the effects that it can have on (2) and (3) are not irrelevant, for example, gothic literature's discussion of embryos' female origins and associations. For this last chapter, this book's enquiry expands to areas (2) and (3) more broadly by examining the ways in which a contextual approach, based on a liminal lens, can help us consider contemporary discussions surrounding embryos *in vitro* and *beyond* using three case studies: the fourteen-day rule, *in vitro* gametogenesis, and partial ectogenesis via artificial womb technologies (AWTs). The first case study, the fourteen-day rule, is important as it is the principal manifestation of law's attempt to reflect 'special status' on the embryo, and because it is also an example of legal attempts to deal with embryonic processes. The discussion does not presuppose any normative claims about what should be done with the rule itself. Rather, this example is used to examine what the context-based approach developed in this book could bring to contemporary debate about the nature of such a rule, as well as its retention, reduction, or extinction. Further, it is an example of how a processual analysis helps us to deepen and enrich our understanding of what this legislative attempt to engage with process might mean. And, in contrast to this case study which examines the embryonic phase of *in vitro* life before birth, the second and third case studies look before and beyond the embryonic stage respectively. The second example, *in vitro* gametogenesis, enables us to consider what this book's analysis says about these relatively new technologies in relation to their regulation, and the key biological and legal thresholds involved. The final case study, ectogenesis, focuses specifically on partial ectogenesis via AWT, a technology which not only introduces new thresholds but leads us to question our existing understanding of meaningful legal thresholds, most notably birth as the moment in which the fetus/baby attains personhood. By these means, the analysis engages with the entire trajectory of embryonic development as this is driven by scientific possibilities, both current and near future.

The chapter concludes that while a context-based approach does not provide a mode of *ethical* deliberation regarding embryos *in vitro* or other *in vitro* entities and how they should necessarily be treated, it does provide the law, and therefore law and policymakers, with the tools to better embrace the processual and essentially uncertain nature of embryos (and fetuses), as well as the biological, social, and familial processes that surround them. It does so within a framework that can inform contemporary debates on what processual law *could* look like.

7.2 The Fourteen-Day Rule

In early 2016, research published in *Nature*[1] and *Nature Cell Biology*[2] reported on the first successful culturing of embryos *in vitro* for thirteen days. In light of this development, which introduced the possibility of learning more about the early stages of human life beyond the two-week stage, calls have been made to revisit the fourteen-day time limit on embryo research.[3] Recall that the fourteen-day rule, first recommended in the United Kingdom by the Warnock Committee,[4] is based on the premise that around this stage in development, the 'primitive streak'

---

[1] Deglincerti and others, 'Self-organization of the *In Vitro* Attached Human Embryo'.
[2] Shahbazi and others, 'Self-organization of the Human Embryo in the Absence of Maternal Tissues'.
[3] A. Insoo Hyun and others, 'Embryology Policy: Revisit the 14 Day Rule' (2016), *Nature* 533 (7602), 169–171.
[4] See Chapter 2 of this book.

generally develops.[5] It is also the approximate stage at which the embryonic cells can no longer split (and thus, produce twins or triplets etcetera).[6] As discussed throughout the book, the fourteen-day rule is the key embodiment of the 'special status' and the attribution of legal boundaries (and putative protections) at the early stages of human life. For nearly thirty years this limit was 'largely theoretical';[7] up until this recent breakthrough, no researcher had been able to culture an embryo up to this biological threshold.[8]

7.2.1   Why Revisit the Fourteen-Day Rule?

Studying embryos *in vitro* beyond the fourteen-day mark could improve our understanding of tissue formation, embryo organisation, and the role of specific genes in early development, and could drive an extensive programme of research into disorders that lead to birth defects and early miscarriage. While there is clear potential for *scientific* benefit in extending the rule, it is less clear whether it is ethical to do so, let alone on which justifiable basis.

While the benefits we could reap from this knowledge may ultimately lead to increased access to assisted reproductive services and a better understanding of some diseases,[9] there is some concern that extending the time limit is a step on the 'slippery slope' towards controversial or immoral research practices.[10] Generally, slippery slope concerns may be somewhat allayed in a *legal* context by the fact that it is possible to draw a line (sixteen as the age of consent to sexual intercourse the United Kingdom, for example), even if it is arbitrary in and of itself. These 'lines in the sand' signify a clear legal difference, for example between sexual intercourse at the age of fourteen, and at the age of eighteen; indeed, technically, one day either side of the legal line will make all of the difference between lawful and unlawful behaviour, viz sexual relations

---

[5] See the Warnock Report.

[6] P. Monahan, 'Human Embryo Research Confronts Ethical 'Rule'' (2016), *Science*, 352 (6286), 640.

[7] S. Chan 'How to Rethink the Fourteen-Day Rule' (2017), *Hastings Center Report*, 47 (3), 5–6.

[8] Monahan, 'Human Embryo Research'.

[9] Chan, 'How to Rethink the Fourteen-Day Rule'.

[10] See for example J. S. Freeman, 'Arguing Along the Slippery Slope of Human Embryo Research' (1996), *Journal of Medical Philosophy*, 21(1), 61–81 and; R. Macklin, 'Splitting Embryos on the Slippery Slope: Ethics and Public Policy' (1994), *Kennedy Institute of Ethics Journal*, 4(3), 209–225.

with a minor the day before their 16th birthday and on the big day itself. Indeed, in the case of the embryo at its early stages of development, one day can make a world of difference. Thus, we should be mindful of this kind of concern: 'we still must consider whether shifting a limit in policy is an appropriate adjustment or instead implies a slip down the slope or the abandonment of moral principle'.[11] Indeed, precisely the same types of argument were raised in the 1980s when the 1990 Act was being formulated, yet the limit set then still stands today, despite the scientific and social change that has taken place. Moreover, most proponents of an extension of the limit do not argue for an extension beyond twenty-eight days.[12] Without wishing to get into the ethical niceties, the incremental increase in the time limit is seen here as being offset by the potential benefits to be gained, and the concern about the slipperiness of any moral slopes is partially addressed as a result.[13]

Aside from the potential for greater developmental understanding and the resultant health benefits, there is another reason that it is important to revisit the fourteen-day rule. It is important to recall that this time limit on embryo research was not intended to be 'set in stone' at its inception.[14] All law must be open to discussion, if not revision, if it is to progress with society and societal interests and values. This is not to say that we should revisit and revise laws for *any* reason or in response to every social or scientific change. The key point here is that proposing a review of the core basis of law is not synonymous with proposing a change to that law. The normative aspect of arguing for review lies in the claim that law in this field should not be left untouched for extended periods, lest it become out of touch with what is scientifically possible and socially acceptable. As Hyun and others comment:

> Revisiting the 14-day rule might tempt people to try to rationalize or attack the philosophical coherence of the limit as an ethical tenet grounded in biological facts. This misconstrues the restriction. The 14-day rule was never intended to be a bright line denoting the onset of moral status in human embryos. Rather, it is a public policy tool designed to carve out a space for scientific inquiry and simultaneously show respect for the diverse views on human embryo research ... The alternatives at each extreme – banning embryo research altogether or imposing no

---

[11] Chan, 'How to Rethink the Fourteen-Day Rule'.
[12] See, for example J. B. Appleby and A. L. Brendenoord, 'Should the 14-Day Rule for Embryo Research Become the 28-Day Rule?' (2018), *EMBO Molecular Medicine*, 10(9). www.embopress.org/doi/full/10.15252/emmm.201809437
[13] For a different view, see G. Cavaliere, 'A 14-Day Limit for Bioethics: The Debate Over Human Embryo Research' (2017), *BMC Medical Ethics*, 18(1).
[14] Chan, 'How to Rethink the Fourteen-Day Rule'.

restrictions on embryo use – would not have made for good public policy in a pluralistic society.[15]

There has been considerable and wide-ranging commentary about the possibility of revisiting the rule.[16] As we have seen, the fourteen-day rule is a reflection of the Warnock Committee's emphasis on 'compromise' made in the name of moral pluralism. It emerged as the Warnock Committee's *modus operandi* of navigating the uncertainty/ambivalence surrounding how to treat embryos *in vitro*, legally. Diversity of moral standpoints on this issue, between which this compromise was set, has not changed.[17] The fourteen-day rule was in many ways a new boundary akin to its historical counterparts (e.g. quickening), albeit it was one based on scientific understandings as they stood at the time about the significant stage of embryonic development. While these stages of development remain immutable,[18] the research possibilities have not. Thus, as with any compromise, if there is a material change in circumstances it is not unreasonable to ask whether the terms of the original compromise continue to hold true. There may, therefore, be good reasons for society, science, and law to bring research embryos *in vitro* across that fourteen-day threshold.

And so, if we decide that it is worth re-considering this legal boundary and to ask whether we want to change it, what might this book bring to the debate? As we have seen in Chapter 4, thresholds are a key feature of the liminal process[19] and the following section briefly considers what a focus on these key points in transition might bring to these contemporary debates about the fourteen-day rule.

7.2.2   How to Revisit the Fourteen-Day Rule: The Importance of Thresholds

Legal instantiation of boundaries at particular biological thresholds and/ or processes play a key role in providing certainty in one way or another.

[15] Hyun and others, 'Embryology Policy: Revisit the 14 Day Rule', 170.
[16] For summaries see Cavaliere, 'A 14-Day Limit for Bioethics', 18–19; M. Pera, 'Human Embryo Research and the 14-Day Rule' (2017), *Development*,144(11), 1923–1925.
[17] i.e. embryos are 'persons' versus the notion that we can/should do whatever we like with embryos.
[18] This is not to say that our understandings of those stages have not changed, nor that we might be importing moral significance in 'the wrong place'. In essence, policymakers guessed at the earliest point at which the central nervous system begins to develop, but science might in the future tell us that this occurs much earlier or later. However, whether, this means we then make the limit even shorter is a separate moral question.
[19] See van Gennep, 'Rites of Passage', pp. 189–190.

That is to say, whether fourteen days turns out to be scientifically 'significant' in terms of the development of the central nervous system and whether this is the most morally relevant point at which to focus attention remain open to question. But the fourteen-day rule carries clarity and fixed certainty, at least for the law. As a direct consequence of this rule, artificially 'freezing' 'the embryo' has become a necessary part of the law's role in securing trust and moral legitimacy: it makes the uncertain more certain by suspending the possibility of unused embryos crossing the threshold into implantation, use for research, or destruction. Attention to thresholds, per this book's analysis, has highlighted the following thresholds in the framework we currently have:[20]

- Once an embryo created *in vitro* passes the threshold of being, deter-minedly, a 'research' embryo, it cannot (legally) be led back past the said threshold and can only come out of this process as something to be disposed of after being utilised.
- In contrast, there are lots of thresholds that embryos are led through for a 'reproductive' path, for example (non)selection after PGD, implantation, freezing and unfreezing, implantation, gestation, etce-tera – indeed, this includes the possibility of crossing the threshold from 'reproduction' to 'research' if, say, PGD tests suggest non-suitability for reproduction.
- When the progenitors of embryos are making decisions regarding what to do with their surplus embryos, they may cross various thresh-olds themselves.

The things that we may wish to consider for the actors leading embryos through liminality might be different for each threshold; we may there-fore consider different sets of factors for different thresholds within the embryonic process. For example, at the third threshold above, many factors come into consideration for donors, including their attitudes towards research and their feelings about and towards their surplus embryos and their future (non)uses.[21]

When considering whether to alter the fourteen-day rule, itself a legal boundary, multiple thresholds come into consideration.[22] As we have seen, the Warnock Committee relied on evidence available at the time,

---

[20] See Chapter 5, section 5.2.
[21] See Jonlin, 'The Voices of the Embryo Donors'; Parry '(Re)constructing Embryos in Stem Cell Research'.
[22] This is not to suggest that we could cross boundaries between research and reproduction, however.

and rigorous ethical deliberation to suggest the fourteen-day mark as a *boundary*, beyond which research could not pass. While the Committee's deliberations did not mention 'thresholds', particular (perceived) biological thresholds played a key part in their recommendations such as the threshold for experiencing pain (which they associated with the formation of the primitive streak), and thus the threshold for causing harm to a (somewhat) sentient being. Consequently, because the fourteen-day rule is a limit or boundary, we may want to consider not only the presence of thresholds in the processes we regulate, but also the importance that we want to attribute to those thresholds, and the boundaries that we wish to place on that basis. If we decide that it is appropriate to *consider* extending the rule, these types of thresholds (i.e. for harm or sentience) may well come into play again if, for example, a '28-day rule' is proposed. Further, debates around extending the fourteen-day limit have already given rise to discussion about another kind of threshold: would extending the rule be of benefit to science and society? Some argue that there is a great deal that we can learn by extending the limit.[23] Yet, the obvious question is: what kind and amount of benefit is enough to justify extension? Therein lies the threshold: a threshold of the prospect of scientific and social 'benefit', which itself will have to be qualified by thresholds such as 'adequacy', 'sufficiency', 'significance', and 'importance'. Moreover, there would also need to be some threshold of 'reasonable prospect of success' in seeking to bring about such benefits. A context-based approach thus has the potential to inform a utilitarian approach here, although this is certainly not the only approach that should be considered in any policy discussions.

There are even more thresholds at play here. These are not only biological or scientific thresholds but also artificial legal thresholds. As we have seen, our current framework for embryo research can be described as permanently liminal, that is remaining on a threshold in many respects. The unacknowledged construction of embryos in law as subject-objects is a result of attempting to regulate an uncertain space. To illustrate this point: if we decide that we want to treat research embryos as objects, with respect to the above, they are also taking the law across a threshold from one state to another. This is not to say that everything under law's ambit must be either subject or object; perhaps, the 'in-betweenness' of the embryos in the current framework must

---

[23] E.g. Wong, 'The Limits to Growth'.

remain.[24] Perhaps we should be honest that the research embryo (once decidedly so, see Figure 6.1) has crossed a threshold into the realm of 'thing'. However distasteful that may sound, as such it requires us to revisit the moral worth of research embryos *in vitro* as entities that will never realise their potential, except as research 'artefact'. Framing research embryos as such might allow and require us to reconsider how they are treated, and perhaps enable us to do more with research embryos. This point is not intend to overlook the key moral concern that lies with each and every embryo *in vitro* that is used for research, however: whether or not there is the prospect of pain. If science continues to inform us that this is very unlikely in the early stages of human life, which at the moment it does, then other thresholds should be considered. Aside from scientific merit, relaxation of the fourteen-day rule may also be supported by enabling the 'parents' of *in vitro* embryos to cross the threshold to becoming involved, informed donors, who get a say in whether their embryos get used in a particular kind of research.[25] In other words, the permanent liminality of the *in vitro* embryo as a legal category of entity might – at the end of the day – best reflect the continued need for compromise between all consider-ations, scientific, social, and moral.

Per this book's analysis, thresholds (or indeed boundaries) are not necessarily 'bad'. Indeed, both moral and legal thresholds are of crucial importance. Rather, this analysis suggests that we should be alive to the presence of moral and legal thresholds within HRR and health research practice. Moreover, we should be aware of their effect(s) on the broader network of actors to whom health research practice relates, so that we may ask questions about the conditions that we require in order to take embryos *across* those thresholds. Considering the multiplicity, variabil-ity, and in many ways subjectivity of these thresholds can enable us to regulate in a more flexible and context-specific way that allows us to recognise the multiplicity of processes occurring within the framework of the 1990 Act. Neither a liminal lens nor this book can definitively say what a revisitation might result in if a context-based framework were used. However, the contributions of this book help us to think about the above by highlighting the following question: what are the conditions for crossing each of these thresholds and what are the ultimate end points that we consider it desirable to reach?

---

[24] See McMillan and others, 'Beyond Categorisation'.
[25] Ibid.

7.2.3 *Summary*

The above analysis is not concerned with the pros and cons of the fourteen-day rule or research and reproductive practices *in vitro* more generally per se, but rather explores the ways in which law could engage with embryonic (and legal) processes through attention to thresholds (as a key facet of these processes). This framing has the *potential* to justify extension, but not without proper public deliberation, sound scientific basis, and, perhaps most importantly, subject to an account of prevalent moral concern that we would not be harming a sentient being if we were to conduct research at later stages of development. The *deliberation* and *revisitation* (not necessarily the revision) of the law is the crucial part to this liminal analysis.

The fourteen-day rule is a key example of an advance in technology that requires us to revisit our scientific trajectory. Other, additional, key advances have also taken place in recent times that require us to consider how we regulate our reproductive trajectory more broadly. The following case studies not only further demonstrate the value of a processual analysis but also demonstrate how the contextual approach advanced in this book can inform discussions beyond the embryo *in vitro* across various stages of its trajectory from creation to birth.

7.3 *In Vitro* Gametogenesis: A Disruption of Process

In vitro gametogenesis (IVG) is a process through which gametes are created from induced pluripotent stem cells (iPSCs). In layman's terms, iPSCs are cells which have the potential to grow into almost any of the cells found in the body, including gametes (i.e. sperm or egg cells). The first research on deriving *in vitro* gametes was limited to deriving gametes from fetal gonads of mice.[26] From there, the technique developed quickly to the ability to derive gametes from embryonic stem cells (ESCs)[27] and

---

[26] K. Nayernia and others, 'In Vitro-Differentiated Embryonic Stem Cells Give Rise to Male Gametes That Can Generate Offspring Mice' (2006), *Development Cell*, 11(1), 125–132. Also see: K. Hayashi and others, 'Reconstitution of the Mouse Germ Cell Specification Pathway in Culture by Pluripotent Stem Cells' (2011), *Cell*, 146(4), 519–532; K. Hayashi and others, 'Offspring from Oocytes Derived from in Vitro Primordial Germ Cell-Like Cells in Mice' (2012), *Science*, 338(6109), 971–975; M. Imamura and others, 'Induction of Primordial Germ Cells from Mouse Induced Pluripotent Stem Cells Derived from Adult Hepatocytes' (2010), *Molecular Reproduction and Development*, 77(9), 802–8011.

[27] S. M. Suter, '*In vitro* Gametogenesis: Just Another Way to Have a Baby?' (2016), *Journal of Law and the Biosciences*, 3(1), 87–119.

eventually to being able to derive gametes from iPSCs. Scientists are now able to produce viable offspring using *in vitro* gametes from either female or male mice.[28] Gamete generation is the precursor to the reproductive processes discussed in this book. While technologies such as IVG are disruptive to particular familial and scientific norms (such as the number of genetic contributors to an embryo), be it processes or thresholds, it does not have to perturb our existing regulatory framework per se; for example, the law might take the position that gametes – however produced – are to be treated within already-established rules. By the same token, it does not follow that IVG should not perturb our framework, as this section discusses. In what follows, this discussion explores: (a) the fact that IVG is an opportunity to bring law and regulation of reproductive technologies more generally out of liminality in at least one important sense, this time relating to family-making, (b) the importance of re-considering regulatory 'lines in the sand', and overall (c) how IVG, as a case study, shows that context is key to how we regulate and calls us to consider what thresholds for reproductive use we want to have in place and why.

    While IVG technology is not new, the potential uses of IVG as a mode of reproduction were severely limited by the requirement that an embryo already exists in order for the technique to take place. However, the introduction of somatic cell programming, and thus the potential for the ability to derive iPSCs[29] from any person, has greatly increased the scope of application of IVG derivation. The research has not, however, progressed to the same extent in humans.[30] As Suter states:

> Researchers have demonstrated the ability to create ESC-like cells – induced pluripotent cells – by dedifferentiating adult somatic cells and then differentiating them into 'haploid spermatogenic cells'. So far scientists have not achieved similar success in creating human oocytes, although they have derived egg-like cells. Given that research on mice has yielded both sperm and oocytes, however, it is probably merely a matter of time before human oocytes can be derived *in vitro*.[31]

If – or perhaps *when* – IVG becomes an effective and safe method of generating gametes for the purposes of human reproduction, one

---

[28] C. Palacios-González, J. Harris and G. Testa, 'Multiplex Parenting: IVG and the Generations to Come' (2014), *Journal of Medical Ethics*, 40(11), 752–758.

[29] See, for example I. H. Park and others, 'Reprogramming of Human Somatic Cells to Pluripotency with Defined Factors' (2008), *Nature*, 451(7175), 141–146.

[30] Suter, '*In vitro* Gametogenesis', 90.

[31] Ibid., 90.

possible technique is likely to involve producing stem cells by taking a somatic cell (i.e. any cell in the body that is not a gamete, germ cell, or stem cell) from an individual and transferring it in modified form into an enucleated egg via CNR (also known as 'SCNT').[32] Alternatively, sperm or eggs could be derived from iPSCs generated from somatic cells, which would completely avoid the need to use embryos for the process.[33] Despite technical challenges that are yet to be overcome, these advances raise some important issues for law and regulation of human reproduction. The development of IVG is part of a broader public and policy discussion that needs to be had about the processes which we do – and do not – want to attribute moral significance to in law and the thresholds, therein, and which we might seek to capture within any governing legal framework(s).

While IVG is, in many ways, just another form of ART, it has the potential to allow for methods of reproduction that have never before been possible.[34] From this, there are several potential positive applications of IVG. For example, it can advance our understanding of gamete formation, which can in turn help to improve fertility services. Moreover, women may be able to avoid egg retrieval if eggs could be made from somatic cells, which would be highly beneficial given how invasive and painful the current procedure is. It would also enable greater reproductive choice for those with fertility issues such as some cancer patients. Further, it has the potential to give further reproductive freedom to those in family structures beyond the heteronormative nuclear family. In particular, it would open up the possibility of genetic reproduction to same-sex couples to have children who are biologically related to both parents; 'multiplex' parenting[35] for polyamorous or polygamous families, where children are genetically related to more than two individuals; and even for single parents to procreate without another person's genetic contribution.[36] Technologies such as this are thus capable of disrupting the 'traditional' familial norms and genetic family-making processes promoted by current legal frameworks. This is not to say, however, that family-making processes are not varied already; on the contrary, it is only

---

[32] Ibid., 91.
[33] Ibid.
[34] Ibid., 88.
[35] Palacios-González and others, 'Multiplex Parenting'.
[36] Although this would be very similar to cloning, see S. Segers and others, 'In Vitro Gametogenesis and Reproductive Cloning: Can We Allow One While Banning the Other?' (2019), *Bioethics*, 33(1), 68–75.

now, with the advent of IVG, that science is keeping up the various forms of kinship[37] that take place in society. In other words, society is often criticised with not keeping up with science, but when it comes to family-making, it is science that has not kept up with society.[38] A considered ethical and policy debate surrounding IVG highlights the need to bring law and regulation governing reproductive technologies out of liminality not only when it comes to un(der)regulated science but also when it comes to family-making and kinship.

There are also reasons why policymakers should not push for this technology to go ahead should it become viable for humans. For example, it reinforces the high value that society holds in genetic relatedness,[39] which is problematic for various reasons (e.g. it can reinforce bias against forms of social parenting such as adoption).[40]

While the ethical pros and cons of IVG are too numerous to cover here,[41] the analysis in this section could inform future policy discussions around IVG. The liminal lens offered in this work, and the context-based approach that is advocated, means that consideration would need to be given to the processes and thresholds that would take place should IVG become viable for human reproduction. In particular, the effect that relationality may have on these processes and thresholds should be a key part in any legal and ethical deliberative process. For example, to view any framework for IVG from an individualistic perspective would miss the broader social context in which new forms of reproduction and family-making would takes place. Suter, for example, draws from a relational account of autonomy 'to suggest that our assessment of IVG and its potential benefits or harms depends entirely on the social, scientific, and legal context in which it is situated and how it is used'.[42] What might a liminal lens and the context-based approach offered in this

---

[37] See M. Strathern, *Kinship, Law and the Unexpected* (Cambridge University Press, 2010).

[38] Palacios-González and others, 'Multiplex Parenting', 752.

[39] See F. D. Ginsburg and R. R. Reiter (eds.), *Conceiving the New World Order: The Global Politics of Reproduction* (University of California Press, 1995).

[40] For more on this see J. McCandless and S. Sheldon, 'Genetically Challenged: The Determination of Legal Parenthood in Assisted Reproduction', in S. Graham and others (eds.), *Relatedness in Assisted Reproduction: Families, Origins and Identities* (Cambridge University Press, 2014), 61–78.

[41] For more on this see A. J. Newson and A. C. Smajdor, 'Artificial Gametes: New Paths to Parenthood?' (2005), *Journal of Medical Ethics*, 31(3), 184–186; Palacios-González and others, 'Multiplex Parenting'; Suter, '*In Vitro* Gametogenesis'; G. Testa and J. Harris, 'Ethical Aspects of ES Cell-Derived Gametes' (2004), *Science*, 305(5691), 1719; G. Testa and J. Harris, 'Ethics and Synthetic Gametes' (2005), *Bioethics*, 19(2), 146–66.

[42] Suter, '*In Vitro* Gametogenesis', 88.

book add to policy discussions surrounding IVG? To build on this, this work suggests that we should not only ask whether we want IVG for reproductive purposes but also question the technology in the broader context(s) in which it would operate:

- If IVG is indeed valuable for reproductive use, *how* do we want that process to take place, and to which reproductive ends?
- Should we consider the welfare of the child in such cases? Are such future persons, born from IVG gametes, 'liminal' to any extent, and if so how should they be supported? On the other hand, would bringing these questions to the fore simply be a re-run of the debates at the time IVF was introduced, or is it nonetheless important to ask these questions?
- Taking the narrow view of liminality as marginality, how should we accommodate third or fourth genetic parents in family law in a way that does not leave them outside of society? Even if we were to bring them in, what might their parental responsibilities be?
- How might disputes over the use of gametes and resultant embryos be resolved? Would the *Evans* case apply here; do we allow a veto to one party over gametes? Do we think it is just that one of four might get the absolute veto? If not, how many of the genetic contributors should count towards a veto concerning gamete use? A majority?
- What, if any, are the counselling and support needs here for persons, current and future (be it the resulting child, or genetic parents), and if they are liminal, who might lead them through and out of this?
- What limits, if any, should be placed on the use and application of IVG, and how would those limits relate to the broader context(s) within which artificial reproduction takes place?

On the final point, for example, embryos created from IVG gametes could, in theory, be fitted into our current regime for reproductive purposes by changing the meaning of 'permitted' gametes under s3ZA of the 1990 Act (as amended). Recall that s3ZA of the 1990 Act (as amended) came about through the aftermath of the *Quintavalle* case, a legal event through which the reproductive and therapeutic distinction for cloned embryos was crystallised in statute, that is embryos made via CNR, a form of cloning, may only be used for research purposes. Considering the potential for IVG to allow 'solo reproduction' in ways that do *and* do not result in 'cloning', it calls us to ask: should the reproductive/therapeutic distinction, crystallised post-*Quintavalle*, continue to stand the test of time if IVG for humans becomes a reality?

If there is value to be found in deriving *in vitro*-generated gametes for the purposes of this advance, it would be intellectually indefensible to attempt to fit that process within a framework that did not predict this advancement, nor account for it in its philosophical underpinnings. As we have seen in earlier chapters, permanent liminality, including the permanent liminality of law, can be dangerous. Even if, after legal and ethical deliberation, it is decided that IVG for reproductive purposes should not take place, like other more recent advances bring to the fore serious questions regarding whether we want our current regime, the 1990 Act (as amended) (along with its intellectual underpinnings), to continue to 'withstand the test of time'. For the reasons advanced in this book, however, policymakers should not rely on the longevity of law and regulation in light of the numerous developments in science since the 1980s. IVG, along with other scientific and technological developments (such as the above discussion of maintenance of an embryo *in vitro* for thirteen days), challenges us to revisit the intellectual basis of the law and regulation surrounding the creation, use, and destruction of the building blocks of human life *in vitro*. More granularly, it challenges policymakers and the public to consider which processes we find important and why we value them, and moreover, what thresholds in those processes we want to reflect (or artificially construct) in any regulatory frameworks.

7.4   Artificial Womb Technology: New Contexts, New Thresholds?

AWT was brought from science fiction into stark reality when, in 2017, a Philadelphia research team successfully sustained the lives of lamb fetuses in 'biobags' (a form of AWT).[43] In this experiment, lambs were removed from the womb at the viability threshold and placed in these artificial womb prototypes until gestation was complete.[44] Ectogenesis is the process by which an embryo or fetus is gestated within the AWT. While full ectogenesis (where the entirety of the gestational process takes place *ex utero*) is not currently viable for human use, it is foreseeable that it will become so in the near future. The use of AWTs on human fetuses, especially for partial ectogenesis (where part of the gestational process, most likely the final stages), is thus also on the horizon. Dubbed the 'third

---

[43] E. A. Partridge and others, 'An Extra-Uterine System to Physiologically Support the Extreme Premature Lamb' (2017), *Nature Communications*, 8, 15112.

[44] Ibid.

era of human reproduction',[45] ectogenesis via AWT has the potential to revolutionise preterm neonatal care in the first instance, if not pregnancy, as well as embryo and fetal research. This technology could provide an environment very similar to that of the uterus, which could aid prematurely born babies. Neonatal intensive care has come on in leaps and bounds in the twenty-first century; babies born around twenty-three weeks, the very edge of viability, are now surviving in neonatal intensive care. Nonetheless, the survival rates of extremely premature babies (less than twenty-eight weeks) are still less than 50 per cent;[46] this rate is even lower in low-income settings.[47] AWT thus has the potential to provide an alternative to, and perhaps revolutionise, neonatal intensive care.

So far this book has argued that in the context of new scientific developments and new understandings of embryonic *process*, we should place context at the forefront of any revisitation of the laws governing the creation and use of embryos *in vitro*. Based on a liminal analysis, this book has posited that law itself should be processual, especially in an area of such rapid scientific development. The prospect of ectogenesis strongly suggests that it is well past time to revise the 1990 Act (as amended). Moreover, the technology's focus on embryos and fetuses who are advancing down the process towards birth suggests, very fittingly, that a processual account of the legal response is required. This is particularly the case in light of new technological advancements, which call for us to revisit, if not revise, normative boundaries and thresholds we currently have in place. In particular, it highlights the importance of asking whether, and how, some long-standing thresholds should remain, as we have seen that the crossing of thresholds are key moments in transformative processes in biology and the law, for example the irreversible legal threshold crossed while changing from 'reproductive' to 'research' embryo.[48]

This final case study focuses on partial ectogenesis for human fetuses, which could be used as something akin to neonatal intensive care, as a more imminent development in reproductive technology. More granularly, this section focuses on one key point of contention in the literature:

---

[45] See S. Welin, 'Reproductive Ectogenesis: The Third Era of Human Reproduction and Some Moral Consequences' (2004), *Science and Engineering Ethics*, 10(4), 615.

[46] H.C. Glass and others, 'Outcomes for Extremely Premature Infants' (2015), *Anesthesia and Analgesia*, 120(6), 1337–1351.

[47] See WHO, 'Preterm Birth' (*World Health Organization*, 19 February 2018) www.who.int /news-room/fact-sheets/detail/preterm-birth .

[48] Once decidedly a 'research' embryo, it cannot be used for reproductive purposes i.e. placed within a woman. See the flowchart on p157.

the meaning and significance of 'birth', a key legal *threshold* in the early stages of human life. First, this section looks at the implications of this new technology for current understandings of the threshold, if not legal bright line, of 'birth' in the common law, and the implications of altering that threshold within the broader context in which the law of 'birth' operates: women's reproductive rights.[49]

7.4.1 The Meaning and Significance of 'Birth'

Ectogenesis disrupts existing legal and biological thresholds and causes us to question them, particularly the meaning and significance of 'birth' in law. The law of birth, and its implications for personhood, is important because personhood lets us know which rights, relationships, and interests are recognised by law. In the United Kingdom, for example, the unborn fetus only attains legal personhood, along with the protections and legal rights that come with the status of 'legal person', *at birth*.[50] However, the introduction of AWT has the potential to make the meaning and legal significance of this bright 'line in the sand' rather complex, as it is unclear as to what point in the process of ectogenesis (i.e. transferral out of the uterus, or removal from the AWT) 'birth' would take place. This is not to say that the common law landscape behind birth, specifically what exactly constitutes birth, is clear. The landmark case on this topic is *Paton* v. *BPAS*,[51] in which Baker LJ affirmed that

> [t]he foetus cannot, in English law, in my view, have right of its own at least until it is born and has a separate existence from its mother. That permeates the whole of the civil law of this country ... and is, indeed, the basis of the decisions in those countries where law is founded on the common law ... America, Canada, Australia.[52]

In the case of *C* v. *S*,[53] another key case on this matter, Heilbron J emphasised that any rights accorded to the fetus are contingent on subsequent birth and thus 'crystallise' at birth[54] in cases of, for example,

---

[49] See Chapter 1 of this book.
[50] For the US, see *Roe* v. *Wade*, 410 U.S. 113 (1973); for Canada see *Tremblay* v. *Daigle* [1989] 2 S.C.R. 530; for Australia see *Attorney-General (ex rel Kerr)* v. *T* [1983] 1 Qd R 404.
[51] [1979] QB 276.
[52] Ibid., 279.
[53] [1987] 1 All ER 1230.
[54] Ibid., at 1234.

claims for prenatal injury.[55] In *Re F (in utero)*,[56] the Court of Appeal had to decide whether an unborn child could be made a ward of the court. On this matter Staughton LJ stated: 'the court cannot care for a child, or order that others do so, until the child is born; only the mother can'.[57] Furthermore, there is the crucial question of what point in the birth *process* is legal personality obtained? We can glean some clarification from the very old English cases of *R* v. *Trilloe*[58] and *R* v. *Reeves*[59] where it was held that a baby is born even if still attached by umbilical cord. However, there has been little clarification on the meaning of birth beyond these cases. Moreover, as Romanis points out, it is clear in English law that a child must be 'born alive' to obtain legal personality,[60] as stillborns cannot bring actions in tort[61] nor be the victim of homicide.[62]

'Birth' is not significant for all areas of law, however. In Scotland, personhood is also acquired at birth (as held in the case of *Kelly* v. *Kelly*),[63] but as Mason points out there is a 'difference between the rights of the fetus per se, and the rights of the fetus which devolve on the neonate'.[64] As for the 'rights of the fetus', while the finer details of what 'birth' constitute are unclear (as the aforementioned shows), we have a clear legal 'born/not born' dichotomy for the purposes of legal personhood in the United Kingdom.[65] However, the 'rights of the fetus which devolve on the neonate' is less clear in English law. Once again, Mason suggests that Scots law can provide some clarity on this.[66] Through the application of the *nasciturus* principle – a legacy of the influence of Roman law in

---

[55] The court also ruled that although fetuses between 18 and 21 weeks old showed signs of movement, they are not capable of being born alive under the Infant Life (Preservation) Act 1929 (which notably does not extend to Scotland or NI, s3(2)), to which the Abortion Act 1967 provides defences.

[56] [1988] 2 All ER 193.

[57] Ibid., at 201.

[58] (1842) Car & M 650.

[59] (1839) 9 Car & P 25.

[60] E. C. Romanis, 'Challenging the "Born Alive" Threshold: Fetal Surgery, Artificial Wombs, and the English Approach to Legal Personhood' (2020), *Medical Law Review*, 28(1), 93–123.

[61] See *Burton* v. *Islington Health Authority* [1993] QB 204.

[62] See *Attorney General's Ref No3 of 1994* [1998] AC 245, and; *CP (A Child)* v. *First-Tier Tribunal (Criminal Injuries Compensation)* [2014] EWCA Civ 1554.

[63] 1997 SC 285. Here, the judgment cited the decision in *Paton* v. *BPAS*, holding that was held that the plaintiffs had not set out a prima facie case.

[64] Mason, 'Life Before Birth', 144.

[65] Romanis, 'Challenging the "Born Alive" Threshold'.

[66] See Mason, 'Life Before Birth', 144.

Scotland[67] – which is that unborn children may sue for title on the death of their relative, as long as they are born alive,[68] as held in the case of *Cohen* v. *Shaw*.[69] Here the court applied the *nasciturus* principle (traditionally only applied in the context of succession) and held that provided that the child is born alive, an unborn child *in utero* is treated as though he had already been born for the purposes of awarding damages.[70] A similar decision was made in the case of *Stuart* v. *Reid*.[71] Although English law does not follow the *nasciturus* principle, *some* redress may be brought in England under the Congenital Disabilities (Civil Liability) Act 1976.[72] As an aside, in both of these cases, the unborn child was already *in utero* at the time of their relatives' passing, so it is dubious as to whether a not-yet-conceived child would have the same title in Scotland. Legal recognition of any legal rights before birth have not extended beyond this principle, however. From Scots law we can glean that if an ectogenic fetus was subsequently 'born alive',[73] it would have inheritance rights if a relative died while *in utero*. For the latter to be clear, however, the law would require clarification on (a) what 'born alive' means for an ectogenic fetus and (b) whether for the purposes of inheritance *in utero* and *in artificial utero* should be treated the same.

To attain legal personhood in both jurisdictions, birth must have taken place and the child must have been born *alive*. This is one of the key issues where AWT adds further complexity to this issue; neonates in intensive care are clearly 'born alive' but are not capable of sustaining independent life. A question for future policy consideration then is: do we wish for AWT to be treated the same as neonatal intensive care in law? Should birth continue to be a matter of location, an *in utero/ex utero* dichotomy? How might we class those transferred from the womb to AWT; are they 'born', and moreover, 'born alive'?[74] Might they, too, be

---

[67] Ibid.

[68] Ibid.

[69] 1992 SLT 1022.

[70] See also *McWilliams* v. *Lord Advocate* 1992 SLT 1045, esp para 1048.

[71] 2014 Rep LR 107.

[72] See Mason, 'Life Before Birth', 145.

[73] See Scottish Law Commission, 'Liability for Antenatal Injury: Report on a reference under section 3(1)(e) of the Law Commissions Act 1965' (Scot Law Com No. 30) Cmd 5371.

[74] For a thorough, in-depth discussion on this and other key policy questions on this topic see Romanis, 'Challenging the "Born Alive" Threshold' in which she offers policy for AWTs in context of fetal operations. The arguments made in this section of the book complements this work by offering a liminal analysis of key policy questions that need to be considered should AWT for neonatal care become a reality.

liminal beings unless and until we resolve their status in law? With the scientific advances such as fetal surgery,[75] improvements in neonatal intensive care, and now AWTs, calls have already been made to further clarify what birth, or indeed what 'born alive', means. Brazier and Alghrani argue that the 'born alive' rule needs to be revisited and that current tests such as this cannot be expanded to fit emerging technologies such as AWT.[76] Romanis states that 'the possibility of *ex utero* gestation, for different reasons, provides more ammunition to the argument that the focus on "birth" may be an out-dated approach to affording legal personality'.[77] Yet, as she also points out, 'current academic discussion has not provided in-depth investigation of the legal fine print detailing what birth encompasses from a legal perspective'.[78]

What might a liminal lens and Chapter 6's context-based approach add to policy discussions surrounding ectogenesis? A liminal analysis suggests that we can frame one of the key questions for this discussion as follows: if we replace birth as a legally relevant threshold, which threshold(s) become legally relevant instead? A liminal analysis also suggests that any deliberations surrounding the answer to this needs to reflect the processual nature of embryonic/fetal growth and where those processes take place. This is crucially important in processual and legal terms. Unlike natural child birth, which is a process that takes over the woman's body after a given amount of time, both ectogenesis and the precise moment of 'being born' become entirely artificial processes, in the sense that they are subject to the control of a third party. This raises the prospect of control over timing of birth, subject to technological and not natural factors. Per the core analysis offered in this book, the literature on liminality focuses on the crossing of a threshold as a key phase in the process of *becoming* – in this case, becoming a legal person. Liminality also focuses on the person(s) who lead us through and out of liminality. Ectogenesis, then, has the potential to disrupt the meanings of, and our reliance on, 'birth' as a key legal threshold for law. Not only should we ask whether birth should still act as *the* legally relevant threshold for person-hood, but if we revisit policy in light of ectogenesis and thus disrupt this marker in any way (which scholars such as Romanis argue that we should), what other threshold(s), if any, do we replace it with?

---

[75] For more on this see Romanis, 'Challenging the "Born Alive" Threshold'.

[76] A. Alghrani, and M. Brazier, 'What is it? Whose it? Re-Positioning the Fetus in the Context of Research?' (2011), *The Cambridge Law Journal*, 70(1), 51–82.

[77] Romanis, 'Challenging the "Born Alive" Threshold', 101.

[78] Ibid., 95.

Birth is not only a legal bright line in the sand but also a threshold that requires crossing in order to reach personhood. Moreover, as we have seen, not only must a child be 'born' but 'born alive'. Liminal analysis is not opposed to bright lines such as this – they can be useful legal tools. Instead, liminal analysis helps us to look at the complexity surrounding placing those bright lines. For 'birth', complexity derives from the process of crossing that physical and legal threshold (e.g. *Trilloe* and *Reeves*) – a liminal phase dictated by physical context. Of course, 'birth' does not have to entail personhood and the rights that go with it. 'Birth' is thus not the only 'bright line' that could be prompted to change by the development of AWT. How we legally define that which is within the biobag – be it fetus, neonate, or 'gestateling'[79] – will affect how we treat it and what, if any, its legal rights and protections are.[80] We cannot, and should not, base legal frameworks on such an important and nuanced matter as a definition of birth from existing law and regulation (be it the United Kingdom, the EU, the United States, WHO, or any other definition) without justifying *why we should still use it* when the context in which we use it has changed entirely.

As we have seen, legal definition and moral status are not one and the same in this or any other context. However, in the field of law, they are undeniably intertwined; they inform each other when it comes to enacting biology and ethics into policy. As argued previously in this volume, liminality cannot tell us what to do, nor, as such, resolve the issue of moral status. It can, however, as a lens, give us the tools to think about when and how we ascribe moral status, including personhood status, and, in the context of this work, how we reflect that status *in law*. Moreover, as we have seen, assigning a moral status to an entity does not always tell us how to treat it. We know that the embryo *in vitro* is 'special' and can derive from conversations surrounding the Warnock Report that it requires some sort of 'respect'; yet, as we have seen, we dispose of embryos as 'artefacts'.[81] More holistically, what this book's analysis has shown is that reducing policy discussions to particular aspects of an ethico-legal framework – such as 'status' (morally and/or in law) or 'definition' – ignores the broad range of contexts that the early stages of

[79] E. C. Romanis, 'Artificial Womb Technology and the Frontiers of Human Reproduction: Conceptual Differences and Potential Implications' (2018), *Journal of Medical Ethics*, 44 (11), 751–755.

[80] Ectogenesis is not the only reason to consider the matter of legal personality for fetuses *ex utero*. We also have fetal surgery and the recent push to the limits of viability.

[81] Mason, 'Human Life'.

life can now, in the twenty-first century, be led *into, through*, and *out of.* It is therefore intellectually indefensible, when considering any framework for AWTs, whether for premature neonatal care or for full gestation, to consider any factor in isolation without context. Context (for this work) is a relational consideration of origins, physical context, and ends. A liminal lens points us to look at process, that is each stage of the process, including the context(s) in which it takes place and that stage's significance therein. For example, any policy discussions should, regarding this threshold, ask: does the emergence of an entirely new physical context, where the fetus' life is maintained *ex utero*, mean that we need to revisit the legal significance of birth? In other words, do we need to clarify what 'birth' means in law? And if so, by what means? As a context that enables the fetus to exist as physically separate from the mother, should the thresholds for birth and personhood be changed for the purposes of ectogenesis? If this is to happen, what then becomes the new legally significant threshold?

Process – especially the nature of gestation as a process – is important for reproductive law. The legal requirement of being 'born alive' is reflective of this in that it marks the (near) completion of that process. However, technologies and modern medicine change what 'born alive' means. Life/death is another seemingly clear dichotomy, but this too has been further blurred by technologies such as life support machines and now AWTs. Technologies such as AWT (and indeed IVG) also blur the distinction between 'natural' and 'artificial' or 'synthetic'. AWT throws a new, synthetic physical context into the mix, and for some, this removes the key moral reasoning behind 'birth' being the moment that legal personhood is attributed, physical separation from the mother's body. It is this important legal moment, a key 'natural' threshold that has been attributed significance by law, that a liminal lens can require us to consider more closely.

As with the advent of IVF, AWT (and indeed IVG) further disrupts the normative trajectories of 'natural' reproductive processes. At the moment, despite the proliferation of reproductive technologies, law still relies on a natural process to decide motherhood and legal personality: birth. With ectogenesis, however, we do not rely on a natural process – we have to rely on an artificial process. An intervention is still required to give birth to that child, but a processual analysis highlights that *when* and *how* that intervention occurs in the context of ectogenesis becomes morally and legally significant. The new, additional[82] threshold to be crossed by the fetus into personhood is entirely 'artificial'/human-made, not 'natural'. Should AWT come into fruition, the ectogenic fetus will need to be led out of its liminal state – yet *when* in the process of gestation this occurs (be it *in utero* or *ex utero*) is key here. A liminal analysis thus suggests the following key question for any regulatory discussion:

- At what point does the liminal entity, the *ex utero* fetus, become legally significant and a bearer of rights?

The point at which the fetus is led across that threshold from fetus/unborn child to 'person' is crucial for the clarification of various rights. Presently, the unborn child/fetus has to be 'born alive', but if the application of this threshold becomes even more unclear as a result of AWT, it is uncertain as to how this test would apply to the ectogenic fetus, if at all. As discussed earlier, the answer to this has important implications for rights involved more generally, one example being the law of succession and another being the rights of the woman.

7.4.2   'The End' of the Abortion Debate?

For some, the advent of partial ectogenesis via AWT might constitute a compromise between pro-choice and pro-life parties[83] and mark the end of the abortion debate, because it would enable the transfer of fetuses into the AWT to gestate to full term. Partial ectogenesis through AWT involves moving the fetus from one liminal state (*in utero*) to another (*ex utero/in* AWT). This raises questions regarding (a) *when,* (b) *how,* and (c) *by whom* the embryo will move *out of* liminality. A context-based approach highlights that all three of these factors need to be considered from a regulatory perspective, even if for (c) *some* of the arguments regarding the bodily integrity of women are 'taken out of the picture' by ectogenesis. The following discussion briefly discusses why this is the case.

   If we accept that physical context is a key consideration, especially for the policy considerations discussed previously, then any policy discussions also need to consider the importance of relationality,[84] that is *who* leads the ectogenic fetus *into, through,* and *out* of liminality. For the

---

[82] In addition to the physical threshold of leaving the mother's body.

[83] See for example W. Simkulet, 'Abortion and Ectogenesis: Moral Compromise' (2020), *Journal of Medical Ethics*, 46(2), 93–98.

[84] See Chapter 5, section 5.4.4 of this book.

ectogenic fetus, two key parties to lead the fetus through this process would be the unborn child's mother(s) and/or father(s). Some of the discussions on ectogenesis and abortion have centred on the question of whether genetic parents have the 'right to the death of a fetus'. For some, a right to abortion is not a right of termination but a right of evacuation.[85] Räsänen, on the other hand, argues that there is a right to the death of a fetus, but it is not a woman's right alone; it is the right of both genetic parents.[86] These arguments are rooted in the notion of the right to *not* become a biological parent.[87] Indeed, the right not to become a biological parent has been supported in several legal cases in the United Kingdom,[88] ECtHR under Article 8,[89] and the United States.[90] Any forced transfer should certainly engage the right to privacy,[91] as the ECtHR held in *Evans*:

> The Court agrees, since 'private life', which is a broad term, encompassing, *inter alia*, aspects of an individual's physical and social identity including the right to personal autonomy, personal development and to establish and develop relationships with other human beings and the outside world (*Pretty*, § 61), incorporates the right to respect for both the decisions to become and not to become a parent.[92]

As an aside, *Evans* notably raises the issue of whether or not parental consent for full gestation can be revoked once implanted in the artificial womb,[93] as here consent was revoked at an earlier stage in the process (pre-implantation). Questions regarding revocation of consent, and indeed other issues such as succession, are unlikely to be answered by current law(s). Ectogenesis is an interruption of the reproductive trajectory that challenges us to reconsider key legal thresholds and limits to those processes, including 'birth', 'born alive', and questions of consent.

---

[85] See J. J. Thompson, 'A Defense of Abortion' (1971), *Philosophy and Public Affairs*, 1(1), 47–66.

[86] J. Räsänen, 'Ectogenesis, Abortion, and a Right to the Death of the Foetus' (2017), *Bioethics*, 31(9), 607–702.

[87] Ibid., 698. As an aside, I suggest that arguments such of these should be broadened to 'right not to become a parent', removing the 'biological', in order to include those who are using donated eggs/sperm in an AWT context.

[88] *Evans* v. *Amicus Healthcare Ltd*, [2004] EWCA Civ 727

[89] Evans v. UK *Application no.* 6339/05, para 57.

[90] See *Davis* v. *Davis*, 842 S.W.2d 588, 597 (Tenn. 1992); *Kaas* v. *Kaas* 91 N.Y.2d 554 (N.Y. Ct. App. 1998).

[91] A. Alghrani, 'The Legal and Ethical Ramifications of Ectogenesis', *Asian Journal. WTO & International Health Law and Policy*, 2(1), 189–212, 198.

[92] *Evans [2004]*, paras 23–27.

[93] Alghrani, 'The Legal and Ethical Ramifications', 203.

As discussed in Chapter 6, intentions are an important *part* of a context-based approach (as informed by a liminal lens). Bringing relationality to the fore here highlights the importance of the reproductive rights of the mother. If, for example, we want AWT to be an 'equalizer' for those that cannot gestate, then, as with pregnancy, those aims should be at the fore of any governing framework. The intentions of the (non)intending parent(s) should not necessarily be foregrounded above all other considerations here, but they are a key part of looking at the context of reproduction holistically. Relationality is important here because it generates an awareness of process that does not solely look at the 'free-floating' embryo/fetus, but at what and *who* is required for that process to take place. It highlights some of the key steps in the gestational process that have taken place; it is thus 'not nothing' (per the judgment in *St George's*) but importantly that it is not yet born, either. This is not to deny that the physical proximity aspect (i.e. the physical placement of the fetus inside the woman's body) of relationality is not 'taken out of the picture'. Yet, a liminal lens highlights that physical proximity is not the *only* part of the picture, for the purposes of legal enquiry, either.

The gestational mother's intentions are a key part of the 'success' of the gestational process. Therefore, looking at process and the importance of time in that process (i.e. as a timeline), this intentionality highlights the interests of the mother and her effect on the context of gestation and birth. As recognised in the gradualist approach of the 1967 Act, at the stage at which an ectogenic fetus may be transferred a lot has to happen within the woman's body for the fetus to be capable of being 'born alive'. It is worth noting, however, that if partial ectogenesis were to be made available for NIC only, it is unlikely to immediately require discussions surrounding abortion; to state the obvious, many pregnant women who reach that stage of pregnancy and require NIC are unlikely to want to terminate their pregnancy. Moreover, if an intervention in pregnancy is required and consented to (rather than an unexpected premature birth), at what point in the gestational process would fetuses be *led out* of their liminal *in utero* state: twenty weeks, twenty-four weeks, twenty-six weeks?

As the limits of viability are brought forward by current NIC (and eventually AWT), it is almost certain that the issue of whether a fetus from a terminated pregnancy can and should be transferred into AWT – the reasons given above strongly suggest that it should not – will urgently need to be resolved. It is thus unclear whether terminating gestation of an ectogenic fetus would fall under the framework of the 1967 Act. For these reasons, among contemporary calls to de-criminalise abortion,[94] AWT adds further pressure to revisit whether abortion law itself is fit for purpose.

AWT by no means ends the abortion debate. While the keystone of the abortion debate for those that are pro-choice is a woman's bodily integrity and autonomy, this is not the only factor proffered by those that are pro-choice. Indeed, in the wording of the (amended) Abortion Act 1967 itself, the risk to any existing children[95] and health of the fetus itself[96] are also grounds for termination. As Alghrani argues:

> Ectogenesis should not signal a green light to those hoping to set out on acts of foetal rescue, unless the law regarding the legal status of the unborn alters. Whilst it is located in a female womb, any attempts to force the pregnant woman to have the foetus transferred in to an ectogenetic device would violate her bodily autonomy and be unlawful.[97]

Arguments that suggest that the abortion debate would be 'settled'[98] by AWT are therefore too narrow, as they fail to take account of the broader, multifaceted context in which decisions about termination of pregnancy take place. As we have seen in the analysis of the creation and use of embryos *in vitro* in reproduction or research, multiple processes take place at once. Oftentimes, these processes interlink (see Figure 6.1). It is no different *in utero*. Pregnancy and gestation are processes through which the embryo/fetus goes through rapidly transformative change within the body of a woman, which itself also goes through a transformative process (in terms of physical appearance, but also internally by, for example getting ready for breastfeeding). Birth is a process, as is becoming a parent – one that for some starts during pregnancy and for others at birth.

Once a fetus has been implanted in the AWT, however, different considerations come into play. Liminality casts ectogenic fetuses, once in the AWT, as yet another form of liminal entity, as a lens it forces us to ask *who* should be the ones to lead them out of liminality. On the one hand, this may be the mother, who may lead it to termination if she is no

---

[94] See S. Sheldon and K. Wellings (eds.), *Decriminalising Abortion in the UK: What Would It Mean?* (Policy Press, 2020).

[95] Abortion Act 1967 s1(1)(a)

[96] Ibid., s1(1)(d)

[97] Alghrani, 'The Legal and Ethical Ramifications', 206.

[98] For a summary of these see S. Langford, 'An End to Abortion? A Feminist Critique of the "Ectogenetic Solution" to Abortion' (2008), *Women's Studies International Forum*, 31(4), 263–269.

longer in a position to have a child. Some, however, might advocate that we always lead the ectogenic fetus to life where medically possible. There are clear social and economic differences between the two positions, but it is self-evident that there is a huge moral difference between leading the ectogenic fetus to death and to being born alive.

7.4.3   Summary

Some key issues need to be considered in relation to the wider, relational context that will occur with AWT, sooner rather than later (not all could be considered here): consent, withdrawal of consent, applicability/suitability of Abortion Act, liability, meaning of birth, and meaning of 'born alive'. A processual analysis thus highlights not only the importance of the processes that take place but also the importance of thresholds for law, the legal problems that AWTs pose for law, especially whether the threshold 'birth' needs to be crossed in order to attain legal personhood. Not only does it highlight the presence and importance of process for law regulating the early stages of human life, but also of the multiplicity of processes that occur (whether naturally, or through technological intervention).

7.5   Conclusion

Overall, if one accepts that the United Kingdom's approach to the regulation of reproduction (and use of embryos for research) is processual and morally relative, then the arguments put forward in this book suggest that there are ways in which any future framework(s) might better do so, and have thus offered a context-based approach. This approach, informed by a liminal lens, has the potential to inform the provision of a more robust intellectual basis and suggests framework to inform contemporary debates on what processual law *could* look like.

The following outlines/summarises *some* of the possible questions that a context-based approach (rooted in the analytical framework laid out in Part II) might raise in relation to novel reproductive technologies at three distinct stages of the reproductive trajectory (gamete, embryo, and fetus):

- First, if there are thresholds within reproductive and/or research processes beyond which embryos or IVG gametes cannot be returned (to another pathway), should we more explicitly delineate 'research' embryos from 'reproductive' embryos in law? If so, how might this be done? Is the reproductive and therapeutic distinction, a clear line in the sand for gamete (and embryo) research, still desirable?

• Second, if we deem it appropriate to bring research embryos out of liminality, is there an imperative to assiduously pursue something valuable for scientific reasons? For example, should law lead embryos out of liminality as 'valuable' research objects in themselves? Relatedly, if 'research embryos' are only ever going to be as such once given that label, then law can only ever lead them to disposal.[99] Does this mean that they should be given a different status from reproductive embryos? If so, would this support extending the fourteen-day rule, and if so, to what extent? Further, would it support treating 'research' embryos (once on that pathway) as 'objects'? If so, what would that entail? Would it necessarily mean abandonment of the moral meaning attached to 'research embryos'? A relational view of this liminal entity would suggest not.

• Third, because the ectogenic fetus is decidedly outside the physical context in which we attribute moral significance – the mother's body – in what ways, if at all, do these relational ties remain significant? This is especially important when a woman seeks to terminate a fetus in ectogenesis.

Finally, more generally speaking:

• If we want to bring the areas of law discussed in this book out of liminality, in order to reflect the three strands of human life that they affect (the embryo, science, and family units)[100] in which contexts do we want to do so, and with what intellectual and philosophical bases? For example, do we want to move away from promoting the nuclear family? If so, does enabling genetic connection help or hinder this?

• Relatedly, what conditions do we consider important enough to cross (or not cross) a particular legal, biological, and moral threshold, for example the fourteen-day rule, or 'permitted' gamete or embryo?

A context-based approach, informed by a liminal lens, allows us to consider how we can embrace the potential for legal change through explicitly distinguishing between embryos that are to be used for reproduction and embryos that are to be used for research. If we want law to

---

[99] This is not challenging the rule that research embryos should not be implanted in a woman.

[100] See the introduction to this book.

reflect process and change, in a way that continues to be morally relative, we cannot expect or want law to be durable in its embodiment of a set of rules that fail to reflect the processual and practical realities of what currently happens with and to human embryos.[101] In the near future, these considerations will also need to be extended to developments involving the human reproductive trajectory more broadly, including IVG, ectogenesis, and abortion. This approach embraces the potential for change by introducing a nuanced, yet important demarcation between 'types' of embryo that the law has already created and facilitated. *In vitro* embryos are quintessentially liminal beings. Yet all the above of course leaves another key question, which is perhaps objectively unanswerable:

- When exactly is the right time to (re)open the above debates on the fourteen-day rule, IVG, and ectogenesis, and more broadly, the intellectual underpinnings of the 1990 Act (as amended)?

---

[101] See Jacob and Prainsack, 'Embryonic Hopes'.

Conclusion

This book, concerned with the regulation of human embryos *in vitro*, and their use for reproduction and research, has explored the ways in which law does and can regulate processually. As we have seen, the 1990 Act (as amended) is static and unchanging with respect to the moral status of 'the embryo', yet our societal understandings and perceptions of *embryos* are not. The 1990 Act (as amended) is, as we have seen, permanently liminal. A 'gothic' framing of embryos and the use of a liminal lens have each revealed a key facet of embryo regulation. All of the practices that law currently allows are, in essence, regulating for uncertainty, process, and change. Here, the truism coined by Thomassen that 'liminality is'[1] has been explored and unpacked with reference to what this means for embryos that are subject to the legal architecture that is the 1990 Act (as amended). It has been argued that the reality of liminality still has much to say about the way we regulate *in vitro* embryos. The overarching contribution of this book is to provide the reader with ways to think about the ways we navigate law and processes governed by law *into*, *through* and *out* of liminality in ways that bring greater insights into the sensitive enterprise of regulating for uncertainty, when our focus of attention is an entity as fluid and remarkable as the human embryo.

Science contains a juxtaposition of certainty and uncertainty. On the one hand, it provides us with explanations for almost everything; it organises our knowledge through research and evidence that assure us of how our world was, how it is, and in some cases how it might be in the future. The future is uncertain, however, as is the 'true'/objective nature of how things are and our knowledge of how things once were. Public wants and needs from science are not always unified, and furthermore, these wants are also evolving, changing, pluralistic, and often uncertain too. The key feature of the analysis offered here is determinedly *not* a particular normative claim about the 'moral status' of embryos (gametes, or

---

[1] See Laurie, 'Liminality and the Limits of Law', 57; Thomassen, *Liminality and the Modern*.

foetuses). Rather, its contribution lies in its claim to provide a deeper understanding of law and society's relationship with embryos *in vitro*, set against historical legal developments, and a greater appreciation of the processes to which embryos are subjected, both biologically and relationally.

The (re)conceptualisations of the 'legal embryo' offered in this book have the potential to inform reform of the legal framework governing this area of science of technology that is increasingly fraught with concerns surrounding its suitability. The law has fixed embryos in time, and in some ways in substance. All embryos *in vitro* fall under the Warnock Report's 'special status'; they are thus conceptually severed from the multiplicity of futures that the law has regulated for. Conceptually disconnecting them from these possible, legally provided destinies is not only confusing, but also intellectually indefensible. New ontological boundaries (not only scientific but also social and moral) require the law to re-orient itself. The embryo *in vitro* thus required significant reconfiguration of the law. Not only did it have to provide a framework for the use of embryos for reproduction and/or research but construct it in a manner that was morally, intellectually, and legally defensible. It has been argued that the processual nature of embryos *in vitro*, tied up with scientific possibility, is thus disruptive for the law's normative boundaries and its intellectual underpinnings. If the law is to adequately and justifiably meet the challenge that advances in technology bring, it must evolve in order to cope with the normative and conceptual challenges that transgressive entities such as embryos *in vitro* pose for it.

Contrary to the legal climate of the past ten years or so, the law must directly confront embryos *in vitro*, rather than 'tinker at the margins'[2] to better understand the challenges that they provide and consider legal futures that can navigate these new boundaries. This is important not only for the improvement of human health as it relates to embryos *in vitro* or embryos more generally but for the multiplicity of legally liminal persons, objects, and subject-objects in the field of health research as a whole. It is therefore time to break the legal stalemate surrounding embryos *in vitro*.

---

[2] See Fox, 'The Human Fertilisation and Embryology Act 2008'.

BIBLIOGRAPHY

Alghrani, A., 'The Legal and Ethical Ramifications of Ectogenesis' (2007), *Asian Journal of WTO & International Health Law and Policy*, 2(1), 189–212.

Alghrani, A. and Brazier, M., 'What is it? Whose it? Re-positioning the Fetus in the Context of Research?' (2011), *The Cambridge Law Journal*, 70(1), 51–82.

Alghrani, A., *Regulating Assisted Reproductive Technologies: New Horizons* (Cambridge University Press, 2019).

Alighieri, D., *The Divine Comedy* (Vintage Books, 2013).

Appleby, J. B. and Brendenoord, A. L., 'Should the 14-Day Rule for Embryo Research Become the 28-Day Rule?' (2018), *EMBO Molecular Medicine*, 10(9), e9437. www.ncbi.nlm.nih.gov/pmc/articles/PMC6127884/

Atkinson, P., 'Book Review: Gothic Imaginations' (2005), *Social Studies of Science*, 35(4), 653–664.

Baldwin, R. and others, *Understanding Regulation: Theory, Strategy, and Practice*, 2nd ed. (Oxford University Press, 2012).

Bateson, G., *Naven* (Stanford University Press, 1958).

Baxter, A., 'Edmund B. Wilson as a Preformationist: Some Reasons for His Acceptance of the Chromosome Theory' (1976), *Journal of the History of Biology*, 9(1), 29–57.

Baylis, F. and Krahn, T., 'The Trouble with Embryos' (2009), *Science and Technology Studies*, 22(2), 31–54.

Becker, G., *The Elusive Embryo: How Women and Men Approach New Reproductive Technologies* (University of California Press, 2000).

Beyleveld, D., *Human Dignity in Bioethics and Biolaw* (Oxford University Press, 2001).

Bibbings, L., 'Legal Commentary- R v Bourne: A Historical Context' in Stephen Smith and others (eds.), *Ethical Judgments: Re-Writing Medical Law* (Bloomsbury, 2017).

Blackstone, W., *Blackstone's Commentaries*, 4th ed. (Clarendon Press, 1770).

Blackstone, W., *Commentaries on the Laws of England* (Chicago University Press, 1765).

Botting, F., *Gothic* (Routledge, 1996).

Botting, F., *Limits of Horror: Technology, Bodies, Gothic* (Oxford University Press, 2010).

Brownsword, R., 'Stem Cells and Cloning: Where the Regulatory Consensus Fails' (2004), *New England Law Review*, 39(3), 535–571.

Burns, J., *The Anatomy of the Gravid Uterus* (Glasgow University Press, 1799).

Callus, T., 'Omnis definitio periculosa est: On the Definition of the Term "Embryo" in the Human Fertilisation & Embryology Act 1990' (2003), *Medical Law International*, 6(1), 1–11.

Cavaliere, G., 'A 14-Day Limit for Bioethics: The Debate Over Human Embryo Research' (2017), *BMC Medical Ethics*, 18(1), 38.

Chan, S., 'How to Rethink the Fourteen-Day Rule' (2017), *Hastings Center Report*, 47(3), 5–6.

Chesney, E., 'Concept of *Mens Rea* in the Criminal Law' (1939), *Journal of Criminal Law and Criminology*, 29(5), 627–644.

Coke, E., *Institutions of the Laws of England* Vol. III (Printed by M. Flesher, for W. Lee, and D. Pakeman, 1622).

Cole G. and Frankowski, S., *Abortion and Protection of the Human Fetus: Legal Problems in a Cross-cultural Perspective* (Martinus Nijhoff, 1987).

Connor, S., 'Inside the Black Box of Human Development', *The Guardian* (5 June 2016). www.theguardian.com/science/2016/jun/05/human-development-ivf-embryos-14-day-legal-limit-extend-inside-black-box.

Creed, B., *The Monstrous-Feminine: Film, Feminism, Psychoanalysis* (Psychology Press, 1993).

Deglincerti, A. and others, 'Self-Organization of the Attached Human Embryo' (2016), *Nature*, 533(7602), 251–254.

Denman, T., *An Introduction to the Practice of Midwifery*, vol. I (J Johnson, 1794).

Department of Health, 'Human Fertilisation and Embryology Act 2008' (Department of Health, 26 July 2010), www.webarchive.nationalarchives.gov.uk/+/http://www.dh.gov.uk/en/Publicationsandstatistics/Legislation/Actsandbills/DH_080211.

Department of Health, 'Review of the Human Fertilisation and Embryology Act' (White Paper, Cm6989, 2006). https://assets.publishing.service.gov.uk/government/uploads/system/uploads/attachment_data/file/272391/6989.pdf.

Devaney, S., *Stem Cell Research and the Collaborative Regulation of Innovation* (Routledge, 2013).

Devlin, H., 'Artificial Womb for Premature Babies Successful in Animal Trials', *The Guardian* (25 April 2017), www.theguardian.com/science/2017/apr/25/artificial-womb-for-premature-babies-successful-in-animal-trials-biobag.

Diatkine, G, 'Le Séminaire, X: L'angoisse de Jacques Lacan' (2005), *Revue française de psychanalyse*, 69(3), 917–931.

Dickens, B., *Abortion and the Law* (MacGibbon and Kee, 1996).

Dickenson, D., *Property in the Body: Feminist Perspectives*, 2nd ed. (Cambridge University Press, 2017).

Eriksson I. and Webster, A., 'Governance-by-Standards in the Field of Stem Cells: Managing Uncertainty in the World of "Basic Innovation"' (2008), *Science and Culture*, 27(2), 99–111.

Ford, M., 'Nothing and Not Nothing: Law's Ambivalent Response to Transformation and Transgression at the Beginning of Life' in S. Smith and R. Deazley (eds.), *The Legal, Medical and Cultural Regulation of the Body: Transformation and Transgression* (Routledge, 2009).

Fox, M., 'Pre-persons, Commodities or Cyborgs: The Legal Construction and Representation of the Embryo' (2000), *Health Care Analysis*, 8(2), 171–188.

Fox, M., 'The Human Fertilisation and Embryology Act 2008: Tinkering at the Margins' (2009), *Feminist Legal Studies*, 17(3), 333–344.

Fox M. and Murphy, T., 'Can Law Facilitate Embryonic Hopes?' (2010), *Social and Legal Studies*, 19(4), 498–505.

Fox M. and Murphy, T., 'Response to Sarah Franklin' (2010), *Social and Legal Studies*, 19(4), 510–513.

Franklin, S., 'Making Representations: The Parliamentary Debate on the Human Fertilisation and Embryology Act' in J. Edwards and others (eds.), *Technologies of Procreation: Kinship in the Age of Assisted Conception*, 2nd ed. (Routledge, 1999).

Franklin, S., 'Postmodern Procreation: A Cultural Account of Assisted Reproduction' in F. Ginsburg and R. Rapp (eds.), *Conceiving the New World Order: The Global Politics of Reproduction* (University of California Press, 1995).

Franklin, S. , 'Response to Marie Fox and Therese Murphy' (2010), *Social Legal Studies*, 19(4), 505–510.

Freeman, J. S, 'Arguing Along the Slippery Slope of Human Embryo Research' (1996), *Journal of Medical Philosophy*, 21(1), 61–81.

Freud, S., *The Uncanny* (Penguin, 2003).

Gamble, D., 'Potentialism and the Value of an Embryo' (2005), *Public Affairs Quarterly*, 19(4), 271.

Gieryn, T. F., *Cultural Boundaries of Science* (University of Chicago Press, 1999).

Gilbert, S., *Developmental Biology*, 6th ed. (Sinauer Associates, 2000).

Ginsburg F. D. and Reiter R. (eds.), *Conceiving the New World Order: The Global Politics of Reproduction* (University of California Press, 1995).

Glas, H. C. and others, 'Outcomes for Extremely Premature Infants' (2015), *Anesthesia and Analgesia*, 120(6), 1337–1351.

Gogarty, B., 'What Exactly is an Exact Copy? And Why It Matters When Trying to Ban Human Reproductive Cloning in Australia' (2003), *Journal of Medical Ethics*, 29(2), 84–89.

Grubb, A., 'Abortion Law in England: The Medicalization of a Crime' (1990), *Journal of Law and Medical Ethics*, 18(1–2), 146–161.

Haimes E., and others, '"So, What Is an Embryo?" A Comparative Study of the Views of Those Asked to Donate Embryos for hESC Research in the UK and Switzerland' (2008), *New Genetics and Society*, 27(2), 113–126.

Hammond-Browning, N., 'Ethics, Embryos and Evidence: A Look Back at Warnock' (2015), *Medical Law Review*, 23(4), 588–619.

Hanafi, Z., *The Monster in the Machine: Magic, Medicine, and the Marvelous in the Time of the Scientific Revolution* (Duke University Press, 2000).

Hansen, G., *The Trickster and the Paranormal* (Xlibris, 2001).

Haraway, D., 'Manifesto for Cyborgs: Science, Technology, and Socialist Feminism in the 1980s' reprinted in L. Nicolson (ed.), *Feminism/Postmodernism* (Routledge, 1985).

Harris, J., '"Goodbye Dolly?" The Ethics of Human Cloning' (1997), *Journal of Medical Ethics*, 23(6), 353–360.

Harrison E. and Midori, I., 'Women's Responses to Child Loss in Japan: The Case of "Mizuko Kuyō"[with Response]' (1995), *Journal of Feminist Studies in Religion*, 11(2), 67–100.

Hartouni, V., *Cultural Conceptions: On Reproductive Technologies and the Remaking of Life* (University of Minnesota Press, 1997).

Hayashi, K. and others, 'Offspring from Oocytes Derived from in Vitro Primordial Germ Cell-like Cells in Mice' (2012), *Science*, 338(6109), 971–975.

Heilbron, J., *The Oxford Companion to the History of Modern Science* (Oxford University Press, 2003).

Hellsten, L., 'Dolly: Scientific Breakthrough or Frankenstein's Monster? Journalistic and Scientific Metaphors of Cloning' (2000), *Metaphor and Symbol*, 15(4), 213–221.

Helyer, R., 'Parodied to Death: The Postmodern Gothic of American Psycho' (2000), *Modern Fiction Studies*, 46(3),725–746.

Hennette-Vauchez, S., 'Words Count-How Interest in Stem Cells Has Made the Embryo Available: A Look at the French Law of Bioethics' (2009), *Medical Law Review*, 17(1), 52–75.

Herring, J., *Medical Law and Ethics* (Oxford University Press, 2016).

Hilhorst, M. and others, 'Nudge Me, Help My Baby: On Other-Regarding Nudges' (2007), *Journal of Medical Ethics*, 43(10), 702–706.

Hinds, E., 'The Devil Sings the Blues: Heavy Metal, Gothic Fiction and "Postmodern" Discourse' (1992), *The Journal of Popular Culture*, 26(3), 151–164.

House of Commons Science and Technology Committee, 'Human Reproductive Technologies and the Law: Report of the Fifth Session 2004–5' (2005). https://publications.parliament.uk/pa/cm200405/cmselect/cmsctech/7/7i.pdf.

Human Fertilisation and Embryology Authority, 'How We Regulate' (HFEA), www.hfea.gov.uk/about-us/how-we-regulate.

Hurley, K., *Gothic Body* (Cambridge University Press, 1996).

Hyun I. and Jung, K., 'Human Research Cloning, Embryos and Embryo-like Artefacts' (2006), *Hastings Centre Reports*, 36(5), 34–41.

Hyun I. and others, 'Embryology Policy: Revisit the 14 Day Rule' (2016), *Nature*, 533(7602), 169–171.

Imamura, M. and others, 'Induction of Primordial Germ Cells from Mouse Induced Pluripotent Stem Cells Derived from Adult Hepatocytes' (2010), *Molecular Reproduction and Development*, 77(9), 802–8011.

Ingram-Waters, M., *Unnatural Babies: Cultural Conceptions of Deviant Procreations* (ProQuest, 2008).

Istvan, Z., 'Artificial Wombs are Coming and the Controversy is Already Here', (Motherboard, 4 August 2014), www.motherboard.vice.com/read/artificial-wombs-are-coming-and-the-controversys-already-here.

Jackson, E., 'The Human Fertilisation and Embryology Bill' (2008), *Expert Review of Obstetrics and Gynaecology*, 3(4), 429–431.

Jackson, E., *Regulating Reproduction* (Hart, 2001).

Jacob M. A. and Prainsack, B., 'Embryonic Hopes: Controversy, Alliance, and Reproductive Entities in Law and the Social Sciences' (2010), *Social and Legal Studies*, 19(4), 497–517.

Jacob M.A. and Prainsack, B., 'Unfreezing Embryos?' (2010), *Social and Legal Studies*, 19(4), 513–517.

Jaworska, A. and Tannenbaum, J., 'The Grounds of Moral Status', The Stanford Encyclopedia of Philosophy (10 January 2018), https://plato.stanford.edu/entries/grounds-moral-status/.

Jentcsh, E., 'On Psychology of the Uncanny' (1906), *Angelaki: Journal of the Theoretical Humanities*, 2(1), 7–16.

Jha, A., 'Winston: IVF Clinics Corrupt and Greedy', The Guardian (21 May 2007). www.theguardian.com/science/2007/may/31/medicineandhealth.health.

Johanson, R. and others, 'Has the Medicalisation of Childbirth Gone Too Far?' (2002), *British Medical Journal*, 324(7432), 892–895.

Johnson, M., 'Escaping the Tyranny of the Embryo? A New Approach to ART Regulation Based on UK and Australian Experiences' (2006), *Human Reproduction*, 21(11), 2756–2765.

Jonlin, E., 'The Voices of the Embryo Donors' (2015), *Trends in Molecular Medicine*, 21(2), 55–58.

Karpin, I., 'The Legal and Relational Identity of the "Not-Yet" Generation' (2010), *Law, Innovation and Technology*, 4(2), 122–143.

Karpin, I., 'The Uncanny Embryos: Legal Limits to the Human and Reproduction Without Women' (2006), *Sydney Law Review*, 28(24), 599–623.

Karpowicz, P., Cohen, C. B., and Van der Kooy, D., 'Developing Human-Nonhuman Chimeras in Human Stem Cell Research: Ethical Issues and Boundaries' (2005), *Kennedy Institute of Ethics Journal*, 15(2), 107–134.

Keown, J., *Abortion, Doctors and the Law: Some Aspects of the Legal Regulation of Abortion in England from 1803 to 1982* (Cambridge University Press, 2002).

Kittler, F. A., *Literature, Media, Information Systems* (Routledge, 2013).

Langford, S., 'An End to Abortion? A Feminist Critique of the "Ectogenetic Solution" to Abortion' (2008), *Women's Studies International Forum*, 31(4), 263–269.

Latour, B., *We Have Never Been Modern* (Harvard University Press, 1993).

Laurie, G., 'Liminality and the Limits of Law' (2017), *Medical Law Review*, 25(1), 47–72.

Law, J., 'The Materials of STS' in D. Hicks and M. Beaudry (eds.), *The Oxford Handbook of Material Culture Studies* (Oxford University Press, 2010).

Macklin, R., 'Splitting Embryos on the Slippery Slope: Ethics and Public Policy' (1994), Kennedy Institute of Ethics Journal, 4(3), 209–225.

Madden, D., *Medicine, Ethics and the Law in Ireland*, 2nd ed. (Bloomsbury Professional, 2011).

Maienschein, J., 'Epigenesis and Preformationism' (The Stanford Encyclopedia of Philosophy, first published 11 October 2015), www.plato.stanford.edu/archives/spr2017/entries/epigenesis/.

Mason, J. K., 'Discord and Disposal of Embryos' (2004), *Edinburgh Law Review*, 8 (1), 84–93.

McCandless J. and Sheldon, S., 'Genetically Challenged: The Determination of Legal Parenthood in Assisted Reproduction' in S. Graham and others (eds.), *Relatedness in Assisted Reproduction: Families, Origins and Identities* (Cambridge University Press, 2014), 61–78.

McGuinness, S., 'Judgment 1- R v Bourne [1939] 1 KB 687' in S. Smith and others (eds.), *Ethical Judgments: Re-Writing Medical Law* (Bloomsbury, 2017).

McGuinness, S. and Thompson, M., 'Medicine and Abortion Law: Complicating the Reforming Profession' (2015), *Medical Law Review*, 23(2), 177–199.

McKie, R., 'Row over Allowing Research on 28–Day Embryos' (Guardian Online, 4 December 2016). www.theguardian.com/society/2016/dec/04/row-over-allowing-research-on-28-day-embryos.

McLean, S., 'The Moral and Legal Boundaries of Fetal Intervention: Whose Right/ Whose Duty' (1998), *Seminars in Neonatology*, 3(4), 249–254.

McMillan, C. and others, 'Beyond Categorisation: Refining the Relationship Between Subjects and Objects in Health Research Regulation' (2021), *Law, Innovation and Technology*, 13(1) (forthcoming).

Meikle, J., 'Axe IVF Watchdog, Says Fertility Expert', *The Guardian* (11 December 2014). www.theguardian.com/society/2004/dec/11/health.medicineandhealth.

Monahan,P., 'Human Embryo Research Confronts Ethical "Rule"' (2016), *Science*, 352(6286), 640.

Mulkay, M., *The Embryo Research Debate: Science and the Politics of Reproduction* (Cambridge University Press, 1997).

Mulkay, M., 'Frankenstein and the Debate over Embryo Research' (1996), *Science, Technology and Human Values*, 21(2), 157–176.

Nayernia, K. and others, 'In Vitro-Differentiated Embryonic Stem Cells Give Rise to Male Gametes that can Generate Offspring Mice' (2006), *Development Cell*, 11 (1), 125–132.

Needham, J., *A History of Embryology*, 2nd ed. (Cambridge University Press, 2015).

Newson, A.J. and Smajdor, A.C., 'Artificial Gametes: New Paths to Parenthood?' (2005), *Journal of Medical Ethics*, 31(3), 184–186.

Novaes, S. B. and Salem, T., 'Embedding the Embryo' in J. Harris and S. Holm (eds.), *The Future of Human Reproduction* (Clarendon Press, 1998).

Nuffield Council on Bioethics, 'Council to Consider "14 Day Rule" in Embryo Research', (Nuffield Council on Bioethics, 5 May 2016), www.nuffieldbioethics.org /news/2016/council-14-day-rule-embryo-research/.

Palacios-González, C., 'Human Dignity and the Creation of Human-Nonhuman Chimeras' (2015), *Medicine, Health Care, and Philosophy*, 18(4), 487.

Palacios-González, C., Harris, J., and Testa, G., 'Multiplex Parenting: IVG and the Generations to Come' (2014), *Journal of Medical Ethics*, 40(11), 752–758.

Park, I. H. and others, 'Reprogramming of Human Somatic Cells to Pluripotency with Defined Factors' (2008), *Nature*, 451(7175), 141–146.

Parpart, J., 'Who is the "Other"?: A Postmodern Feminist Critique of Women and Development Theory and Practice' (1993), *Development and Change*, 24(3), 439–464.

Parry, S., '(Re) Constructing Embryos in Stem Cell Research: Exploring the Meaning of Embryos for People Involved in Fertility Treatments' (2006), *Social Science and Medicine*, 62(10), 2358.

Partridge, E. A. and others, 'An Extra-Uterine System to Physiologically Support the Extreme Premature Lamb' (2017), *Nature Communications*, 8, 15112.

Pera, M., 'Human Embryo Research and the 14-Day Rule' (2017), *Development*, 144(11), 1923–1925.

Punter, D., *Gothic Pathologies: The Text, the Body and the Law* (Springer, 1998).

Quigley, M. and Ayihongbe, S., 'Everyday Cyborgs: On Integrated Persons and Integrated Goods' (2018), *Medical Law Review*, 26(2), 276–308.

Rabinow, P., *Anthropos Today: Reflections on Modern Equipment* (Princeton University Press, 2003).

Rabinow, P., *French DNA: Trouble in Purgatory* (University of Chicago Press, 1999).

Räsänen, J., 'Ectogenesis, Abortion, and a Right to the Death of the Foetus' (2017), *Bioethics*, 31(9), 607–702.

Report of the Committee of Inquiry into Human Fertilisation and Embryology (Cmnd 9314, 1984).

Romanis, E. C., 'Artificial Womb Technology and the Frontiers of Human Reproduction: Conceptual Differences and Potential Implications' (2018), *Journal of Medical Ethics*, 44(11), 751–755.

Romanis, E. C., 'Challenging the "Born Alive" Threshold: Fetal Surgery, Artificial Wombs, and the English Approach to Legal Personhood' (2020), *Medical Law Review*, 28(1), 93–123.

Rothman, B., 'Pregnancy, Birth and Risk: An Introduction' (2014), *Health, Risk and Society*, 16(1), 1–6.

Sage, V. and Smith, A. L. (eds.), *Modern Gothic* (Manchester University Press, 1996).

Sample, I., 'Clone Research Hampered by Red Tape Says Fertility Expert', *The Guardian* (2 March 2007). www.theguardian.com/politics/2007/mar/02/genet ics.immigrationpolicy.

Saunders, P. and Watts, G., 'Should MPs Sanction Three-Parent Babies?', *The Guardian* (12 June 2012). www.theguardian.com/commentisfree/2012/jun/12/ head-to-head-three-parent-babies.

Schroeder, M., 'Value Theory' (The Stanford Encyclopedia of Philosophy, Fall 2016 Edition), Edward Zalta (ed.) https://plato.stanford.edu/archives/fall2016/ entries/value-theory/ accessed 20 January 2018.

Scully, J. L., *Disability Bioethics: Moral Bodies, Moral Difference* (Rowman & Littlefield, 2008).

Scottish Law Commission, 'Liability for Antenatal Injury: Report on a Reference under Section 3(1)(e) of the Law Commissions Act 1965' (Scot Law Com No. 30) Cmd 5371. www.scotlawcom.gov.uk/files/5112/7989/6877/rep30.pdf.

Segers, S. and others, 'In Vitro Gametogenesis and Reproductive Cloning: Can we Allow One while Banning the Other?' (2019), *Bioethics*, 33(1), 68–75.

Seymour, J., *Childbirth and the Law* (Oxford University Press, 2000).

Shahbazi, M. and others, 'Self-Organization of the Human Embryo in the Absence of Maternal Tissues' (2016), *Nature Cell Biology*, 18(6), 700–708.

Sheldon, S., '"Who is the Mother to Make the Judgment?": The Constructions of Woman in English Abortion law' (1993), *Feminist Legal Studies*, 1(1), 3–22.

Sheldon, S., *Beyond Control: Medical Power and Abortion Control* (Pluto, 1997).

Sheldon, S. and Wellings, K. (eds.), *Decriminalising Abortion in the UK: What Would It Mean?* (Policy Press, 2020).

Shelley, M., *Frankenstein* (Penguin Classics, 2003).

Shildrick, M., *Leaky Bodies and Boundaries: Feminism, Postmodernism and (Bio) Ethics* (Routledge, 2015).

Simkulet, W., 'Abortion and Ectogenesis: Moral Compromise' (2020), *Journal of Medical Ethics*, 46(2), 93–98.

Solter, D. and others, *Embryo Research in Pluralistic Europe*, vol. XXI (Springer Science & Business Media, 2003).

Squier, S., *Liminal Lives: Imagining the Human at the Frontiers of Biomedicine* (Duke University Press, 2004).

Stanley, T., 'Three Parent Babies: Unethical, Scary and Wrong', *Telegraph* (03 February 2015), www.telegraph.co.uk/news/health/11380784/Three-parent-babies-unethical-scary-and-wrong.html

Stanton, C. and Harris, J., 'The Moral Status of the Embryo Post-Dolly' (2005), *Journal of Medical Ethics*, 31(4), 221–225.

Star S. L. and Griesemer, J., 'Institutional Ecology, Translations and Boundary Objects: Amateurs and Professionals in Berkeley's Museum of Vertebrate Zoology 1907–39' (1989), *Social*, 19(3), 387–420.

Star, S. L., 'This is not a Boundary Object: Reflections on the Origin of a Concept' (2010), *Science, Technology, and Human Values*, 35(5), 601–617.

Stenner, P., 'Liminality: Un-Wohl-Gefühle und der affective turn' Transcript Verlag (2016), 45–68.

Storrow, R., 'Quests for Conception: Fertility Tourists, Globalization and Feminist Legal Theory' (2005), *Hastings Law Journal*, 57(2), 295–330.

Strathern, M., *Kinship, Law and the Unexpected* (Cambridge University Press, 2010).

Suter, S. M., 'In Vitro Gametogenesis: Just Another Way to Have a Baby?' (2016), *Journal of Law and the Biosciences*, 3(1), 87–119.

Svendsen, M. and Koch, L., 'Unpacking the "Spare Embryo": Facilitating Stem Cell Research in a Moral Landscape' (2008), *Social Studies of Science*, 38(1), 93–110.

Szakolczai, Á. , 'Liminality and Experience: Structuring Transitory Situations and Transformative Events' (2009), *International Political Anthropology*, 2(1), 141–172.

Szakolczai, Á. , 'Permanent (Trickster) Liminality: The Reasons of the Heart and of the Mind' (2017), *Theory and Psychology*, 27(2), 231–248.

Taylor-Alexander, S. and others, 'Confronting the Liminal Spaces of Health Research Regulation: Beyond Regulatory Compression' (2016), *Law, Innovation and Technology*, 8(2), 149–176.

Tesarik, J. and Greco, E., 'A Zygote is not an Embryo: Ethical and Legal Considerations' (2004), *Reproductive Biomedicine Online*, 9(1), 13–16.

Testa, G. and Harris, J., 'Ethics and Synthetic Gametes' (2005), *Bioethics*, 19(2), 146–66.

Testa, G. and Harris, J., 'Ethical Aspects of ES Cell-Derived Gametes' (2004), Science, 305(5691), 1719.

Thomas, Y., 'Fictio Legis: L'empire de la fiction Romaine et ses limites Medievales' (1995), *Droits*, 21, 18.

Thomassen, B., *Liminality and the Modern: Living Through the In-between* (Ashgate, 2014).

Thompson, J. J., 'A Defense of Abortion' (1971), *Philosophy and Public Affairs*, 1 (1), 47–66.

Thorne, S. (tr), *Bracton on the Laws and Customs of England*, vol. II (Belknap, 1968).

Toumey, C., 'The Moral Character of Mad Scientists: A Cultural Critique of Science' (1992), *Science, Technology and Human Values*, 17(4), 411–437.

Tudor, A., *Monsters and Mad Scientists: A Cultural History of the Horror Movie* (Wiley-Blackwell, 1991).

Turner, V., 'Frame, Flow and Reflection: Ritual and Drama as Public Liminality' in M. Benamou and C. Caramello (eds.), *Performance in Postmodern Culture* (Coda Press, 1977).

Turner, V., *The Forest of Symbols: Aspects of Ndembu Ritual* (Cornell University Press, 1967).

Turner, V., *The Ritual Process: Structure and Anti-Structure* (Aldine Transaction, 1969).

van Gennep, A., *The Rites of Passage* (University of Chicago Press, 1960).

Vibert, F., *The New Regulatory Space: Reframing Democratic Governance* (Edward Elgar, 2014).

Waldby, C. and Squier, S., 'Ontogeny, Ontology, and Phylogeny: Embryonic Life and Stem Cell Technologies' (2003), *Configurations*, 11(1), 27–46.

Warnock, M., 'The Warnock Report and the 14-Day Rule' (Rethinking the Ethics of Embryo Research: Genome Editing, 13 Days and beyond, London, 7 December 2016).

Warnock, M., *A Question of Life: The Warnock Report on Human Fertilisation and Embryology* (Blackwell, 1985).

Webster, K., 'Whose Embryo is it Anyway? A Critique of Evans v Amicus Healthcare [2003] EWHC 2161 (Fam)' (2013), *Journal of International Women's Studies*, 7(3), 71–86.

Welin. S., 'Reproductive Ectogenesis: The Third Era of Human Reproduction and Some Moral Consequences' (2004), *Science and Engineering Ethics*, 10(4), 615.

WHO, 'Preterm Birth' (World Health Organization, 19 February 2018), www .who.int/news-room/fact-sheets/detail/preterm-birth.

Willett, J. and Deegan, M., 'Liminality and Disability: Rites of Passage and Community in Hypermodern Society' (2001), *Disability Studies Quarterly*, 21 (3), 137–152.

Williams, G., *The Sanctity of Life and the Criminal Law* (Knopf, 1957).

Winter, G., 'The Future of Artificial Wombs' (2017), *British Journal of Midwifery*, 25(7), 416.

INDEX

Lightning Source UK Ltd.
Milton Keynes UK
UKHW022011230321
380890UK00005B/245